e-Business Fundamentals

The main issues surrounding e-Business are often difficult to untangle. *e-Business Fundamentals* is a comprehensive textbook that considers all of the key business, management and technical issues of e-Business, examining and explaining how technologies can help organizations in both the public and private sectors conduct business in new ways.

The book begins by addressing the changing nature of the e-Economy and the impact of the dotcom 'bubble' of the late 1990s, going on to analyze key software developments and the impact these have had on organizational practices, such as Human Resource Management. It then outlines the legal and ethical frameworks of e-Business, and considers how companies use various e-Commerce tools to enter new markets. Finally, it traces the progress public sector organizations have made in adopting e-Business practice.

This is an accessible, jargon-free and focused textbook that offers readers both a technical and managerial overview of the issues surrounding e-Business. It uses illustrative cases and discussion questions to help students and managers in organizations not only to familiarize themselves with e-Business but also to equip themselves with the skills to challenge and analyze the changing environment in which we work.

Paul Jackson is e-Government Forum Manager for the Institute of Public Finance.
Lisa Harris is Lecturer in e-Business at Brunel University.
Peter M. Eckersley is an e-Government Research Officer for the Institute of Public Finance.

Routledge e-Business series

Routledge e-Business is a bold new series examining key aspects of the e-Business world, designed to provide students and academics with a more structured learning resource. Introducing issues of marketing, Human Resource Management, ethics, operations management, law, design, computing and the e-Business environment, it offers a broad overview of key e-Business issues from both managerial and technical perspectives.

Marketing the e-Business
Lisa Harris and Charles Dennis

e-Business Fundamentals
Edited by Paul Jackson, Lisa Harris and Peter M. Eckersley

e-Retailing
Charles Dennis, Bill Merrilees and Tino French

e-Business Fundamentals

Edited by Paul Jackson,
Lisa Harris and
Peter M. Eckersley

Routledge
Taylor & Francis Group

LONDON AND NEW YORK

First published 2003 by Routledge
11 New Fetter Lane, London EC4P 4EE

Simultaneously published in the USA and Canada
by Routledge
29 West 35th Street, New York, NY 10001

Routledge is an imprint of the Taylor & Francis Group

Typeset in Perpetua and Bell Gothic by
Florence Production Ltd, Stoodleigh, Devon
Printed and bound in Great Britain by
The Cromwell Press, Trowbridge, Wiltshire

British Library Cataloguing in Publication Data
A catalogue record for this book is available from the
British Library

Library of Congress Cataloging in Publication Data
e-business fundamentals/edited by Paul Jackson,
Lisa Harris, and Peter M. Eckersley.
      p. cm. – (Routledge e-business series)
   Includes bibliographical references and index.
      1. Electronic commerce.   I. Jackson, Paul J.
   II. Harris, Lisa.   III. Eckerlsey, Peter M.   IV. Series.
   HF5548.32 E1738 2003
   658.8'4–dc21   2002153078

ISBN 0–415–25594–5 (hbk)
ISBN 0–415–25595–3 (pbk)

Contents

Illustrations

FIGURES

TABLES

Contributors

LESLIE BUDD is Reader in Social Enterprise at the Open University Business School. He has published widely in the field of regional and urban economics in the context of international financial markets. He has produced consultancy reports for UK public bodies on benchmarking regional competitiveness and modelling training and entrepreneurship in small businesses.

FINTAN CLEAR is a Lecturer at the School of Business and Management, Brunel University, where he teaches business strategy for electronically mediated trading. He hails from Worcester, and after cutting his academic teeth in geography and communications policy went on to gain extensive experience in industry, working on large-scale supply chain systems in food retailing. He has taught on three continents, worked as a consultant for a number of small firms in the United Kingdom, and also for larger bodies such as the European Space Agency, Italcable Telecommunications (Italy) and the BBC World Service. His recent research has been concerned with examining the inhibitors and promoters of e-Business adoption among small firms in the west London catering trade. He is working on an EU-sponsored project looking at the adoption problems of telework by small firms. His other interests include archaeology, speaking rusty Italian and proselytizing the health-giving benefits of olive oil.

GERALDINE T. COHEN, Dipl. Ing., MBA (INSEAD), MCIM, Chartered Marketer, is a Lecturer in Marketing at the Brunel School of Business and Management, Brunel University. Her main research interests lie in the areas of marketing for professional services and corporate branding. She is a member of the Chartered Institute of Marketing and has been a Chartered Marketer since 1998.

MICHAEL COLLINS, BA (Hons), DipM, MCIM, MIDM, MInstD, a CIM Chartered Marketer and accredited Institute of Direct Marketing consultant and trainer, has more than twenty-eight years' marketing experience, with the last eighteen spent specializing in data-driven marketing. An internationally acknowl-edged writer, speaker and award-winning marketing consultant, he has wide experience in developing data-driven strategies, in data analysis and interpreta-tion and the integration of business intelligence for clients in both consumer and business-to-business markets. He is a Visiting Lecturer in Database Marketing at Brunel University and has delivered his seminars and workshops on database marketing in the United Kingdom, Europe, North America and the Far East.

NELARINE CORNELIUS is Senior Lecturer in Human Resource Management and Organizational Behaviour in the School of Business and Management at Brunel University. She is also Senior Honorary Research Fellow, King's College Hospital Medical School, University of London. Her research areas include learning and change in organizations, workplace diversity and quality of life and emotional labour. In addition to her work with Lisa Harris, she has published in *Human Resource Management Journal, Journal of General Management, Business Ethics: a European Review,* and *Soundings: Journal of Politics and Culture.* Her books include *Human Resource Management: a Managerial Perspective*; *Building Workplace Equality: Ethics Diversity and Inclusion*; *Challenging the Boundaries: Personal Construct Psychology Perspectives for the New Millennium* (with John Fisher). She is editing with Nigel Laurie and Paul Griseri the forthcoming book *Reason in Practice: an Introduction to the Philosophy of Management.*

NOAH CURTHOYS is a doctoral student in the School of Business and Management at Brunel University. Prior to this he studied international rela-tions at the London School of Economics, followed by public policy at University College London. He has written on the subjects of public sector management reform and on regional and international aspects of e-Government. Current research interests include e-Business in the public sector, e-Government in the United States and European Union, and governmental and constitutional reform.

PETER M. ECKERSLEY is an e-Government Research Officer with the Institute of Public Finance. Since its inception in 2001 he has undertaken research, analysis and report writing for the CIPFA e-Government Forum, which promotes and shares e-Government best practice among public sector practitioners. He holds undergraduate and postgraduate degrees from the University of Newcastle upon Tyne and has also studied at the University of Leipzig. He contributes to CIPFA's Financial Information Services volume on information technology and previously worked for the City of Edinburgh Council.

LISA HARRIS, ACIB, MBA, MCIM, PhD, Chartered Marketer, is a Lecturer in the School of Business and Management, Brunel University. She is Course Director of the BSc e-Commerce and has management responsibilities for the

Brunel MBA. Lisa worked in retail banking for ten years, and her PhD research examined the management of change in the banking industry in the early days of the Internet. She is a Chartered Marketer, Education Officer for the Royal Counties branch of the Chartered Institute of Marketing, Associate Lecturer for the Open University and External Examiner for the Oxford Brookes University MBA. Lisa also teaches marketing courses for the Student Support Group and Oxford College of Marketing. Her research interests are focused upon the management challenges of e-Banking, mobile marketing and e-Learning. Lisa is also running a research project reviewing emerging trends in the ethics of e-Marketing and has just published *Marketing the e-Business* with Charles Dennis (Routledge, 2002).

PAUL JACKSON is the Manager of the e-Government Forum at the Institute of Public Finance (http://www.ipf.co.uk/egov). IPF is the commercial arm of the Chartered Institute of Public Finance and Accountancy (CIPFA). He worked for several years as an academic, producing a number of books and articles on information technology and new ways of working. His current interests lie in the area of e-Business, with a particular focus on public sector change.

NANDISH V. PATEL is a Lecturer in Information Management in the School of Business and Management, Brunel University, where he co-ordinates the Information Management stream on the Brunel MBA. He has published research papers on information technology governance and e-Business, and he has originated and led research on deferred systems design. Dr Patel has edited and contributed to a book titled *Evolutionary Adaptive Information Systems*. His previous Department of Information Systems and Computing entered him in the British government's Research Assessment Exercise 2001 to judge quality of research. The department was awarded Grade 5.

LAURA J. SPENCE is the co-ordinator of Brunel Research in Enterprise Sustainability and Ethics (BRESE) at the School of Business and Management, Brunel University. Her publications include articles in *Business Ethics Quarterly*, *Journal of Business Ethics* and *Business and Society Review*. Her specialist research area is ethics in small firms. Laura was an executive member of the European Business Ethics Network from 1998 to 2002. She has published on the ethics of e-mail use and using bulletin boards in the teaching of business ethics, and her teaching includes Ethics of e-Commerce.

DAVE WADSWORTH teaches legal aspects and applications in the School of Business and Management at Brunel University. He has taught business for over thirty years, initially in further education but most recently at Brunel and the University of Westminster. He was for many years a Moderator and then a Chief

Examiner for the LCCI. He teaches undergraduate, postgraduate and MBA students on various legal aspects, ranging from the business legal environment, labour law and company law to the legal and ethical environment of e-Commerce. He is a Member of the Institute of Learning and Teaching and was responsible for Learning and Teaching Quality within the School of Business and Management at Brunel.

Preface

This book, and the Routledge series of which it is part, were first conceived of during the heady days of the 'dotcom boom'. This was a time, not so long ago, when the belief was strong that the organizational and economic order was soon to be overturned by the application of Internet-related technologies. Established business models, we were told, were threatened. Internet start-ups were emerging that would rewrite the rules on how customers purchased products and services, and how companies produced and delivered them. While recent history has found such prognostications somewhat overstated – with many getting their fingers burnt in the financial speculations that ensued – we are now perhaps facing the opposite danger: *underestimating* how much things have and are changing.

Today, few organizations remain untouched by Internet-related devices. But perhaps more significant is the fact that, as time goes by, such technologies are penetrating ever deeper into processes and services. And it's not just private companies; the public sector too is steadily remoulding its *modus operandi*, thanks in part to the support of the new technologies. If not a revolution, then, there is a steady evolution taking place, resulting in new organizational structures, changes in working practices and innovations in service delivery.

So while many of the tenets in established management textbooks remain intact, there are still numerous developments that today's managers and students need to understand and master. As they do they must also recognize that the strict dualism between 'managers' and 'techies' will have to disappear. Given the importance of new information technology (IT) to all aspects of organizations, some technical understanding must become part of the contemporary manager's toolkit. Likewise, IT managers themselves can no longer assume a mainly operational or supporting role but must increasingly engage with the business issues surrounding the development and application of emerging technologies.

The book, and the series as a whole, are therefore written with these two audiences in mind: to be accessible and relevant to students and managers in both technical and business departments. The book's main purpose is to improve understanding of the organizational issues raised by 'e-related' developments.

While the electronic world may not call for the wholesale abandonment of old frameworks and toolkits, it does ask us to be cautious about when and where we use them. Some tools will need sharpening and refining, while others may indeed need replacing. A number of new tools and ideas are therefore needed if we are to manage organizations effectively in the electronic age. It is in the face of this latter challenge that the present volume should play an important role.

Paul Jackson
Lisa Harris
Peter M. Eckersley

Acknowledgements

This book would not have been completed without the hard work and commitment of the contributors. As editors we would like to thank them again for their dedication to the project and trust they are glad to be on board. As so often with books, but doubly so in this case, we need to thank the team at Routledge for their patience and forbearance, in particular Catriona King and Rachel Crookes. Finally, we would like to thank IPF for giving us the time and space to pursue this project through to fruition.

Please note that the editors and the publishers have made every possible effort to verify all the web site addresses mentioned in the book. However, readers should be aware that organizations often change their web sites and we cannot be held responsible for any such changes.

Paul Jackson
Lisa Harris
Peter M. Eckersley

Abbreviations

3G	third generation
A&E	Accident and Emergency
AC	Audit Commission
AOL	America Online
ARPA	Advanced Research Projects Agency
B2B	business to business
B2C	business to consumer
B2G	business to government
BACS	Bankers' Automated Clearing Service
BBC	British Broadcasting Corporation
BI	business intelligence
C2C	consumer to consumer
C2B	consumer to business
CCTV	closed circuit television
CD-ROM	compact disc – read-only memory
CEO	chief executive officer
CGI	common gateway interface
CISG	UN Convention on Contracts for the International Sale of Goods
CMC	computer-mediated communication
COD	cash on delivery
CPA	comprehensive performance assessment
CRM	customer relationship management
DIY	do it yourself
DNS	domain name system
DoH	Department of Health
DTI	Department of Trade and Industry
e-	electronic
EDI	electronic data interchange
EFT	electronic funds transfer
ESD	electronic service delivery

ETL	Extraction, Transformation and Load
EU	European Union
FTP	file transfer protocol
HMSO	Her Majesty's Stationery Office
HR	human resources
HRM	human resource management
HTML	hypertext mark-up language
HTTP	hypertext transfer protocol
ICANN	Internet Corporation for Assigned Names and Numbers
ICT	information and communication technology
IEG	Implementing Electronic Government
IETF	Internet Engineering Task Force
IP	Internet protocol
IPRs	intellectual property rights
IS	information systems
ISOC	The Internet Society
ISP	Internet service provider
IT	information technology
ITU	International Telegraphic Union
JIT	just in time
LAN	local area network
MEMEX	memory extension
MEP	Member of the European Parliament
MIME	multimedia internet mail extensions
MP	Member of Parliament
NAO	National Audit Office
NAP	national access point
NCOA	National Change of Address File
NHS	National Health Service
NHSIA	National Health Service Information Agency
NPM	New Public Management
OBI	Open Buying Consortium
ODPM	Office of the Deputy Prime Minister
OLAP	online analytical processing
OSI	International Standards Organization
P2P	peer-to-peer
PC	personal computer
PCT	primary care trust
PDA	personal digital assistant
PK	public key
PKI	public key infrastructure
PR	public relations

QoS	quality of service
RSI	repetitive strain injury
SHRM	strategic human resource management
SME	small or medium-size enterprise
SSL	secure socket layer
SWIFT	Society for Worldwide Interbank Financial Telecommunications
TCP	transmission control protocol
TDA	Trade Descriptions Act
TNC	transnational corporation
UK	United Kingdom
UN	United Nations
UNCITRAL	United Nations Committee on International Trade and Law
URL	uniform resource locator
US	United States
VAT	value-added tax
W3C	World Wide Web Consortium
WAN	wide area network
WAP	wireless application protocol
WDM	wave division multiplexing
WIPO	World Intellectual Property Organization
WTO	World Trade Organization
WWW	World Wide Web
XML	extensible mark-up language
Y2K	Year 2000

Part I

Introduction

Chapter 1

Organizations in the Electronic Age

PAUL JACKSON AND PETER M. ECKERSLEY

KEY LEARNING POINTS

After completing this chapter you will have an understanding of:

- The meanings of e-Commerce, e-Business and e-Government
- The reasons why e-Business demands new skills and thinking
- The structure of the book and the role of each chapter

ORDERED LIST OF SUB TOPICS

- e-Commerce, e-Business, e-Government
- Structure of the book

We live today in a world much beyond the hype of the dotcom bubble. It is a world in which even the most staid and traditional businesses, such as banks and insurance companies, would not be without their online and telephone service channels. In the United Kingdom the government is committed to putting all suitable public services online by 2005. Put simply, e-Business is now a mainstream part of most organizations.

This doesn't mean, of course, that all organizations have thrown off the shackles of Industrial Age business models and ways of working. In many factories and offices life goes on, seemingly unchanged. But peer beneath the surface and a lot has happened. Purchasing clerks may still spend their days staring into a computer screen, but nowadays that computer is as much a communication tool as a word-processing or computational device. While paper may still exist, more and more processes are now handled electronically. With links to the Internet, the clerks

3

in question may spend most of their time exchanging e-mails with remote suppliers, ordering goods via electronic catalogues and tracking those orders through the whole procurement cycle.

Beyond the purchasing department, senior manager and marketing departments will be pulling together a range of newly integrated, up-to-date information (not least about customers and products) and using it to perform more effective analysis and decision making. That same infrastructure is also allowing closer links with suppliers and collaborating organizations, and enabling personnel to operate more flexibly and remotely – in the field (with clients), at home (as teleworkers) or with other colleagues and partners (in virtual project teams).

Slowly but surely the old approach is giving way to a new way of doing things. But, as it does, most organizations are still trying to fathom the implications and opportunities this presents. As managers increasingly recognize, the Electronic Age calls into question many established 'good' business practices while also creating new challenges and dilemmas.

How, for instance, can organizations make the most effective use of the data that e-enabled processes now produce on customers and their buying habits? Inside the organization, what use should be made of electronic information systems to improve internal communications? And, in both cases, what safeguards should be put in place to insure against invasions of (e-)privacy?

These and other questions will be addressed in the chapters that follow. Each one examines the fundamental aspects of life in the Electronic Age. Whether it's the nature of the e-Business environment, or the intricacies of Internet technology; ethics and the law, or maybe database marketing, there are few 'e-issues' that managers can now afford to ignore. Big or small, public or private, today's organizations have some challenging times ahead. But with the guidance of the chapters below, we trust they'll be able to face them with a little more skill and confidence.

e-COMMERCE, e-BUSINESS, e-GOVERNMENT

In a moment, we'll look at an overview of the book. Before we do, let us clear up some of the basic conceptual issues underlying the chapters that follow. Most people know that the prefix 'e' commonly denotes something to do with ICT (information and communications technology) and the Internet (the worldwide network of computer networks that link together, using common ICT standards). Nandish Patel in Chapter 3 of this volume deals with the key hardware and software components that make up Internet systems; we shall therefore leave a detailed discussion of the more technical issues to him.

For now, let us clarify some of the differences between ideas of e-Commerce and e-Business. As Harris (2002) discusses in another volume in this series, there are numerous definitions of e-Commerce and e-Business, with many people treating them somewhat synonymously. For most, though, e-Commerce has a more restrictive meaning and is concerned with the buying and selling of goods online. This may also extend to 'back-end' processes where supply chains are managed through electronic stock ordering systems (which, as Harris points out, pre-date the Internet in the form of EDI, or Electronic Data Interchange).

e-Business is therefore a broader concept and describes arrangements where organizations have redesigned their business structures, processes and services to take advantage of Internet capabilities. The essential features of an e-Business are that it:

- Makes greater use of electronic devices in the processing and communicating of data.
- Allows increased integration of databases and hardware devices (thanks largely to the 'open protocols' that govern the transfer of data between systems).
- Enables users to engage 'interactively' with systems and services – for instance, to purchase goods, check on orders or collaborate in virtual teams or communities.

Realizing the full benefits of the Internet, as well as the e-Commerce functions it supports, is not easily done using traditional systems of work and organization. It is therefore an e-Business orthodoxy that organizations need to 'reinvent' their business processes or entire business models if they are to see the full dividends from their Internet investments (see, for example, Chaffey 2002).

The same principles apply equally well to the public sector, of course. Indeed, many parts of government might be seen as archetypal bureaucracies that could benefit significantly from a rethink and redesign. When talking about the public sector, though, it's common to discuss such 'e' developments under the banner of 'e-Government'. This of course does not disguise the fact that most e-Commerce and e-Business issues and theories are just as relevant to the public sector as they are to the private.

ACTIVITY

Take a look at some books and articles that discuss e-Commerce, e-Business and e-Government. Do they treat these concepts synonymously or quite separately? Are they implicit or explicit about what the concepts mean? Why do you think different sources may define these concepts differently?

STRUCTURE OF THE BOOK

The book has eight main chapters, which cover the essential economic, technical, organizational, ethical, legal and marketing issues raised by e-Business.

In Chapter 2, 'The business environment for e-Commerce' by Leslie Budd and Fintan Clear, we look at the similarities and differences between e-Commerce and traditional ways of doing business, some of which led commentators to proclaim the 'end of economics' during the 'dotcom boom' at the end of the

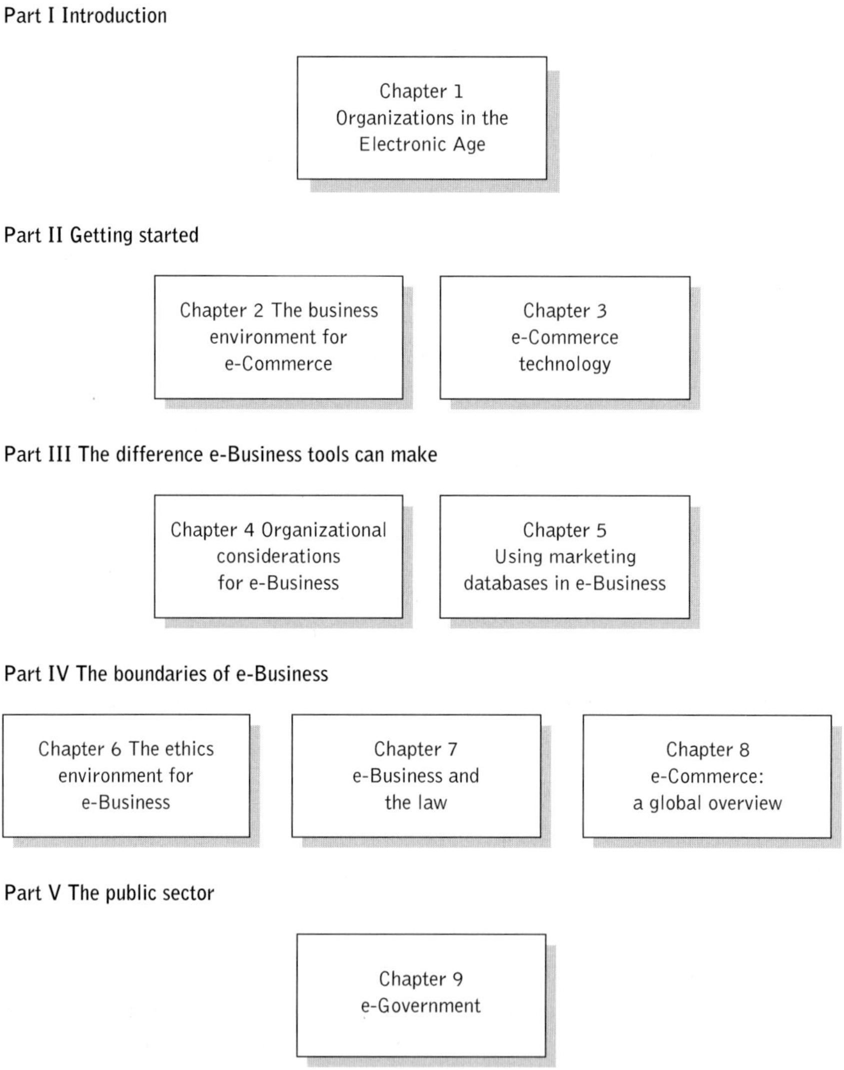

Part I Introduction

> Chapter 1
> Organizations in the
> Electronic Age

Part II Getting started

> Chapter 2 The business
> environment for
> e-Commerce

> Chapter 3
> e-Commerce
> technology

Part III The difference e-Business tools can make

> Chapter 4 Organizational
> considerations
> for e-Business

> Chapter 5
> Using marketing
> databases in e-Business

Part IV The boundaries of e-Business

> Chapter 6 The ethics
> environment for
> e-Business

> Chapter 7
> e-Business and
> the law

> Chapter 8
> e-Commerce:
> a global overview

Part V The public sector

> Chapter 9
> e-Government

Figure 1.1 *Structure of this volume*

twentieth century. The chapter outlines some of the technology that has made e-Commerce possible, whilst cautioning that technology cannot overcome a number of older obstacles (such as transport costs). It also highlights other difficulties, for example low Internet access levels in the developing world and the World Wide Web's (WWW) complicated governance structure.

Although e-Commerce's original economic drivers (the desire to break out of traditional market places) remain, Budd and Clear remind us that many people (a large number of stockbrokers as well as companies) got their fingers burnt during the late 1990s Internet 'bubble'. As they argue, the Internet is a very useful medium through which one can conduct business and social transactions and disseminate information, but it has not heralded the arrival of a 'new economy' in the true sense of the term.

Chapter 3, 'e-Commerce technology' by Nandish Patel, provides a useful introduction to how the Internet and World Wide Web can be used to facilitate e-Commerce transactions. It traces the development of the technologies that make up the Internet and World Wide Web, and explains much of the terminology that sometimes acts as a deterrent to those people and organizations that would otherwise embrace them.

Patel goes on to explain how these technologies complement each other to create an architecture that enables online trading. Other tools, such as databases and evaluation software, are able to improve the customer's experience of e-Commerce. Although concern still exists over the security of some transactions, the chapter outlines some of the methods available to prevent unauthorized parties accessing customers' data and credit card details. It finishes by outlining how newer technologies, such as eXtensible Mark-up Language (XML), will benefit e-Businesses in future.

Chapter 4, 'Organizational considerations for e-Business' by Lisa Harris and Nelarine Cornelius, traces the development of traditional personnel responsibilities into modern strategic Human Resource Management (HRM). The authors argue that this must now also be updated to be relevant for e-Businesses. 'e-HRM' is necessary because of the extra communication, IT, customer service and networking skills that e-Business demands, as well as the recruitment and retention problems that many companies encounter. Harris and Cornelius address the extent to which 'clicks and mortar' organizations (large, traditional companies which have introduced e-Business methods) have adopted e-HRM, as well as global 'dotcom' corporations.

In a similar way, new marketing techniques must also be developed to respond to modern business methods. New forms of communication and information dissemination, such as Internets and intranets, have radically altered external and internal marketing strategies. Increasingly, organizations initiate contact with potential clients *on*line and then seek to form longer-term 'relationships' with them *off*line, rather than view them as one-off customers. This approach

7

requires strong internal branding, because organizations must maintain their image in all forms of communication, and for a much longer time than previously. The chapter concludes by outlining some of the barriers to introducing e-Business practices in traditional organizations.

Chapter 5, 'Using marketing databases in e-Business' by Michael Collins, emphasizes the importance of databases to e-Commerce and traditional ways of doing business. It explains how organizations can acquire different types of data from primary or secondary sources, and advises on ways to ensure that the information is of good quality. He also warns of potential data decay (between 8 per cent and 10 per cent of the UK population move home or die every year) and recommends methods of appraisal to ensure that the information held by organizations is up-to-date and relevant. This last point also has legal implications for all organizations under the Data Protection Act.

The chapter then addresses data manipulation and analysis tools, including storage mechanisms like warehousing or marting and other techniques such as mining or campaign management, which interpret the data in a way that is more useful to marketers. Companies are now able to use their databases to improve the customer experience, by providing the 'front office' with extensive information about their profile and previous experiences with the organization. This also puts them in a much better position to reach their target customers in marketing campaigns.

Chapter 6, 'The ethics environment for e-Business' by Laura Spence, points out that global e-Business recognizes few legal boundaries, leaving ethics as the most useful guide for determining the behaviour of organizations involved in the 'new economy'. The chapter suggests useful tools that transcend traditional business ideas of profit maximization and explains how ethical guidance can be applied to individual and organizational behaviour in the electronic age. She describes how approaches such as ethical egoism, utilitarianism, Kantianism, discourse ethics theory and virtue theory can provide decision makers with a more rounded and sustainable perspective.

New technology introduces many different ethical issues into business activities: one notable advantage is the removal of potentially prejudicial barriers through electronic (rather than face-to-face) communications. However, it also enables other, more controversial, behaviour, such as increased monitoring of customers, competitors and employees, often without their express consent. The law is unclear on this and many other issues, such as data ownership and the personal use of ICT in work time. Such lack of clarity serves to highlight the need for a detailed, professional code of conduct or computer use policy in order to maintain mutual trust in employer–employee, business–customer and business–business relationships.

Chapter 7, 'e-Business and the law' by Dave Wadsworth, examines the combination of cross-border agreements, UK legislation and case law that forms the legal framework of e-Business transactions and Internet behaviour. Echoing

Spence's point about the problems caused by the Web not recognizing traditional legal boundaries, he outlines some of the battle lines between anarchic Netizens and states attempting to jealously guard their jurisdictions. This conflict has encouraged states to reach a number of international agreements, which form the basis of governance in cyberspace. Wadsworth goes on to describe the various pieces of legislation that inform criminal or civil prosecutions and protect citizens' privacy under English law, and the chapter also addresses issues of copyright, trade marks and patents.

Although much of the relevant legislation and case law dates from before the technological revolution, the chapter illustrates how the Internet has led to new problems with these old issues. When compared with traditional ways of conducting transactions, business–client relationships in e-Business can be far more complex, subject as they are to outside interference by third parties such as hackers, cyber-squatters or Internet service providers. Web posting allows individuals to broadcast information to far more people than was previously possible, leading to increased claims of defamation, for example. This chapter charts the law's success in trying to keep abreast of these developments and questions where the line should be drawn between respecting the anonymity of the Internet and protecting the rights of individuals and organizations that may be targeted as a result.

Chapter 8, 'e-Commerce: a global overview' by Geraldine Cohen, looks at how new technology has transformed business practice in recent years, benefiting from and accelerating the process of 'globalization'. As domestic markets have become saturated, large businesses have tried to expand into other countries, eventually becoming 'multinational' or even 'transnational' companies, and the Internet enables them to reach potential consumers all over the world. However, Cohen points out that e-Commerce is not limited to these corporations, since the Web is the perfect market place for selling 'niche' commodities, which may have numerically limited but geographically disparate customers. Her chapter addresses a number of important issues for organizations wishing to enter the realm of international e-Commerce.

First, they have to ensure they get the balance right between specialist, country (or even regional) specific marketing, and standardized, general, brand-based approaches. Although two-thirds of the Web is in English, less than half of all Internet users have English as their mother tongue. This is likely to have significant implications for anglophone companies attempting to sell in other countries, since online translation facilities are notoriously bad and consumers are unlikely to buy something if they do not know exactly what it is. Cohen also highlights other problems that need to be addressed, such as payment methods, exchange rates, distribution and legislative differences across boundaries. As her chapter shows, e-Commerce has evolved in different ways across the world, reflecting local diversity.

9

Finally, Chapter 9, 'e-Government' by Noah Curthoys, Peter Eckersley and Paul Jackson, begins with an overview of the e-Government concept and traces its development in the United Kingdom. They explain the difference between e-Govern*ment* (essentially using ICT to improve the delivery of public services) and e-Govern*ance* (how technology can change the way important decisions are made by enabling better engagement with stakeholders, greater transparency and more democratic legitimacy). The British government has been the most important driver of change within local authorities, the health, police and fire services, as well as its own central departments. Developments in Germany, Sweden and the United States have followed similar patterns and are also discussed.

In particular, the chapter addresses some of the problems and issues that e-Government practitioners must tackle in order to reap its full benefits. These include managing the change from traditional to modern working practices and 'joining up' service delivery across and between agencies, involving both public bodies and private partners. This often requires the sharing of databases and personal information, and the use of 'entitlement cards' to enable easier access to services. Such issues lead in turn to ethical issues about privacy and 'ownership' of data and accusations of a 'Big Brother' state.

REFERENCES

Chaffey, D. (2002) *e-Business and e-Commerce Management*, London: Prentice Hall/ Financial Times.

Harris, L. (2002) 'History, Definitions and Frameworks', in L. Harris and C. Dennis, *Marketing the e-Business*, London: Routledge.

 WEB LINKS

www.dti.gov.uk/insight_information_age.html

www.ukonlineforbusiness.gov.uk

www.ipf.co.uk/egov

Part II

Getting started

Chapter 2

The business environment for e-Commerce

LESLIE BUDD AND FINTAN CLEAR

KEY LEARNING POINTS

After completing this chapter you will have an understanding of:

- The similarities and differences between e-Commerce and traditional business practices
- Various e-Commerce models
- The history and basic technology behind the Internet and World Wide Web
- The extent to which business transactions are Internet-based
- The importance of potential barriers to the growth of e-Commerce

ORDERED LIST OF SUB TOPICS

- Definitions and models
- The technical environment for e-Commerce
- Trust and governance: who governs the Internet?
- Measuring e-Commerce
- Drivers and barriers for e-Commerce take-up
  - Drivers
  - Barriers
- e-Commerce policy
- New business models?
  - Problems of valuing companies
  - Defining frameworks and models
- Conclusion

By the middle of 2001 the business revolution promised by the 'new economy' and the functions of the Internet had come to naught. The promise of a new business model based on e-Commerce or e-Business (as the term has been used interchangeably) failed to deliver as the dotcom phenomenon imploded into that of the dot-bomb. Simon Caulkin, management correspondent for the *Observer*, described it as follows:

> So, farewell then death of the business cycle, the end of inflation and above all the myth of the New Economy: slain by revisions to US figures that show that, far from lifting the economy permanently to the sunny uplands of unending productivity growth, the great Internet binge has given us levels of improvement that haven't been seen since, er, the 1930s.
>
> (Caulkin 2001)

This quotation brings to mind the cultural revolution promised by punk in the mid-1970s. According to the then manager of the infamous Sex Pistols, Malcolm McClaren, punk would sweep away all hitherto popular culture into the dustbin of history as it represented a new Situationist adventure.[1] In reality, punk was a speeded-up version of good old rock 'n' roll and ironically corresponds to the Pistols' most famous album, *Never Mind the Bollocks*. Similarly, the Internet, instead of promising a business revolution, speeds up the rate of transactions rather than their primary nature. *Never Mind the Bollocks* seems to be making a comeback, nearly thirty years on, but in a different guise.

Where did it all go wrong? Why hasn't the move 'from capitalism to knowledge society', as in the essay title by the management theorist Peter Drucker, become our everyday reality? According to Drucker (1993), economic history can be divided into three eras:

- The *industrial revolution*. From the late eighteenth century onwards, knowledge was applied to tools, processes and products.
- The *productivity revolution*. From 1880 until World War II knowledge was applied to work.
- The *management revolution*. From World War II onwards, knowledge applied to knowledge itself.

For Drucker, we now effectively live in a 'knowledge society'. For other contemporary theorists we inhabit 'the information society' in which the 'spirit of informationalism' drives all economic and social transactions (Castells 1996). There are concepts derived from the same root: the 'weightless economy' (Coyle 1997), the 'thin economy' and the 'weightless society' (Leadbeater 1999) and the 'death of distance' (Cairncross 1998). The factor common to all these conceptions is the role of technology. In fact, all these accounts can be said to be technologically determinist. That is, it is the technology that is transforming economy and society, rather than the business processes to which technology is put to use. In Drucker's account, technology and the invention of calculating machines, in particular the computer, are central to the progress of society through the three revolutions outlined above. Traditional factors of production – land, capital and labour – have become secondary to knowledge. As long as there is specialized knowledge these factors can be obtained. In this view, company transactions become weightless. For example, the value of Coca-cola is tied not to the value of production of a fizzy drink, but the power the brand exercises in the market place.

A more salutary account is given by Robert Schiller in his book *Irrational Exuberance* on stock market volatility (Schiller 2000). He compares the building of the interstate highway system in the United States between 1956 and 1976 and the Internet as innovations. He argues that the Internet is 'notable for its visibility and vividness, and not unprecedented prospects for promoting economic growth and profits' (2000: xxiv). The interstate and Internet are both network innovations. The former transformed the economic geography of the United States, promoting lower transport costs, greater market access, outward mobility into the suburbs and the rise of the local shopping mall. Schiller notes that while the Internet offers a wider selection and a greater ability to search, the delivery of goods is not immediate. Consequently, Internet marketing may not be superior to the marketing of the conventional shopping malls.

The Internet remains part of the long march of creating innovations, but like all technology it is the nature of human inventiveness that makes them beneficial. The period of building the interstate system coincides with an annual average 1.6 per cent growth in real earnings on the Standard & Poor's 500 index of the financial performance of the top 500 US companies. Despite the enormous impact of the interstate on the economic geography of the United States why were these earnings not higher? The answer according to Schiller was that the interstate system was just another innovation along the path of inventiveness. Similarly, evidence from McKinsey & Co., the international consultancy, shows that the impact of new technology, including the Internet, on productivity in the United States in the late 1990s was much less than was believed at the time (McKinsey 2001).

The relationship between technological change, economic growth, increased productivity and profits is much more complex and indirect than the easy direct relationship suggested by some popular commentators. In the past decade the service sector has been in the forefront of investment in new technologies in the advanced economies. The benefits of these investments, however, have been decidedly uncertain:

Over the past decade senior managers in banking, insurance, health care, and other services have invested billions of dollars in computers and

15

communications equipment – technology investments that promise to hone operations into an acute competitive weapon. But executives have been deluded: the payoffs have not been fully realised . . .

The primary reason is that technology alone does not determine corporate performance and profitability. Employee skills and capabilities play a large role, as do the structure of day-to-day operations and the company's policies and procedures. In addition, the organisation must be flexible enough to respond to an increasingly dynamic environment. And products must meet customer requirements.

(Hackett 1994: 21)

These observations act as a health warning to the business environment for e-Commerce. This warning is not posted to suggest that Internet-based trans-actions will fail to deliver *material* benefits to producers and consumers alike. Rather, they act to signpost the difficulties associated with claims that we now live in a new business, economic and social order. This chapter attempts to explain the context in which e-Commerce has developed and the difficulty faced by companies that believe the Internet is the universal solution to all business problems. Furthermore, the chapter seeks to navigate the reader through the complex issues that arise from the development of e-Commerce as a business model.

The structure of this chapter is as follows. First, we examine some defini-tions and models of e-Commerce, and highlight some of the problems that exist to derive an adequate taxonomy for this emerging area. Next comes an examination of the technological underpinnings of the Internet, and its child, the Web. Following this assessment comes a discussion of issues of trust and governance associated with the Internet, and the fact that there is consider-able disquiet in some quarters on leadership. A brief examination of how to measure the Internet economy is followed by an identification of the drivers and barriers to e-Commerce take-up. We conclude by looking at some of the issues that have arisen from the implosion of the dotcom phenomena into the dot-bomb outcome. By doing so, we suggest that the business environment for e-Commerce has not destroyed the possibilities of a new economy, but is one in which the realities of the business cycle and the role of technological innovation are reasserted. In the next section we look at models and definitions of e-Commerce.

DEFINITIONS AND MODELS

There are many definitions of e-Commerce, but they all imply some manner of electronic mediation for business transactions. The UK Department of Trade and Industry (DTI) defines e-Commerce as:

The exchange of information across electronic networks, at any stage in the supply chain, whether within an organisation, between businesses, between businesses and consumers, or between the public and private sectors, whether paid or unpaid.

(HMSO 1999)

Though the word *commerce* carries with it a sense of activities being undertaken for payment, this definition gives the term *e-Commerce* a broad informational scope to also include activities for which no direct payment is made within a supply chain. A supply chain describes the distribution of goods, services and information flows between market participants within or between industries. For example, a vehicle manufacturer is at the heart of a variety of supply chains, including parts, raw materials, services, etc., supplied to it by other firms. The optimal management of a supply chain reduces transaction costs. As a result, the competitive advantage of the vehicle manufacturer is enhanced. This explains why many prefer the term *e-Business* rather than *e-Commerce* to describe such electronically mediated activities. The DTI definition does not just place the scope of e-Commerce as being Internet- or Web-mediated, but includes electronically mediated activities undertaken outside the Internet and/or which pre-date the Internet.

Earlier forms of e-Commerce, prior to the term being coined, include Electronic Data Interchange (EDI). This is the exchange of information by trading partners, for example orders, using technically defined templates whose origins go back to 1969. The succeeding decades have seen many large corporations taking up EDI based on value-added networks. Value added is the process whereby each successive stage of production adds more value than the previous stage. Examples include private sector organizations such as IBM and GEIS (part of the US giant General Electric). Another major sphere is that of Electronic Funds Transfer (EFT) through which the banking system facilitates financial settlements. Prominent amongst EFT systems is SWIFT (Society for Worldwide Interbank Financial Telecommunication), which has handled international inter-bank settlements since the 1960s. The BACS system is one such that handles inter-bank settlement for the UK banking sector. Finally other industries have created their own forms of EDI such as the airline reservation system, SABRE.

There is a distinct difference between the Internet and these other forms of electronic transactions:

- The Internet uses protocols that are *open* and *non-proprietary*. That is, these protocols are published so that theoretically any user can use them to hook up to the Internet
- EDI systems are *closed* or *proprietary* systems, which are open only to paying participants.

17

The fact that systems are closed means a greater guarantee of security for all transactors. Open systems are by definition open to potential fraudulent activity. So though the economic transactions may be alluring, the potential threat to the integrity of global payment systems is too great at present for the major international banks to shift towards Web-enabled systems. One of the major challenges to examining, analysing and explaining the business environment for e-Commerce is the confusion of terms. Perhaps more importantly, the lack of appropriate models by which to examine, analyse and explain it inhibits clarity of thought and interpretation. One possible solution is offered by the taxonomy set out in Figure 2.1.

Central to any market transaction, whether in a geographical or virtual location, is the exchange of information. In a market economy, prices signal information about transactions between consumers and producers and between producers themselves. The equivalent in e-Commerce is Business-to-Consumers (B2C) and Business-to-Business (B2B). The advantage of e-Commerce to consumers is greater access to fuller information on prices of goods and services. The advantage to producers is they can directly access a greater market potential for their goods and services.

However, e-Commerce does not overcome the problem of transaction costs (particularly transport costs) and immediacy in purchasing goods and services at

TO:	B2C	C2C
Consumer	*Organizational sites* (Dell, Amazon) *Consumer market places* (Kelkoo.com, Shopsmart.com)	*Auctions* (QXL, Ebay) *Consumer reviews* (Bizarre.com)
	B2B	**C2B**
Business	*Organizational sites* (Dell) *Business market places* (CommerceOne, VerticalNet)	*Customer bids* (LetsBuyit.com, PriceLine.com)
FROM:	Business	Consumer

Figure 2.1 *Taxonomy of transactions between businesses and consumers*
Source: Chaffey (2002)

18

designated locations, although it may reduce search costs in some general instances and shift them from producers to consumers in others. Essentially, e-Commerce does not alter the nature of exchange and transactions in a market economy.

Moreover, given the relatively low level of Internet commerce in most advanced economies, the heroic assumption that the Internet is now the universal market transactor is not vindicated by evidence. Given the United States had first-mover advantage, and the size of its economy (which is only slightly less than the whole of the European Union), it may come as no surprise that e-Commerce revenue in the United States in 2000 was twenty-three times that of the United Kingdom, thirty-three times that of France and seventeen times that of Germany. The ratio of B2B to B2C for the same year in the United Kingdom, France and Germany was 7.04, 7.06 and 7.09 respectively, compared with 7.07 for the United States (Connectis 2001). If one looks at the contribution of total e-Commerce to national income, measured by Gross Domestic Product (GDP), the results do not stand up to many of the hyped claims. These figures are given in Table 2.1.

Notwithstanding the rise and then fall in e-Commerce revenues in 2000 and 2001, and allowing for the size of the US economy, e-Commerce represents a small proportion of all economic transactions. The essential issue is that the dominant virtual medium is television and is likely to remain so for a long time, so that adaptations of this technology to the demands of e-Commerce are more likely to generate longer-term benefits and greater market access. There is also a tendency to conflate goods and services that can be downloaded via a modem, for example software and music, with more physical goods that have to be delivered to the home or pick-up point. In other words, there is as much variability in e-Commerce transactions as there is in conventional ones.

Examples of B2C include Amazon.com, the on-line retailer of books, music and games. Amazon started achieving profitability ($5 million) only in the last quarter of 2001 after having invested $3 billion in its short life, much of which has been spent establishing itself as an on-line brand and creating a fulfilment system. The disadvantage for many B2C companies dealing in tangible goods is the lack of a distribution system that is reliable and economically efficient. These firms to date have difficulty obtaining the economies of scale and scope[2] derived by large retail outlets in conventional shopping malls.

Table 2.1 *e-Commerce revenue as a percentage of GDP, 2000 (%)*

UK	France	Germany	USA
0.62	0.41	0.57	2.36

Source: Connectis (2001).

Much of B2B activity is associated with the operation and management of supply chains. Advances in information and communications technology (ICT) have facilitated the development of real-time supply chains, that is, orders for goods and services that are activated immediately. For example, the Ford Motor Company had proposed to link its suppliers of car parts to Ford's production sites through their Web sites so that adjustments in demand for parts could occur instantaneously. However, rather like Just-in-Time (JIT) inventory systems, instantaneous delivery of large items of inventory from anywhere in the globe was not realizable owing to size and cost restraints. The technology does speed up the turnover time of production through instant receipt and processing of orders. What these changes produce is an electronic continuum along which supply chains find themselves in terms of the two types of flow:

- Those which use electronic mediation to organize their supply chains, but whose tangible goods require physical transportation, and whose payment is handled using traditional inter-company means.
- Products whose entire supply chain can be mediated by electronic means, in terms of product, payment and its mediation. So digital artefacts, for example computer programs can be developed, and then searched for, ordered, invoiced, paid for and delivered to customers using wholly electronic means.

Chaffey's taxonomy includes other less well cited e-Commerce models such as C2C and C2B. Consumer-to-Consumer (C2C) implies the sale of goods and services between individuals, often via auction sites such as eBay. Consumer-to-Business (C2B) implies individuals selling goods and services to companies. Examples include the sale of cars by individuals to companies. Conceptually in these cases, it is difficult to define who is the consumer and who is the producer. By definition, a consumer does not sell. Such models persist even though the semantic irregularities demand otherwise, partly because no better descriptions currently exist, and that these are part of marketing strategies and ploys by particular companies.

A more concrete model is Business-to-Public Institution, or, more commonly in the United Kingdom, Business-to-Government (B2G). This relates to the trade in goods and services between the private sector and the different forms of government, whether local, regional or national. This particular description is gaining greater resonance as governments in the advanced economies seek to promote the concept of e-Government (see Chapter 9 of this volume). A final model is the User-to-User or Peer-to-Peer, which is styled P2P. This implies a relationship between two individuals that is electronically mediated but not via any central body. Freenet is an example of a network that promotes the digital exchange of music artefacts on a P2P basis.

THE TECHNICAL ENVIRONMENT FOR e-COMMERCE

Many of the claims for a significant break with the past stem from the more sceptical accounts of post-industrialism and the information-based economy, for example by the sociologist Daniel Bell. Other more enthusiastic and technologically determinist accounts include those of the futurologist Alvin Toffler, who coined the phrase 'Third Wave' to imply an impending information revolution. What they share is the prediction and formulation of the concept of an 'information society'. The problem for commentators like Bell and Toffler (in common with almost everybody else) was an inability to predict the physical agency that would bring the 'information society' to fruition. This agency was the Internet.

The Internet began life in 1969 as a demonstration project linking up four university campuses in the United States. It showed how a primitive file-sharing system worked. Today the Internet boasts in excess of 300 million users, offering the most rapid take-up of any technology in history. For a relatively small outlay on a computer, a suitable telecommunications link (e.g. via a phone line and modem) and an on-line account provided by an internet service provider, individuals located across the globe can access this massive network which has grown at an exponential rate. The network – the Internet – hooks up the physical infrastructure of computers via cable and wireless links so that users can access rich informational sources (e.g. via the Web) and use interactive forms of communication (e.g. e-mail). However, though the population of Internet users across the globe has grown exponentially, their dispersal is not uniform internationally. According to Figure 2.2 (which notes Internet hosts *per capita*), the relative density of hosts across the globe is variable. It may be unsurprising to note that the higher concentrations of users are in North America and Europe.

Levels of computers and data services can be shown by measuring Internet access. Network Wizards provide a longitudinal study of the growth of Internet nodes (computers with unique 'Internet Protocol' (IP) addresses) from the network's earliest days. Growth between 1980 and 1987 shows numbers of hosts in the tens of thousands. After 1987, when the US funding body NSF (National Science Foundation) started to work with the Internet, the growth leapt into the hundreds of thousands: many non-US academic sites and scientific and research bodies linked up at this point. The next pulse of acceleration of this growth came when the World Wide Web appeared in 1990. Rapid growth rates ensued, especially after 1993, when the graphical browser called Mosaic appeared, and the scale of change moved into the millions. From an almost unknown medium at the beginning of the 1990s, the Internet by the year 2000 was heading for 100 million *hosts* (i.e. unique computers linked up) across the world. Gartzen (2001) estimates that in broad terms the number of users is due to grow from around 300 million in 2001 to around 1 billion in 2005.

In addition to these *fixed* hosts that link individual desktop computers to the Internet there will be *mobile* hosts linking up mobile phones to it using wireless

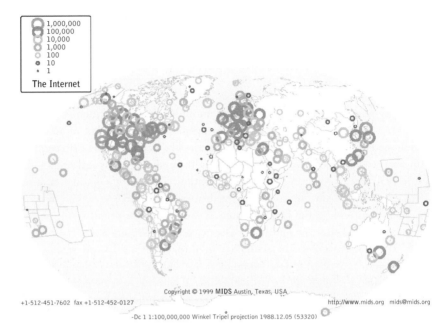

Figure 2.2 *Relative global densities of Internet hosts in July 1999*
Source: Matrix Maps Quarterly (1999), copyright © 1999 MIDS, Austin TX

technology. In predictions offered in May 2001, phones labelled as 'Third Generation' (3G) in Gartzen's 'ball park' are due to amount to 1 billion by 2005. This potential rapidity of the Internet's growth creates problems for its continued deployment, as discussed below. Notwithstanding the assumptions underlying these forecasts, even the current global downturn does not detract from the problems associated with the growth of Internet usage. This issue will become sharper if the 'digital divide' is not overcome. That is, between countries that are hardly wired, as in the developing world, and those with maturing virtual infrastructure, for example in the advanced economies.

As the next chapter demonstrates, the Internet – an *inter*connected series of *net*works – began life as a project supported by the US Department of Defense's Advanced Research Project Agency (ARPA). Based on an original concept (the use of a multi-nodal network) developed by the Rand Corporation in the early 1960s and added to by bodies such as the UK National Physical Laboratory (which had developed packet switching ideas), the objective of the research was to provide the United States with a communications network that would survive in the event of a nuclear conflagration. This product of the Cold War was a network purposely designed to offer resilience during a hot war of massive destruction such that it would continue to function whilst 'in tatters'.

Up to this time, network paradigms had offered a central node by which messages could be routed (on a circuit-switched basis). A paradigm is defined as a set of theories, concepts, methodologies and practices usually associated with particular forms of knowledge. For example, the natural sciences and social sciences have complementary but sometimes opposing paradigms. So the implication was that if this one central node were to be destroyed, then communications on a continent-wide US basis would have been impossible. In order to circumvent such an emergency, the need was established for a network whose technical architecture was based on multiple nodes, and whose messages could be distributed as packets of data. As long as every computer linked to the network could be uniquely identified, then messages broken up into packets (each with a header detailing message destination and source) could be routed across the network via diverse nodes and could be reassembled at the destination computer. In-built system resilience meant that if elements of a message were not present for reassembly (identified through gaps in packet sequences), an automatic request would be generated for retransmission. The events of 11 September demonstrated the robust nature of the Internet: where fixed and mobile telephony failed to function in parts of Manhattan after the deadly attacks on the World Trade Center, e-mail continued to get through.

One notable feature of the Internet's tremendous growth is based on the fact that core software elements were given away by suppliers for free. Mosaic – the first graphical browser – was distributed via the Internet and magazine CD-ROMs to all who wanted to use it at no charge. Its authors (who worked at a university department in Illinois) received no royalties for this work. In the same manner, the underlying software operating system of the Internet – TCP/IP – was also available free to anybody who could hook up to the Internet. TCP/IP is a set of protocols or technical definitions, developed by Vinton Cerf, which, when rolled out across a number of networks in 1983, allowed their inter-linkage and the coining of the term 'Internet'. TCP (Transfer Control Protocol) and IP (Internet Protocol) handle packet disassembly/reassembly and computer addressing respectively.

Central to the development of the Internet is the root democracy. The ARPAnet was developed for operation under cataclysmic conditions. Whatever remnant nodes that existed on a network were required to function. One way of helping to maximize success was to keep any processing tasks as simple as possible. So once the interrogation of a packet's destination is adduced, a routing computer does little more than pass it on. At root, therefore, the Internet evinces 'packet switching democracy': all packets are equal under TCP/IP. In the event of a network disruption, therefore, all packets would be delayed equally.

This inherent lack of packet prioritization has significance for any time-critical or contiguous operations, and thus the efficacy of the Internet can be called into question, not least by commercial interests. This treatment of message packets is defined by the IP protocol in its fourth version (known as IPv4). Though a new version, IPv6, allows packet prioritization, it is not yet pervasive. For some commercial interests, delay in introducing this prioritization will be significant, and ultimately have an impact on the growth of e-Commerce.

While TCP/IP has provided the 'glue' of the Internet, until 1993 it was mainly the preserve of a 'high priesthood' of academics and scientists who used detailed knowledge of protocols to exploit Internet applications. Only with the emergence of the World Wide Web – or 'the Web' – did individuals with little knowledge of such protocols manage to participate in this electronic medium. Initially the Web was text-based only.

The relative simplicity with which new users can hook up to the Internet, given telecoms access, has meant its vast and dispersed take-up, such that demand peaks can lead to network congestion and the so-called 'World Wide Wait'. Innate human perception of delays in response times means that 'waiting' for more than a second can be intolerable for some. Nevertheless, the response of suppliers has not been slow, as the vast investments in Internet connectivity make clear. However, the very success that the Internet enjoyed in its rapid take-up led to so much conceptual and financial hyperbole during the late 1990s that speculative activities intended to reap vast profits from vast investments reaped vast losses instead.

On so much technical configuration does human response lie. If nothing else, the dotcom crash had the effect of sharpening the eye for the detail of the Internet's case. In a fundamental degree that case is shaped by technical protocols. Where once the examination of such arcane documents may have been the preserve of technical departments, now they are examined in boardrooms. Many are aware that technical protocols govern the way they undertake business, and that tiny changes to protocols, for example, can have disproportionate effects on business prospects. The ability to influence the technical standards of Internet technologies is therefore to permit some control over financial destinies.

TRUST AND GOVERNANCE: WHO GOVERNS THE INTERNET?

Trust and governance are seen as key concepts in the contemporary business environment. Trust is crucial in businesses that act as intermediaries. For example, when we write or receive a cheque, we take it on trust that the intermediary between the issuer and the recipient of the cheque will honour the payment. In this case, the intermediary is a commercial bank. Similarly, when we buy goods or a service via the Internet, we take it on trust that the goods or service will be delivered at the price quoted. *Governance* is a slippery concept that has become current in a number of fields. Essentially, governance refers to the manner in which activities are governed through a set of institutions, practices and procedures. For example, corporate governance refers to the way in which companies are governed in respect of fulfilling obligations to the various stakeholders. Governance will often include legal obligations, but can be distinguished from *government*, which is the formal organization of legally binding functions operated on the behalf of a population, be it local, regional or national. Government includes legally imposed regulations, practices and procedures.

The governance of the Web and the Internet started from the view that it should be a universally available and free resource. However, as the Internet has developed, there is an implication that its governance will shift towards more formal regulation as large corporations come to dominate its activities. No single entity owns the Internet or is wholly responsible for its functioning. It is a decentralized network, whose operation is influenced by a number of bodies and forces, not least large commercial interests such as Cisco and Microsoft which help drive ICT standards and innovation in the market place itself, and as members or otherwise of the various bodies.

Between 1987 and 1995, however, one of the most dominant influences on the Internet and Web was the US National Science Foundation (NSF), which subsidized its use, along with scientific and academic institutions that paid for servers and created Web content. The ethos underpinning the Internet at this point was one of not-for-profit, and the lack of packet prioritization underpinned an essentially democratic spirit amongst its user communities.

However, with the 'Boucher amendment' of 1992 the US Congress permitted this not-for-profit medium to extend its remit to include for-profit activity. This had an impact in 1995 when the publicly funded NSFNET (whose 'charter' precluded direct commercial activity) withdrew from network backbone responsibilities in the United States to be replaced by private and commercial funding. In the same year Netscape, which had launched its Navigator browser the previous year, sought share capital through an Initial Public Offering (IPO) and staggered the markets with a 'Day 1' capitalization in excess of $2 billion. It is the year 1995 therefore that can claim to be the birth date of e-Commerce – at least in popular imagination – and from this point the rapid colonization of the network by commercial interests began.

The operation of the Internet in hardware and software terms is based on technical standards produced by a plethora of bodies. Telecommunication standards and other technical specifications have been set by the International Telegraphic Union (ITU) and OSI (representing the French for 'International Standards Organization') for a number of decades. Principal among the bodies that have a prescribed influence on the development of the Internet and the Web are IETF, W3C and ICANN.

The IETF (Internet Engineering Task Force) was created in 1986 to be responsible for drawing up the technical standards for the Internet and comes under the aegis of the Internet Society (ISOC) – created in 1992 – which assumes overall responsibility for the organization of its development. The World Wide Web Consortium (W3C) focuses on the development of the Web (a subset of the Internet) and was created in 1994. It is chaired by the Web's original creator, Tim Berners-Lee. The Internet Corporation for Assigned Names and Numbers (ICANN), created in 1998, controls the accreditation of domain name registrars that undertake the business of registering Web sites. Decisions made by these bodies determine how Internet and WWW operations take place, and by definition what products and/or services are to be successful in the market.

Indicative of the self-view of these organizations is a statement from ICANN:

> ICANN has no statutory or other governmental power: its authority is entirely a consequence of voluntary contracts and compliance with its consensus policies by the global Internet community. It has no power to force any individual or entity to do anything; its 'authority' is nothing more than the reflection of the willingness of the members of the Internet community to use ICANN as a consensus development vehicle.
>
> (ICANN 1999)

Other than in their own terms, no major legal statutes charter these bodies or determine their membership or procedures. ISOC, IETF, ICANN and W3C are bodies that determine their own existence, their own charters and their own procedures, and tend to have memberships composed of established figures in the Internet world, whether from academia or from industry. The claimed ethos of these groups is to further the development of the Internet on the basis of consensus.

ICANN, however, has attracted conflicting views since its incorporation in 1998, when it took responsibility for the Domain Name System (DNS), IP address space allocation and the Internet root server. The significance of this is highlighted by David Post, who observes:

> Any entity responsible for, and exercising control over, the root server databases possesses immense power over the future development of the Internet itself, and will, accordingly, be subject to immense pressure to act in ways that may be contrary to the best interests of the Internet community as a whole. Devising ways to prevent arbitrary, oppressive, or self-interested actions by this entity is a task of deep, of truly constitutional importance to that community.
>
> (Quoted in Mueller 1999)

Whilst the technology creates the physical mechanism by which the Internet functions, the determining of domain names (e.g. www.abc.com) along with their unique numerical identities (e.g. 234.5678.901.234) gives ICANN the power to create definitive and addressable electronic spaces, central to the establishment of Internet and Web entities. Without them commercial enterprises would be unable to establish any Web presence.

The issue of trust and governance is central to the business environment for e-Commerce. From a system of governance that was essentially self-regulating we are moving towards a market structure in which a few large firms are starting to dominate. From economic theory, this is akin to market structures that are oligopolistic – markets dominated by a few large firms that formally or informally collude – and monopolistic – markets dominated by one large firm. Despite the low cost of entering Internet-based markets, the resources and infrastructure needed to sustain larger volumes of business suggest that firm size and market consolidation in the form of mergers and take-overs will become characteristic features. In this scenario, some form of government regulatory intervention is inevitable – the admirable roots of the Web as a free resource then being undermined by the imperative of avoiding monopolistic dominance of the Web and the Internet by large corporations.

The other side of the regulatory governance coin is trust. Given that the Internet establishes a new set of intermediaries between consumers and producers, producers and producers, trust is essential for sustaining the basis of e-Commerce and e-Business. Consumers can inspect, check and then buy goods at their local mall at a given price instantaneously, whereas there is the virtual intermediary of purchasing on the Internet and the physical intermediary of getting goods delivered. There is also the issue of credit and payment card security, which at present is higher in conventional shopping outlets. The beauty of the Internet for the consumer is that it reduces search costs. One can search various outlets to compare the availability and prices of goods and then visit one local mall to purchase them. Similarly, for producers, transaction costs are transferred to the consumer as the latter provides details of preferences, tastes and prices he or she is willing to pay, thereby allowing producers to identify their markets more clearly. The issue of trust and governance is thus central to developments in the business environment for e-Commerce as the Internet and other media, particularly television, are increasingly adapted for B2B and B2C transactions.

MEASURING e-COMMERCE

Measuring the value of electronically mediated business has become an important activity in its own right. Fraught with difficulty, it is one which has to date produced wide divergences in terms of predictions, many of them prepared by those with a material interest in promoting e-Commerce and e-Business. It is also one where the danger of double counting is most frequently encountered. One source of data is the University of Texas at Austin, where Barua et al. identify four levels of the 'Internet economy', as shown in Table 2.2.

Table 2.2 *Estimated revenues and jobs in the Internet economy, 1999*

Internet layer	Estimated revenue ($million)	Attributed jobs
Infrastructure	114,983	372,462
Applications	56,278	230,629
Intermediary	58,240	252,473
Commerce	101,893	481,990
Economy total	301,393	1,203,799

Source: Adapted from Barua *et al.* (1998).

- *Layer 1: The Internet infrastructure layer.* This includes trade in products and services that provide for the electronic infrastructure. It encompasses Internet backbone providers (e.g. Nortel Networks), Internet service providers (e.g. AOL), networking hardware and software (e.g. Cisco), PC and server manufacturers (e.g. Dell), security vendors (e.g. Norton) and fibre optic manufacturers (e.g. Corning).
- *Layer 2: The Internet applications layer.* This includes products and services that build upon the infrastructure layer and make it technologically feasible to undertake business activities online. Categories include all software applications such as browser and server software (e.g. Netscape, Microsoft), multimedia (e.g. Macromedia), Web building (e.g. Adobe), search engines (e.g. Google), databases (e.g. Oracle), on-line training (e.g. Assymetrix, ilearn.to) and consultancy (e.g. Scient).
- *Layer 3: The Internet intermediary layer.* Internet intermediaries seek to increase the efficiency of electronic markets by facilitating the meeting of buyers and sellers and their interaction. Categories include Web portals (e.g. Yahoo), brokerages (e.g. Schwab), content aggregators (e.g. ZDNet), market makers (e.g. IFX) and online advertising brokers (e.g. Doubleclick).
- *Layer 4: The Internet commerce layer.* This layer concentrates on Web-based commerce transactions. It includes the new 'e-tailers' (e.g. Amazon.com), manufacturers (e.g. Dell), fee/subscription-based providers (e.g. Forrester) and online entertainment (e.g. AOL Time Warner) and professional services (e.g. KPMG).

This is a useful approach to measuring the Internet economy. The difficulty is untangling what is attributable to the 'new economy' and what is attributable to the 'old economy'. In fact, this example is as problematic as trying to separate out manufacturing from services: a common mistake among politicians and journalists.

28

There is also the problem of double counting. In national income accounting, each successive stage of production adds value to the previous stage. For example, coal is mined and then sold to make steel. Steel is made from the combination of coal, iron ore and lime. Steel is used in the production of, say, beams for buildings, which are manufactured and then sold to construction companies to be used in buildings which are then sold or leased to clients. At each stage in the production value is added. The value of the coal, iron ore and lime is added to the net increase in value of the steel, what it is sold at less the cost of the material inputs. The value of the steel beams less the cost of the steel inputs is then added and finally the value of the buildings less the cost of the steel beams is added to produce final national income made up of the value added at each production stage. This method avoids double counting and it is this kind of approach that should be used in measuring the value of the Internet economy, notwithstanding the general problem of disentangling conventional economic transactions from those associated with the Internet.

Although the taxonomy of Table 2.2 is a useful way to think about measuring the 'Internet economy', Table 2.1 provides the necessary corrective. It shows that the contribution of B2B and B2C to national income was very small in 1999, just before the peak of the so-called productivity miracle in the United States. The significant slowdown from the end of 2000 and subsequent recession in the United States, the fall-out from dot-bomb phenomena and events after 11 September 2001 show that the brave new world of the virtual economy was as susceptible to the business cycle and political shocks as the so-called old economy. In the words of Public Enemy, the US rap band, 'Don't believe the hype.' In the next section we return to the problem of measurement in examining the absurd market valuations given to many dotcom companies.

DRIVERS AND BARRIERS FOR e-COMMERCE TAKE-UP

Drivers

The principal driver for the take up of e-Commerce is economic. If we accept what corporate forecasters such as Forrester and IDC predict, then more than 80 per cent of the growth of electronically mediated trade in the period 1999–2004 will be via B2B e-Commerce. At root, this take-up is driven by transaction costs. As an example, banks feel that the cost of processing a financial transaction via the Web can be as little as 1 per cent of that performed at a branch using traditional paper methods. So once fixed costs such as equipment and telecommunication lines are found, the marginal cost of servicing transactions on the Web can be very low.

For a relatively small outlay, companies and individuals can hook up to the Web and access sites that are dispersed across the globe. This fact has contributed to an explosion of infrastructural and service provision on the Internet and prompted many commentators to enthuse about the potential it holds for the traditional economics of location. Frances Cairncross (1998), for example, asserts that the communications revolution removes geographical boundaries to trade. 'No longer will location be key to most business decisions. Companies will locate any screen-based activity anywhere on the Earth, wherever they can find the best bargain of skills and productivity.'

However, though the Internet can facilitate market growth for individual companies, commentators point to more complex factors at work in terms of location. Pratt cites New York's 'Silicon Alley' as a cluster of software developers that could locate in a disaggregated manner if they wished but choose to retain close physical proximity. Whatever the reasons for this and the nature of the particular business function, it suggests that commentators such as Cairncross are ignoring the potential value of social interaction and informal face-to-face networks that clustering might imply. In the case of the City of London, Europe's largest financial centre, large international financial institutions, law and accounting firms and business services providers seek to locate in close proximity.

The underlying logic is associated with external versions of economies of scale and scope. That is, the ability to explore large and different transactions in the same place (Parr and Budd 2000). Other key factors are the ability to easily recruit specialist labour, access to informational and transport infrastructure and, perhaps more important, the development and sustaining of a powerful innovation environment in which new financial products are developed. Richard Sennett, the American sociologist, has pointed out that in an apparently global era, the leading international economic and business activities are still crowding into the world's major cities (Sennett 2000). Whatever the claims made for an imagined virtual future, place still matters to business and society.

The cost of computing power has declined over the past thirty years to such an extent that claims are made that the power of the multi-million-dollar mainframes supporting the Apollo mission to the moon at the end of the 1960s can now be contained within a desktop computer costing less than $1,000. The precipitous increase in the power of 'microchips' has followed a pattern first predicted by Gordon Moore, a co-founder of Intel, in 1965. 'Moore's law' reckoned that the power of chips would double at intervals of every eighteen months to two years.

The effect has been that, in relative terms, the cost of ICT is now so low and its power so great that companies have little financial reason to avoid taking up Web-mediated business if they so wish. Once installed, all that a user needs is an account with an Internet service provider (ISP). At the height of the dotcom boom, there were hundreds of ISPs on the UK market offering access to the Internet, and pricing reflected their relative quality of service.

Case study:
FREESERVE

In 1998, at a point when dotcom valuations were accelerating wildly, the radical new pricing formula – *it's free!* – was extended into the UK ISP market when *Freeserve* (www.freeserve.com) launched. Owned by Dixon's, a large UK multiple retailer group that sold PCs amongst other items, it got very large market penetration quickly when it launched in September. A number of other UK ISPs quickly followed suit. Though Freeserve were effectively subsidizing the cost of user access, their rationale for this was linked with the value of a subscriber base to which they could direct advertising and to act as leverage with retailers wishing to gain privileged access to it. User surveys have consistently pointed to the high proportion of individuals with large disposable incomes amongst those with Internet access. Nevertheless, its rapid growth did appear to justify faith in the 'digital revolution', and the 'Follow the free!' mantra that had been espoused by writers such as the editor of *Wired* the year before (Kelly 1997). Freeserve gained a membership in excess of 2 million in a matter of months. This rapid take-up seemed to reflect a kind of 'network fever' in which all that appeared to matter was to get a club of Internet users up and running a.s.a.p. Whether this network fever and associated activities could be sustained in a declining economic environment seems to have been answered by subsequent events.

Globalization and competition

Globalization has engendered as much debate about the new economy. For some, it represents a cleavage with the past (Leadbeater 2000; Giddens and Hutton 2000). For others, the hype does not measure up to the reality and is merely a different version of the past, this difference being due almost entirely to the evolution of information and communications technology (ICT) and the subsequent speeding up of economic transactions (Hirst and Thompson 1996; Boyer and Drache 1996; Drache 2001). Leaving aside the influences that pervade under the notion of 'global culture', economic globalization can be defined in the following way:

- The development of and access to markets, the organization of production, corporate decision making and consumer strategies on a global scale.
- Capital markets operating through electronic media twenty-four hours a day.

31

- The development of transnational corporations (TNCs) in which there is significant foreign ownership and whose board of directors has a large proportion of foreign members.

The reality is a little more mundane. The world appears to be made up of three large economic blocs, the Americas, Europe and East Asia, each accounting for around a third of the world's income, and the United States, Germany and Japan being the largest constituent national economies. If one looks at a mapping of Internet traffic, its volume and frequency tend to mirror telephone and airline traffic, the largest amounts being between the three largest economic blocs. Large parts of Asia, Africa, Latin America and Eastern Europe are bypassed. For these regions of the world, the 'digital divide' is more appropriate than the 'digital revolution'. It also suggests that the world's economy is characterized more by regionalism than by globalization (Albert 1993; Thurow 1993).

What has afforded a more global perspective is the manner in which ICT developments, deregulation and liberalization have opened new markets and productions sites around the world. The general level of production costs has been lowered, and increased international take-overs and mergers by large corporations have generated large economies of scale and scope. As a result, there has been a tendency towards the over-supply of goods, partly rendering a low inflationary environment and a much more intensively competitive environment. In such an environment, new modes of market access with the possibility of lower transaction costs, such as the Internet, have been beneficial to firms' international strategic position, at least in the short term. The key issue for international firms' strategies is still the development of new business models arising from the development of technology rather than market change being driven by the technology itself. Like the proclamations of the new economy, globalization is long on promise and short on delivery.

Political imperatives

The political imperatives that both drive and arise from the prospect of the Internet economy are relatively easy to understand. Political cycles and the longevity of politicians' careers tend to rest on achieving economic growth and full employment. Any prospect of short-cutting the achievement of these twin goals, for example by the evolution of the new or Internet economy, is often greeted with quasi-religious fervour. By also embracing the ideology of globalization the political elites can escape blame for any of the local social costs, whilst taking credit for the creation of local benefits in the form of inward investment, employment creation, innovation generation and so on.

Added to these aspects is the development of e-Government in which many of the public administration's operations could be transferred to online media.

In the United Kingdom, the government has set up the Office of the e-Envoy to encourage and develop e-Government activities. In the United States, the federal government's Office of Commerce has undertaken similar activities. In the European Union, politicians and business proponents have been arguing for the speeding up of further telecoms liberalization so that high-speed Internet access is provided directly to small and medium-size enterprises (SMEs) and individual subscribers. An EU summit held at Lisbon in March 2000 created an over-ambitious timetable when Member States demanded that incumbent telcos should allow access to rival service providers from 1 January 2001. Incumbent telcos have been laggard in this. At the same summit, the UK Prime Minister, Tony Blair, boasted of the United Kingdom becoming the leading knowledge economy in the European Union by the end of the decade.

Apart from these examples, governments in general in the advanced economies account for about 40 per cent of national income. They are large purchasers of private goods and services, invest heavily in infrastructure and information systems and employ large numbers of people. They also initiate and underwrite big technology research and innovation programmes and projects under the rubric of building and sustaining the knowledge economy. Therefore, the political imperative driving the Internet economy is both concrete and abstract.

Barriers

Access

Physically, before users can begin to address linking up to access the Internet via an internet service provider they must have a telephone line (or some other kind of communications link). In many economies, telecoms provision has increased significantly as the result of deregulatory policies that have seen competition introduced into telecom markets. Once physical connectivity is possible, you can begin to exchange electronic communications across a global network by virtue of an account with an ISP. Initial ISP hook-ups provided speeds of data transfer of nine kilobits per second (kbps) – or 9k – but successive jumps via 14k and 28k generations have seen the establishment of a 56k standard.

Computers work at a digital granularity with all messages and their modes of communication (text, audio, still and moving images) being decomposed into streams of noughts and ones. The telephone system though was originally designed for voice. So, for data transfer to take place, computers were obliged to communicate via the network using sound. Thus the 56k modem converts a digital signal from the computer (composed of noughts and ones) into an analogue signal – sound – for delivery along the telephone system as a stream of sounds of two discrete pitches. The fact that further modem standards have not been developed is indicative of the apparent physical limit of 'acoustic coupling'.

33

While the demands of asynchronous communications such as e-mail, on-line chat and simple Web pages can be accommodated satisfactorily within 56k, such data transfer rates are not sufficient for synchronous communications such as video-conferencing or 'video on demand'. Thus wholly digital transfer technologies such as ISDN (128k) and ADSL (from 500k) have come into focus and are seen as the means of opening up multimedia – and hence e-Commerce – delivery to domestic premises and small firms. Such bandwidth had only been available to large companies using leased lines before this.

Though deregulation of telecoms markets had seen the development of digital communications in trunk networks, their extension to the 'last mile' of telecom networks (i.e. from local exchange to domestic or small firm premises) occurred only in the late 1990s. For competition to prevail, two physical developments must occur. At the exchange the physical unbundling of copper wires is required. This 'unbundling the local loop' allows digital equipment to be hooked up to individual lines by alternative telecom providers. At the domestic or small firm premises, the installation of a digital adaptor is required.

However, political imperative has not led to the desired opening up of the local loop market, with ex-monopolist telcos such as BT and France Télécom failing to act with the speed the regulators envisaged. As a result, high-speed services are not as prevalent as proponents of e-Commerce desired. With 20:20 hindsight, it seems clear that incumbent telcos would not vote for reductions in their revenue streams with gusto. In the United States, however, where unbundling began in the mid-1990s, the liberalized telephony and data services regime was to allow regional telcos to enter long-distance markets and permit long-distance telcos to enter the local loop market, so long as access could be gained to individual subscribers by any service provider. Purton (2001) observes that while US service providers were allowed to enter each other's markets in exchange for giving up exclusive service provision in their own markets, in the European market there had been no such *quid quo pro*.

Further comparison of US *v*. European markets shows that in the United States, subscribers pay a flat fee to their telecoms provider for line rental. After paying this fixed cost, there are no further charges for calls using local exchanges. In Europe, on the other hand, local market practice saw the establishment of per-minute charging on local networks from the 1960s onwards. There is an impact on Internet use of 'unmetering' and 'metering'. Metering inhibits Internet use owing to the ongoing financial penalty of maintaining a presence on a line. An unmetered approach promotes potential Internet use owing to a user's indifference to the quantity of time spent maintaining a presence on a line – at least in financial terms.

Technical problems

The Internet protocol IPv4 was not designed either to handle very large numbers of unique addresses or the different levels of 'Quality of Service' (QoS) that different forms of media and hence e-Commerce require. The Internet has become a victim of its own success, and it is assumed that all IPv4 addresses will be exhausted by the 2005–11 period (Pouffary 2001) if predictions about the total number of devices that will be attached become true. This includes extra fixed links such as printers, cookers and fridges and mobile links including 3G phones, vehicles, ships and planes. Whereas businesses with the necessary resources can avoid traffic problems on the public switched telephone network by leasing telecom lines to guarantee QoS levels, the Internet works on a 'one size fits all' approach. Mathy *et al.* (2000) note that it was originally designed primarily to move files between computers. For this there were no strict time requirements – termed *elastic* – and a 'best effort service' was adequate for the task of delivering e-mail and Web pages. However, applications such as video-conferencing are much more demanding and require on-demand, guaranteed and immediate delivery of data packets. These have *inelastic* service requirements, and imply a more complex set of service quality attributes than IPv4 can offer. IPv6 has been designed, however, to allow service discrimination, and data packets are forwarded depending on their prioritization.

e-COMMERCE POLICY

There are bodies at international, regional and national levels that seek to promote the take-up of e-Commerce. The principal international bodies come under the auspices of the United Nations and include the World Trade Organization (WTO), the World Intellectual Property Organization (WIPO) and the United Nations Committee for International Trade and Law (UNCITRAL). This latter body has drawn up the UNCITRAL Model Law for Electronic Commerce that supports the commercial use of international contracts in e-Commerce, and offers technical advice to governments on this. The Model Law creates rules and norms validating the practice of electronic commerce, seeks to make electronic documents and signatures legal and supports the admission of electronic evidence into court proceedings and arbitration.

At a European level, the European Union has drawn up a number of directives that aim to provide a legal framework for e-Commerce within the European Union. The member countries are obliged to follow these directives by creating new legislation in order to harmonize the legislative framework across the single market. These directives include:

- *The Electronic Signatures Directive.* This defines the requirements for electronic signatures and their certification in order to ensure a minimum level of security in e-Commerce dealings. The United Kingdom passed the Electronic Communications Act in 2000 that amended in the region of 300 laws so that any reference to documents, writing and signatures

35

would now include their electronic equivalents. However, to get this Act through Parliament, the UK government was obliged to remove controversial provisions on encryption keys. Public Key Cryptography has both public and private keys that allow the encryption and decryption of data and is seen as critical in the provision of secure e-Commerce transactions.

- *The Conditional Access Services Directive.* This aims to safeguard against the unauthorized use of conditional access services, and to make illegal, for example, technology that allows decryption of satellite television services when no contract exists with a service provider.

- *The Data Protection Directive.* This seeks to harmonize the rights of individuals and the obligations placed on organizations with regard to the use of 'personal data' gathered in e-Commerce activities. Additionally a prohibition was created on the export of such data to organizations in countries without similar provision. A potential problem that would have seen much of the trade between the European Union and the United States being deemed illegal was averted by use of a 'Safe Harbor Agreement' which sought to bring some level of accommodation in data protection terms between the two bodies. The United States places greater emphasis on the 'freedom of information' in its legislative framework and this comes into conflict with a European focus on the right of an individual to relative privacy. The United Kingdom's 1998 Data Protection Act updated the 1984 Act of the same name in line with this.

- *The Misleading Advertising Directive.* This seeks to prohibit the use of advertising on EU Web sites that is either misleading or likely to mislead consumers.

- *The Distance Selling Directive.* This seeks to protect those buying products or services on the Internet within the European Union, and to provide seven day 'cooling off periods' during which consumers may choose to withdraw from agreed transactions. The directive does not apply to financial services or a number of product types and services such as auctions or short-life products. In October 2000 this directive was mirrored in the United Kingdom when the Consumer Protection (Distance Selling) Regulations Act was brought into force.

Chapter 7 of this volume discusses the legal environment for e-Business in further detail.

NEW BUSINESS MODELS?

Problems of valuing companies

One of the popular confusions of e-Commerce is the valuation problem, that is, the proper valuation of companies on stock markets. The hype surrounding the arrival of the dotcom phenomenon and the development of e-Commerce led to extraordinary claims that the laws of economics had been overthrown. Moreover, that the business cycle itself had been abolished. In this new world, perfectly competitive markets would ensue the lowest 'just prices'.[3] The realities are market structures dominated by oligopolists and monopolists as stated above. The real concern at the height of the dotcom phenomenon was the accounting conventions that distorted the market value of companies. This can be seen in Table 2.3.

The US Internet system provider Cisco Systems was the largest company in the world, by stock market valuation, compared with the 'old economy' companies General Electric and Exxon Mobil in March 2000. This valuation appears to be seriously out of line with turnover and net income as shown in Table 2.3. Similarly, in the United Kingdom, Lastminute.com was floated on the London stock exchange at a value of £350 million in February 2000, on cumulative revenues of £1 million from its establishment in April 1998 (Kay 2001). The start of the fall of the House of e-Usher began in 2001 when Amazon the on-line bookseller's market capitalization fell from £22.8 billion in March 2000 to $3.7 billion exactly one year later.

The logic of these valuations partly came from the supposed benefits of networks being natural monopolies and Metcalfe's law that the value of a network rises in proportion to the square of the number of agents connected to it (*ibid.*). The reality, as described above, was a little more straightforward. It did lead, however, to a conceptual challenge to conventional accounting principles. For believers in the new economy, these principles were inappropriate to the new world order. As Kay nicely puts it:

> Arthur Miller's description of the witch-hunt in *The Crucible* is a forceful demonstration of the mechanisms by which misinformation can be spread.

Table 2.3 Market capitalizations at March 2000 ($ billion)

Company	Turnover	Net income	Market capitalization at Cisco peak (27 March 2000)	Market capitalization (27 March 2001)
Cisco Systems	19	3	548	132
General Electric	130	13	520	416
Exxon Mobil	233	18	266	280

Source: Kay (2001).

Note: Market capitalization measures the price of shares and stocks multiplied by the number on offer in stock markets.

Insistence that non-believers pose a threat to believers imposes an irresistible pressure for conformity which enforces belief throughout a population.

(Kay 2001: 67)

Defining frameworks and models

The Web does offer a new medium by which vendors can bring their goods and services to the market. Though there are many accounts that describe the business models evident on the Web, there are no definitive and wholly consistent frameworks. Some base their definitions on revenue streams, a sub-set that includes advertising, subscription, pay-per-view and transaction (and combinations thereof). Amazon, for example, sells books on which it makes revenue per book sold, and also carries advertising, generally for complementary products and services. Thus if you were to buy a travel book, for example, you might also be linked to holiday companies that offer trips to the book's destination.

Others define models by function. One comprehensive taxonomy is provided by Paul Timmers, who, whilst focusing on B2B e-Commerce, cites eleven different business models. These are *not* mutually exclusive, and through them, he argues, a further set of marketing models can be pursued. The majority of these models, he asserts, are not inherent innovations but merely manifestations of business models existing in the 'off-line' world. Thus an 'e-shop' is merely a shop that uses electronic means of marketing. However, by contrasting degree of innovation with level of functional integration Timmers highlights models that would be unfeasible without the level of electronic mediation offered by the Internet and World Wide Web. These include 'Value-chain integrators', which are 'critically dependent on information technology for letting information flow across networks and creating added value from integrating these information flows' (Timmers 2000: 41–2) and other models such as 'third-party market places', 'collaboration platforms' and 'virtual business communities'.

The promise of a new business model, held out by B2C, has not lived up to expectations. Expectations of the much larger B2B sector as a set of new and large profitable opportunities remain unfulfilled. Many standardized financial products were traded profitably in real time by electronic media before Internet access. In developing new business models based upon Internet access, recognition has to be made of where and how appropriate is the medium for transactions in certain goods and services.

For computer manufacturers like Dell, the Internet provides a very good global marketing application. Similarly, for businesses like low-cost airlines, the transaction costs advantages of Internet transactions are imperative. There are now greater possibilities for e-Learning as a new business model, as universities and other education providers around the world develop strategic alliances with international publishing companies and telcos. It opens up the prospect of their buildings and facilities becoming twenty-four-hour assets. However, strategic alliances are notoriously unstable and believing that technology of itself will transform the education world and the learning environment is riven with the same dangers experienced by the disciples of the dotcom hype. It is management and product innovation, and the delivering technology, that will be the basis of new business models in e-Commerce and not the technology itself.

CONCLUSION

The business revolution underpinning the development of e-Commerce has failed. True believers in the new economy may hold on to the clarion call of 'Long live the revolution!' Like most reality, things are a little more mundane. The Internet is here to stay as a medium for business and social transactions, but not the basis of a new economy in itself. At the end of the 1990s commentators in the United States observed that permanently and miraculously higher levels of productivity driven by Internet transactions had not occurred. The productivity miracle has now turned into a mirage, a point made frequently by economists like Robert Solow and Robert Gordon. The problem is not the technology itself but the proclamations that have been made for each new epochal invention. As Gordon puts it:

> Much less has been said about telecommunications and biotechnology . . . Like many benefits of the 'New Economy', biotech research may boost consumer welfare without having any measurable impact on productivity. But this is an old story – great inventions like electricity and the internal combustion engine delivered unparalleled increases in consumer welfare in the early and mid 20th century as electric light lengthened the day . . . The fruits of innovation in telecom and biotech are wondrous to behold and partly unmeasured, and exactly the same could be said with even greater emphasis of all the great inventions dating back to the dawn of the first industrial revolution in the late 18th century.
>
> (Gordon 2001: 47)

Despite Peter Drucker's optimism, we still have not moved from capitalism to the knowledge economy. The Internet is a wondrous invention but it does not mean that the business model of e-Commerce is global or universal. It holds out prospects of new ways of doing business and enhancing consumer welfare like the great inventions of the past. The difficulty is, as Simon Caulkin reminds us:

> The New Economy was a gigantic computer-aided pyramid scheme, sustainable only as long as the illusion lasted that computers did anything genuinely new. They did a few things, of course, but mostly just existing ones faster or differently . . . Where at the height of the Internet boom, Cisco and Sun could

see no end to the demand for yet more IT from eager dotcoms, now they find themselves in competition with their own second-hand boxes. Let's mark their second half-century by putting computers in their place – under the desk, not on it, as servants, not masters.

(Caulkin 2001)

The business environment for e-Commerce may look less promising in the global recessionary environment as the new century moves into the middle of its first decade. However, if the lessons of the failure of the new economy to mature, the dotcom to dot-bomb implosion and the stock madness are learned, then the Internet and associated media may be part of new business models. This will depend on getting the direction of causality. Three and a half centuries after the claim that supply creates its own demand was first falsely mooted, technology does not create its own business model. This is the fundamental lesson to be derived from the business environment for e-Commerce.

CHAPTER SUMMARY

The chapter has provided a wide-ranging examination of the environment in which e-Commerce has developed, taking in some of the political, economic, legislative and technological underpinnings of the commercial exploitation of the Internet. It has critiqued among other aspects the drivers and inhibitors of the adoption of e-Commerce, the complex issues that arise from the development of new business models, and the role of a series of technical and standards institutions that govern its development. One body, ICANN, which acts as the senior registrar of cyberspace 'real estate', attracts the bile of a number of commentators, who regard its apparent altruism as a sham, pointing to the latent veto of the US Department of Commerce as the true source of commercial governance of the Internet. The chapter has exposed some of the myths that surround the growth and use of this globally dispersed information medium, and concluded that, though the Internet is here to stay, it is ultimately only a technology.

NOTES

1 Situationism was a European art/philosophical/political movement that peaked during the May 1968 Paris student rising. Key ideas include: ruthless critiques of everyday life and experience; opposition to what leading Situationist Guy Debord labelled 'spectacular economies'; hostility to parties, leaders and most organizations;

militant hatred of art establishments. The best-known figure is Guy Debord, whose ideas are exemplified in *Society of the Spectacle.* The manner in which the Internet revolution has been promoted can be seen in the light of 'the spectacle'.

2 Economies of scale refer to the benefits of increased output from a stable cost base. That is, as the output of a firm increases, the cost of producing each successive unit of output decreases. For example, if an airline put a larger aircraft on a route, the unit cost of each seat would decrease, as the same costs, crew salaries, fuel, etc., are being spread over more passengers. Economies of scope refer to the ability to produce more than one good or service simultaneously from the same location. For example, an investment bank buys and sells shares, bonds, foreign exchange and provides corporate finance advice, all under one roof. It can switch between these activities without incurring any extra costs.

3 'Just prices' refer to the prices that should pertain at competitive market equilibrium. In other words, they are determined by the interaction of consumers and producers without the distortion of monopoly power on the producer side and lack of full information on the consumer side.

BIBLIOGRAPHY

Albert, M. (1993) *Capitalism against Capitalism,* London: Whurr.

Barua, A., Pinnell, J., Shutter, J. and Whinston, A. *Measuring the Internet Economy: An Exploratory Study.* Online. Available HTTP: www.crec.bus.utexas.edu (accessed July 2002).

Boyer, R. and Drache, D. (eds) (1996) *States against Markets: the Limits of Globalization,* London: Routledge.

Cairncross, F. (1998) *The Death of Distance,* London: Orion.

Castells, M. (1996) *The Rise of the Network Society,* Oxford: Blackwell.

Caulkin, S. (2001) 'A bubble we need to burst', *Observer,* 19 August.

Chaffey, D. (2002) *E-business and E-commerce Management,* London: Pearson.

Connectis (2001) 'e-Commerce Revenues', *London Financial Times,* 20 June.

Coyle, D. (1997) *The Weightless World: Thriving in the Digital Age,* London: Capstone.

CPSR (1999) *Governing the Commons: The Future of Global Internet Administration,* conference held by Computer Professionals for Social Responsibility, 24–5 September 1999, Alexandria VA. Online. Available HTTP: www.cpsr.org/conferences/dns99/dnsconf99.htm.

Drache, D. (ed.) (2001) *The Market or the Public Domain: Global Governance and the Asymmetry of Power,* London: Routledge.

Drucker, P. (1993) 'From capitalism to knowledge society' in P. Drucker (ed.) *Post-capitalist Society,* New York: Harper.

Gartzen, P. (2001) 'B2B e-Commerce: Issues, Impacts and Evolution', paper presented at 'e-Business for Industry 2001' conference at Earl's Court, London, 5–6 June.

Gordon, R. (2001) 'Technology and Economic Performance in the American economy', Department of Economics Research Paper, Evanston IL: Northwestern University.

Hackett, G. (1994) 'Investment in technology: the service sector sinkhole?' in D. Wield and E. Rhodes (eds) *Implementing New Technologies,* Oxford: Blackwell.

Hirst, P. and Thompson, G. (1996) *Globalization in Question,* Cambridge: Polity Press.

Hutton, W. and Giddens, A. (eds) (2000) *On the Edge: Living with Global Capitalism,* London: Cape.

ICANN (1999) *Background.* Online. Available HTTP: www.icann.org/general/back ground.htm#2 (accessed 16 July 1999).

IPv6 Forum (2001) Global IPv6 Summit, Fairmont Chateau Laurier, Ottawa, 15–16 May.

Kay, J. (2001) 'What became of the new economy?' *National Institute Economic Review,* 177: 56–69.

Kelly, K. (1997) 'New rules for the new economy', *Wired.* Online. Available HTTP: www.wired.com/etc (accessed July 2002).

Leadbeater, C. (2000) *Living on Thin Air,* London: Viking.

Mathy, L., Edwards, C. and Hutchison, D. (2000) 'The Internet: a global telecommunications solution?' *IEEE Network Magazine,* 14, 4: 46–57.

Matrix Maps Quarterly (MMQ) *603: State of the Internet.* Online. Available HTTP: www.mids.org/mmq/603/pub/ii.pop.w.799.sm.c.html (accessed July 1999).

McKinsey Global Institute (2001) *US Productivity Growth, 1995–2000,* New York: McKinsey & Co.

Mueller, M. (1999) 'Commentary: ICANN and Internet regulation', *Communications of the ACM,* 42, 6: 41–3.

Parr, J. and Budd, L. (2000) 'Financial services and the urban hierarchy: an exploration', *Urban Studies,* 37, 3: 593–610.

Performance and Innovation Unit, UK Cabinet Office (1999) *e-Commerce@its.best.uk,* London: HMSO.

Pouffary, Y. (2001) 'IPv6 Advantages', presented at 'Global IPv6 Summit', Seoul, 3–6 July.

Pratt, A. (2000) 'New media, the new economy and new spaces', *Geoforum,* 31: 425–36.

Purton, P. (2001) ' "Trench Warfare" in the European battle to free the last mile', *Financial Times* 'Telecoms' section, 17 January.

Schiller, R. (2000) *Irrational Exuberance,* Princeton NJ: Princeton University Press.

Sennet, R. (2000) 'Street and office: two sources of identity' in W. Hutton and A. Giddens (eds) *On the Edge: Living with Global Capitalism,* London: Cape.

Thurow, L. (1993) *Head to Heads: the coming Economic Battle among Japan, Europe and America,* London: Brearly.

Timmers, P. (1999) *Electronic Commerce: Strategies and Models for Business-to-business Trading,* Chichester: Wiley.

UNCTAD (2000) *Building Confidence: Electronic Commerce and Development.* Online. Available HTTP: www.unctad.org/ecommerce/docs/building.pdf (accessed October 2002).

Chapter 3

e-Commerce technology

NANDISH V. PATEL

KEY LEARNING POINTS

After completing this chapter you will have an understanding of:

■ The Internet and World Wide Web technology that enables e-Commerce
■ The difference between the Internet and the World Wide Web
■ The main elements of an e-Commerce system architecture
■ e-Commerce security technology for confidentiality and payments

ORDERED LIST OF SUB TOPICS

■ The Internet and the World Wide Web
■ Internet and World Wide Web technologies
■ Architecture of e-Commerce systems
■ Future developments in e-Business technology
■ Conclusion

e-Commerce uses the Internet and the World Wide Web technologies. This chapter will cover the evolution of the Internet and World Wide Web to their present state and provide details of the current state of those technologies that enable e-Commerce. These include digital networks and their protocols, which form the basic system technologies required to develop an e-Commerce system, and the client–server architecture and World Wide Web in particular.

As the basis of commerce is transactions between buyers and sellers (whether the exchange of goods for money or the passing of data and information between parties), e-Commerce requires interactive digital technology that can facilitate transactions over the Internet. Consequently, the chapter also introduces inter-active technologies such as JavaScript and methods of exchanging data between systems. It also looks at how the Internet, World Wide Web and interactive technologies need to be configured to enable electronic commerce that is secure. Finally, current developments in Internet and World Wide Web technology are considered in terms of their future impact on e-Commerce.

THE INTERNET AND THE WORLD WIDE WEB

Prior to the Internet, World Wide Web and its associated technologies, the impact of technology for the purposes of business transactions had been peripheral. The Internet and the World Wide Web have fundamentally changed commerce. Commerce's basic mode of communication, written and verbal communication between a business and its customer or business and its suppliers or partners, remained unchanged since Adam Smith's first observations on economic markets. Electronic communication, in the form of digital mainframe computers and microcomputers (personal computers) connected to the Internet, has radically transformed commercial activity for customers and businesses alike. The transformation has been so fundamental that new terms such as 'e-Commerce', 'e-Business', 'e-Markets' and the 'new e-Economy' are freely used to describe the modern phenomenon of Internet-based commercial activity. e-Commerce may be described as the sharing of product and service information, developing and maintaining human commercial relationships, and transacting business over the Internet and the World Wide Web.

Technologies such as telephony have influenced business activity in the past, but their influence has not been revolutionary. Such technologies have not funda-mentally changed how businesses organize themselves and how they interact with their customers, suppliers or partners. In contrast, the Internet and the World Wide Web have revolutionized business activity. The aim of this chapter is to provide an overview of the information technology (IT) and Internet tech-nology used to develop e-Commerce systems. The chapter: (1) provides an introductory description of the current IT, Internet and World Wide Web tech-nology underpinning e-Commerce; (2) comments on its implications for business and e-Commerce; and (3) explores potential future developments in Internet and World Wide Web technology that will affect e-Commerce.

This introductory reading on e-Commerce technology should enable you to describe Internet and World Wide Web technology to enable e-Commerce. Critically, the reading should enable you to state and understand the main elements of an e-Commerce system architecture and assess e-Commerce secu-rity technology for confidentiality and payments.

Memex

The Internet's evolution has encompassed over fifty years of technological and conceptual development. The original concept of the Internet is attributed to Vannevar Bush. He worked in a team of engineers during World War II in the United States. His experience of working in an expert team of scientists led him to think about the problem of processing and sharing information among the team. His solution was the invention of a machine called Memex (MEMory EXtension). He envisaged that Memex would work like the human brain, which finds information by association. His ideas provided the conceptual framework for subsequent work on developing the technology of the Internet and World Wide Web.

ARPAnet

The Internet began in 1969 as a communications medium project of the US Department of Defense, and its associated academic and research agencies. It needed a network of computers to enable collaborative work among the different agencies. In its original form, the Internet consisted of a decentralized digital network that connected defence, research and academic mainframe computers. This network was called the ARPAnet after the agency that led the project, the department's Advanced Research Projects Agency (ARPA). The purpose of the ARPAnet was to connect various government and related computers, and in the event of disaster or war to preserve the integrity of information passing between these important government agencies. ARPAnet was privatized in 1990, and as it was gradually released to the public domain it began to be transformed into the Internet that we know today.

The World Wide Web

Around the same time, Tim Berners-Lee, a research scientist working at the European CERN physics lab in Switzerland, conceived the World Wide Web and released it to the public domain in 1991. The problem that Tim Berners-Lee faced was how to share research knowledge among scientists who used different brands of computers and associated software at CERN. He developed the method of hypertext link for connecting information stored on different computers. In his words, his motive for inventing the Web was: 'I realised that if everyone had the same information as me, my life would be easier.'

The original idea for linking electronic documents was Ted Nelson's. He coined the term 'hypertext' in the early 1960s. Marc Andreessen developed the first graphical browser for the Internet. It enabled people seeking information on the Internet to find it quickly and efficiently.

45

A major effect of the Internet and the Web over the 1990s was to enable executives and business strategists to develop new ways of doing business electronically. These new electronic approaches are termed e-Commerce 'business models'. Business models that combine the use of the Internet and Web technologies with fundamental business transformation are referred to as 'e-Business'. The term e-Business is used to describe a business that shares its production or service information with customers and business suppliers or partners, fosters the development of customer relationships electronically, and enables business to be transacted from personal computers or other electronic devices, such as mobile phones or personal digital assistants (PDAs). One of the most successful e-Commerce business models is the US company Dell Computers. It has a $14 million per day Internet-based revenue stream, or a quarter of its total revenue. Though a survey by NOP in 1999 revealed that only 15 per cent of the companies surveyed used the Internet for making online sales, Gartner Research predict that 97.5 million US users will adopt e-billing and online account management by 2005.

ACTIVITY

Identify reasons why the Internet might not have been as popular as it is today without the invention of the World Wide Web. *Answer* The Internet is a command-based system. It does not have a graphical user interface. The Web has a graphical user interface that makes it user-friendly. The Web has also made it easier to author and transfer information over the Internet using hypertext and hypermedia.

Surf www.w3c.org for details of current developments in the Web.

INTERNET AND WORLD WIDE WEB TECHNOLOGIES

The microcomputer or Personal Computer (PC) forms the basis of e-Commerce. The Internet would not have the wide reach that it has into peoples' homes in the absence of the PC. Most office PCs are linked to a computer network and PCs at home are connected to the Internet via modems or dedicated data transfer cables.

Local area networks and wide area networks

PCs on local area networks (LANs) and wide area networks (WANs) are connected to the Internet. LANs and WANs are digital computer networks that connect PCs to enable sharing of information between separate computers. LANs are limited to a geographical area such as an office, whereas WANs connect computers over a wider geographical area. The computers on a LAN or WAN share information in the form of addressed packets of data. The capacity of a single computer is increased by connecting it to a LAN or WAN, as it can share computer programs and information. A computer that is linked to a network can download and use computer programs and share storage and printing facilities, and take advantage of network capabilities for sending and receiving data and information.

Client–server architecture

A computer on a LAN or WAN that provides resources like application programs or printer connections is known as a 'server'. A server provides other computers known as 'clients' on the LAN or WAN with software and other resources. This set-up is called client–server computing architecture. A server that is linked to the Internet is called a 'host computer'. A server computer is capable of running server software, which needs to be compatible with the network operating system. The client and server are independent and perform specialized tasks to process information and run computer applications. If you use Microsoft Word on your computer, the client, it is probable that a server will have provided the Microsoft Word software for you to use. The client–server architecture is the basis of the Internet too.

The Internet and protocols

The Internet is the sum total connection of LANs, WANs and stand-alone computers around the world. The term 'Internet' is short for 'inter-networking' or an interconnected set of networks. It is the global network of computers, whether the computer is on a LAN in an office, or a WAN in an industry extranet, or an independent computer in a private home. An Internet-connected computer is known as an Internet host computer. The Internet is also known as the 'Net', the 'Information superhighway' or 'Cyberspace'.

The set of rules for moving information over the Internet is called a 'protocol'. The transmission control protocol (TCP) is used for sending large amounts of information between host computers on the Internet. Vinton Cerf wrote the basic ideas for TCP on the back of an envelope over lunch, and in 1983 the core protocols of the Internet transmission control protocol/Internet protocol (TCP/IP) became the standard protocol for transmitting information over the Internet.

Intranet

An intranet consists of networked internal connection of computers owned by an organization and makes use of Web technology. An intranet may be mounted on a LAN or a WAN. An intranet makes use of Internet technology such as TCP/IP, HTML, Java and HTTP to make it interoperable and to provide it with Web capability. The basic elements of an intranet are a computer network, a computer designated as a server containing server software and the Internet protocols TCP/IP.

An intranet offers several benefits to an organization: improved sharing and communication of information, open standards and cross-platform collaboration. For example, a car manufacturing company may connect its information systems on purchasing with its accounting information systems to form an intranet for sharing and processing information between two departments in the company.

An intranet is a company's own internal information transfer system that offers: e-mail, communication among different computers, connection to remote offices, a Web browser interface and special-interest news groups. For e-Commerce, an intranet is used to provide a corporate image and unified 'experience' for a customer that combines product information, ordering and customer care.

Extranet

An extranet is used for business-to-business (B2B) e-Commerce. It is the networked connection of computers of two or more companies. It is a private communication system to support trade and is used for communication and transactions between business partners, suppliers or special customers. For example, a car manufacturing company may connect its computers with its various suppliers of components for the cars it makes. Another example is the airline industry's OneWorld network, which enables customers to transfer seamlessly between airlines to reach their destinations.

Design principles

Intranets and extranets share the same design principles formulated for the Internet. The Internet design principles are:

Interoperability. There are varying operating systems that control computer functions on the many different computers on the Internet. Normally a given operating system cannot communicate with a different one. A standard to enable varying operating systems to communicate with each other was introduced by the US Department of Defense, which originally financed the Internet. Interoperability means that independent implementations of Internet protocols can work seamlessly.

Consequently, operating system developers such as Microsoft or Apple incorporate software into their operating systems that enables them to operate with other computers over the Internet. Internet-compatible systems use the TCP/IP common protocol for communication. Interoperability for e-Commerce means that companies and customers do not have to purchase and upgrade software from the same vendors. Their computers will be able to communicate over the Internet because of the standard protocols.

Layering. The Internet can be regarded as a series of layers of software. The structure of the Internet is layered. It is a five-layer system consisting of: interconnect level (National Access Points, NAPs), national backbone providers, regional Internet providers, local Internet service providers, and the business and consumer market.

The bottom layers of software, interconnect and network, are concerned with operating the computer hardware. The higher layers, business and consumer market, come closer to the needs of the person using the Internet. The most relevant layer is the layer that processes the information required by the Internet user; this is called the 'application' layer. These different hardware and application layers need to communicate with each other and they do so by using well defined interfaces. The Internet layering standard has resulted in increased reliability of Internet software and it is invisible to the Internet user.

Simplicity. The layering has resulted in simplicity of software design. Each layer is concerned only with its own functionality, making its design simpler. For example, the layer concerned with physical devices like mouse operations are hidden from the higher layers that process information. This kind of simplicity has contributed to increased software reliability too.

Uniform naming and addressing. Each Internet host computer has an Internet Protocol (IP) address that uniquely identifies it on the Internet from the millions of other computers also on the Internet. The IP address is expressed in a uniform format or 'dotted quad'. An example is: '17.10.2.3'. As the dotted quad is not meaningful to humans the domain name system (DNS) is used to provide a symbolic name for the dotted quad. An example is: 'sol.brunel.ac.uk'. The DNS is capable of translating the symbolic name into the required IP address to enable Internet operations.

End-to-end protocols. The Internet does not process information. It enables the transfer of 'packets' of information between computers. This is called end-to-end protocol. The Internet enables the transfer of information or 'content' of the packet. The transmitting or receiving computers, known as the 'end' system, do the actual processing of information.

ACTIVITY

For information on the electronic aspects of the Internet visit the IEEE Web site and search on 'Internet' http://standards.ieee.org/

49

The combined use of the Internet, intranets and extranets by companies has resulted in the term 'virtual organization' or 'networked organization'. The virtual organization is to be contrasted with the physical organization; the latter is restricted by geographical, physical space. Companies can combine computer-networking technology with information technology (IT) and information systems (IS) to develop a network of computers that can capture, process and share information and knowledge in virtual or cyberspace, where time and space are defined differently from physical time and space. Amazon.com may be classed as a virtual organization. Virtual organizations tend to be flatter because access to information and knowledge is potentially open to all employees who have access to a PC.

The World Wide Web

The World Wide Web, also known as the 'Web' or 'WWW', consists of pages of information depicted as text, graphics, sound, or video clips. A Web page may contain Java applets – Java programs that are downloaded from the server and run on the local computer. The Web consists of over a million Web servers, and an untold number of Web browsers. What distinguishes the Web from other computer media is its ability to link Web pages dynamically; this is known as hypertext links or simply links. The Web combines computer network technology with hypertext to provide a 'global information system'. One Web page can be linked to another by a hypertext link and the user merely has to click on the link to display related information. A link appears as highlighted on the Web page. It is this hypertext linking capability of the Web that makes it a powerful source of information. The Web is a client–server architecture system, and a Web user can access the Web servers with a Web browser such as Netscape or Microsoft Explorer.

Hypertext

A document on the Web is composed using hypertext technology. Hypertext is an electronic document system that can be read non-sequentially and interactively. The reader does not have to read it like a book, she/he can click on hyperlinks of related information. The Apollo space program to record its documentation used a hypertext system. e-Commerce Web sites are built using hypertext documents, and other hypermedia.

Hypertext transfer protocol

The Web differs from the Internet by the protocol it uses to transfer information between computers. The Web uses the hypertext transfer protocol (HTTP) to connect and transfer hypertext documents stored on Web servers, also known as Web sites. All the computers on the Internet that use the HTTP protocol compose the Web.

The Web browser

A Web browser is a graphical interface for searching, accessing and viewing hypertext and multimedia files on the Web. The first browser, called Mosaic, was invented by the US company Netscape Communications, founded in 1994 by Marc Andreessen. He set himself the problem of transferring sound and pictures over the Web. His solution was the first graphical Web browser. It allowed basic functions such as retrieving and displaying hypertext files. The growth of the Internet and the Web is largely because of the invention of the graphical browser which makes it easier for people to search and view information.

Two popular browsers are Netscape Communicator and Internet Explorer. They are more sophisticated than the original Mosaic browser and enable e-mail messaging, HTML authoring, and extensions such as scripting, plug-in and multimedia.

Internet search engines

The Internet is unarguably the most voluminous information store in the world. Finding information on the Internet requires complex computer algorithms. These algorithms form the backbone of Internet search engines designed to help people find the information they want. Organizations need search engines to find information about customers or business competitors or partners. Search engines are computer programs that locate specific Web pages, files or multimedia items stored on the Internet. Search engines such as Google or Autonomy use different algorithms or techniques to search for Web pages.

Uniform resource locator

The uniform resource locator (URL) is the address of a particular Web site on the Internet. It consists of domain names and a pathway that locates a particular host computer that is connected to the Internet. An example URL is www.yahoo.com or www.dell.com. A URL consists of the protocol that is to be used to make the Internet connection (the WWW in the examples), the name of the host computer ('Yahoo' or 'Dell') and the domain (.com). In the case of commercial companies, the name of the host computer connected to the Internet is usually the registered name of the company.

Hypertext mark-up language

Hypertext mark-up language (HTML) is used to author information on a Web page. HTML documents are text files that are interpreted by a Web browser. The browser reads the HTML file and interprets the HTML instructions. The browser has to do this interpretation each time a hypertext file is loaded.

A Web page can be divided into 'frames' or sub-pages. Each frame is used to display separate but relevant information designed by the Web author. Multimedia can be facilitated by extensions to HTML or by 'plug-ins' or add-on programs that make the Web client more versatile to deal with additional media types. An example of extension is Secure HTTP that enables sophisticated encryption and decryption algorithms for sensitive e-Commerce data like payments for transactions.

It takes time to learn to write HTML code. Authoring tools are available for automatically converting documents in Microsoft Word to HTML files, ready to load on to a Web server. Hot Dog Pro, Adobe PageMill and Microsoft FrontPage are examples.

A Web site consists of one or more Web pages linked together by hyperlinks. The contents of a Web site are known as 'content'. HTML is not capable of processing or interacting with Internet users. To process data captured through a Web form JavaScript is required.

Multimedia

Multimedia is a tool capable of providing the transfer of sound and images like pictures over the Internet. Multimedia applications require lots of memory and bandwidth – the physical capacity of data cables to carry and transfer data. For example, one minute of music requires 5 MB of data. The transfer of sound and images in real time requires special software which is added to TCP/IP and HTTP protocols. On the client end, a player is required to interpret the data and render it into sound or images.

Multimedia Internet Mail Extensions or MIME is an Internet standard for multimedia Internet e-mail. MIME enables e-mail to be cast as types consisting of HTML, text, images or video. Example MIME types are: image/jpeg, video/mpeg or application/pdf.

Java, applets, JavaScript and interactivity

The Internet is popular because it is interactive. Interactivity means that the Internet user (or client) can actively request information from and provide information to the server. Such interactivity is important for e-Commerce applications. CGI script and JavaScript provide interactivity on the Internet.

Java is a programming language originally intended for programming consumer electronic devices like microwave ovens, dishwashers or electronic clocks. As there are many manufacturers of these products, Java's developer, Sun Micro-systems, designed Java to be ubiquitous, meaning that it should be operable on any manufacturer's device. Virtual Java machines that are independent of PC operating systems interpret Java, a feature that makes it ideal for Internet programming. Java programs created for the Internet are called applets. Java applets are embedded in HTML documents.

An applet is a Java program that is executed on the client machine. It is loaded by the Web browser and restricted to prevent security breaches. The applet is executed on a Java virtual machine in the browser.

JavaScript, originally called LiveScript, was developed independently of Java by Netscape to provide interactivity. It is used to process data captured via forms on the Internet and to create interactive Web sites, and both the server and the client side use it. JavaScript is embedded in HTML and is interpreted by a browser. Web pages that contain JavaScript can be transferred around the Internet, because JavaScript is platform-independent or interpreted. ActiveX is a competitor of JavaScript. Scripts can be used in e-Commerce to validate service or product order form entries.

ACTIVITY

1 Summarize the Internet design principles.

2 What is meant by the term 'protocol'?

3 Differentiate between the Internet, intranets and extranets.

4 What particular properties of the World Wide Web make it suitable for use in e-Commerce systems? *Answer* The Web's graphical user interface makes it user-friendly for customers and companies. Hypertext and hyperlinks allow related customer or product information to be linked and displayed.

5 Differentiate between the World Wide Web and the Internet. *Answer* The Internet is the global physical network of computers and the Web is the composition and transmission of hypertext and hypermedia information documents.

6 Differentiate between Java and a Java applet. *Answer* Java is a programming language used for Internet programming. An applet is typically shorter Java code that is transmitted over the Internet in a Web page.

Surf www.sun.com for Java, www.cisco.com for networks and www.ieee.org for standards.

Common gateway interface

CGI programs are text files that consist of line or programming code similar to JavaScript; such programs are called CGI script. Pear is an example of CGI programming. CGI is used to create interactive Web sites that pass information from a Web browser to a server using a form, very useful for organizational needs. A form is a document that is created to interact with a user, take data from the user and send it to the server for processing, usually via a database.

ARCHITECTURE OF e-COMMERCE SYSTEMS

The buying and selling of products and services over the Internet is termed 'online trading'. Online trading or e-Commerce is important to businesses because it provides a flexible source of trading with customers, and with business partners. To enable online trading, companies need to combine existing computerized transaction processing systems and information systems with Internet and Web technology. Existing computerized systems, databases, and Internet and Web technology are the basic components of online trading and form the architecture of e-Commerce systems. Computer system architecture consists of hardware and software components that are configured in terms of the needs of organizations.

Companies connect computers to a LAN, WAN and the Internet, using TCP/IP, based on client–server architecture, to share computer software, printers or scanners. Basic Internet tools such as e-mail, browsers, search engines and protocols such as file transfer protocol (FTP) and Telnet are combined to form the system architecture for e-Commerce.

The systems architecture for a company will depend on its trading activities. A retail company will have a different architecture from a manufacturing company or a service company. As a company changes and evolves its mission or objectives, its e-Commerce system architecture will need to change too. Alternatively, the stimulus to change may come from competitors who use the most modern e-Commerce technology.

Internet, e-Commerce systems and information systems

Some of the terms used to describe a company's involvement with the Internet are that it has 'an online presence' or it has 'a Web site'. Such terms hide the complex IT and IS that form the infrastructure that underpin e-Commerce systems.

An information system is the application of a computer to capture and process data to provide information for managers and executives for the purposes of decision making and management. A company will normally have various information systems, such as an airline reservation system or an inventory control system. These systems will be linked to a corporate database that stores relevant data, like product or customer details. A company's Web site is connected to such information systems and databases to provide the essential product or service information for customer and employee use.

Companies' existing client–server technology and its IS/IT infrastructure is connected to the Internet to form part of an e-Commerce architecture. The e-Commerce architecture is based on a company's business model, consisting of the basic logic of what it wants to produce or sell, how it will market it, how it defines its customers and other fundamental business issues. IT is combined with Internet technology to enable a company to personalize its service to a customer.

Databases

A computer database consists of records on specific items of interest, for example customers' contact details or the products they have bought. It is a collection of data that can be queried for specific purposes such as targeting a particular customer for certain products. Databases are used to market products and services. This is termed *database marketing* and is addressed further in Chapter 5. Databases are used to store data on the purchasing habits of customers and enable a company to develop a tailored relationship with its customers. The data are then processed to provide tailored information on individual customers' prefer-ences that are then sent information about products or services relevant to their current buying habits. Data-mining techniques are used to reprocess existing data in databases to extract previously unrealized information of potential commercial use.

e-Commerce systems and the customer

e-Commerce systems that interface with the customer need to be pragmatic. The selection and evaluation of Internet technology need to be appropriate to both the company's needs and the customer's ability to use the system. A good business model will assume that the customer has little interest in technology and avoid the technology trap.

Avoiding the technology trap. It is not user-friendly to use over-complex Internet and Web technology in e-Commerce systems. The technology needs to be appro-priate to prevent prolonging the time it takes for customers' commands to be executed by the system.

Web site evaluation software

It is possible to measure the popularity of a company's Web site using evalua-tion software that generates log files. Such log files record the number of visitors to the site or page impressions. They record which parts of the Web site are most popular, the times of the day people visit, record which search engines are being used by visitors and how long they spend on the site, known as the 'stickiness' of the site. These log files can subsequently be used to evaluate the performance of the site from a business perspective and the information can be used to make it easier for customers to make transactions.

Internet service providers

A company wanting to trade over the Internet has to agree a contract with an Internet service provider (ISP). ISPs provide communication and hosting services for individuals and companies wanting to access the Internet.

ISPs provide access to the Internet and enable Internet commerce by connecting individuals and companies to the Internet. There are thousands of ISPs that a company can choose from, all of them providing domain name services and electronic mail. The two most popular ISPs are UUNET Technologies and AT&T World Net. Other organizations, like a bank with mainframe computers, may also act as an ISP.

ISPs also provide hosting services for Web sites by installing and operating the server computers and software for a company. The computers and software are located at the ISP's site. Transaction services such as payment systems or order capture and fulfilment are also provided by ISPs.

Example of e-Commerce architecture

The important considerations for designing e-Commerce architecture are the customer, the company, the company's existing information systems and how payment will be made. For example, a company with a Web site that includes an order form would need a Web server that can provide a catalogue, whose details would be retrieved from a catalogue database, and order form. It would need to interface with an existing database to collect and record the order details entered by the customer. The payment might be transacted with a credit card whose details would be captured on the order form utilizing standard security features available on the Web.

ACTIVITY

Surf www.ibm.com and search on 'electronic business' for news of products and services offered by IBM.

This example shows that an e-Commerce system is composed of existing information systems, databases and Internet technology. Other sophisticated e-Commerce architectures are possible for companies that need distributed transaction processing. For example, the Open Buying Consortium (OBI) has proposed a system architecture consisting of six fundamental system components split into buy-side, the customer and sell-side activities. These components are: Browse, Request, Approve, Fill, Receive and Pay.

e-Commerce security technology

The success of e-Commerce depends on the security of data like personal details and credit card numbers transmitted over the Internet. The domain name system Internet protocol that makes IP addresses readable by humans is insecure. Security measures need to be taken in e-Commerce systems to prevent compromising the systems. Some of these measures include building firewalls, incorporating cryptography and authentication, and using secure connections.

Firewall

A firewall is hardware and software that are used to secure a private computer network system from uninvited intruders. A firewall is used to control whether a client is permitted to connect to the private network it protects.

Cryptography

Cryptography is a science that provides secure communication over vulnerable channels. Cryptography is fundamental to the success of the Internet and e-Commerce. Governments regulate cryptographic technology because of its importance to national security.

In cryptography a message, like a credit card number, is encrypted using a key and the encrypted message is transmitted. The receiver uses the key to decrypt the message and convert it back to its original form. The basic elements of a cryptographic system are algorithms, protocols and key management. An example of key management is the secret-key encryption algorithms. These algorithms are 'secret' because only the receiver and sender know the secret key.

Cryptography is used to provide secure transmission of data over the Internet. Private data like credit card details or digital signatures are encrypted and then transmitted over the Internet. Cryptography can keep a message secret and act as a gateway for identifying senders and receivers. It provides the secure electronic transaction technology for credit card transactions on the Internet.

Authentication

Authentication procedures are used to establish the identity of an individual or another computer system. Authentication procedures can be hardware- or software-based. Authentication procedures make use of personal items of knowledge or possession such as secret names or birth dates. Good authentication systems make use of two-factor authentication, such as a place name and memorable date known to the user. Some banking systems make use of three-factor authentication before allowing customers to make online account transfers.

Secure socket layer

The secure socket layer (SSL) is a layer of security between the application and the transport protocol. The purpose of SSL is to enable secure and reliable data transmission and communication over the Internet. The SSL provides private connection, making use of encryption and secret-key cryptography. Authentication in SSL is achieved using public-key cryptography, which consists of a private key that is never made public chosen by one participant in the data exchange, and a public key chosen by the other participant in the exchange. Either key may be used for encryption. Reliability of data transmission is achieved by using secure hash functions like SHA or MD5. Secure hash functions check the integrity of a message. SSL is commonly used in e-Commerce systems.

ACTIVITY

1 What level of key management is sufficient for Internet banking?
2 How can Internet banks authenticate the identity of their clients?

From the list of Web links at the end of this chapter surf www.dell.com or www.amazon.com and think about what technology described in this chapter is used by Dell and Amazon; surf www.oracle.com for database uses; www.ibm.co.uk for security; www.nationwide.co.uk for authentication of clients.

FUTURE DEVELOPMENTS IN e-BUSINESS TECHNOLOGY

The Internet

Just as the internal combustion engine (the motor car) and jet engine (aeroplane) have radically changed our lives, the Internet is beginning to do the same. In the short time of its existence the Internet has greatly affected business and society. The Internet's evolution and future development are set to continue. The TCP/IP protocol is evolving with the development of IPv6, the next generation of the Internet protocol. The improvements in IPv6 are scalability, security and support for real-time media quality. Companies such as Ciena Corporation are working on improving bandwidth. They have a product called Wave Division Multiplexing (WDM) that moves data at the speed of 100 billion bits per second (100,000,000,000 b.p.s.). This contrasts with the standard modem's 36,600 b.p.s.

The World Wide Web

The Web's HTTP protocol is evolving to encompass better performance and flexible interactions between clients and servers.

Companies compete in complex and increasingly competitive markets. They do so by following, for example, competitive strategies of product differentiation or cost reduction. Similarly, as Chapter 4 argues, *relationships* are becoming increasingly important in business models. Current developments in Web technology are best placed to enable companies to exploit their differences and build personal relationships with customers, suppliers or business partners. For example, the eXtensible Mark-up Language, the Semantic Web and other Internet developments are leading the way to providing tailoring capability in e-Business technology.

eXtensible mark-up language

The extensible mark-up language (XML) is gaining popularity over HTML with companies. XML offers companies the ability to define tags that uniquely describe their products, services or customer service culture. Companies can design XML tags to display price or product or service descriptions that cannot be done in HTML. In short, XML allows a company to tailor the feel and look of its Web site and order forms to its needs.

The Semantic Web

Semantic Web is the name given to developments in Web technology by the World Wide Web Consortium (W3C), headed by Tim Berners-Lee, who invented the Web. The Semantic Web enables communication of contextual data and information. Information makes sense to humans only when it is used in context. The Semantic Web enables such context to be captured in Web applications.

ACTIVITY

Surf www.w3c.org 'Semantic Web' for information on technological developments of the Semantic Web.

The primary contribution of the Internet, the Web and associated technologies is to enable collaboration and sharing of information and knowledge among people. The types of collaboration are numerous, ranging from intra-organizational to inter-organizational and across the boundary of the organization with the customer. Future technology development will focus on this collaborative aspect of e-Commerce and will lead to radically different organizational structures and patterns of interaction among and between businesses and their customers.

CONCLUSION

The Internet has fundamentally changed business activity. The buying and selling of products and services, market making, the forging of relationships between companies and customers or between two or more organizations; all these activities are increasingly being digitized. Although the success of these efforts is not guaranteed, the business landscape is now truly digitized. Some types of e-Commerce, for example independent e-Markets, are not likely to succeed. The digital technology that enables e-Commerce is progressing and will continue to offer companies opportunities for further changing their business activities.

CHAPTER SUMMARY

This chapter has traced the recent development of the Internet and World Wide Web and shown how they have transformed the ways in which a huge number of companies conduct business transactions. It has provided an overview of the relevant technologies, explaining in layman's terms their potential for public, private and voluntary organizations. Combined with these other innovations to form an 'architecture', the Internet and World Wide Web can enhance the customer's experience whilst simultaneously improving internal business processes. Although a number of hurdles have yet to be overcome before many people will feel totally at home with e-Commerce, more recent technologies will undoubtedly improve the situation further.

GLOSSARY

Applet A Java program that is executed on the client machine. It is loaded by the Web browser and restricted to the browser to prevent security breaches.

Bandwidth The physical capacity of data cables to carry and transfer data, measured in bytes.

Client–server architecture An arrangement of computers where a main computer, the server, provides the software to other computers, the clients, over a network is called client–server architecture.

Cryptography Cryptography is used to provide secure transmission of data over the Internet. Private data like credit card details or digital signatures are encrypted and then transmitted over the Internet.

Database A computer database consists of records on specific items of interest, for example customers' contact details or the products they have bought. It is a collection of data stored to enable querying of the data for specific purposes such as targeting a particular customer for certain products.

extensible mark-up language XML provides companies the capability to define tags that uniquely describe their products, services or customer service culture. Companies can design XML tags to display price or product or service descriptions that cannot be done in HTML.

Extranet The networked connection of computers of two or more companies. It is a private communication system between two or more companies to support trade between them.

Hypertext mark-up language A Web page is created by authoring information using a Web authoring programming language such as hypertext mark-up language (HTML). HTML documents are text files that are interpreted by a Web browser.

Information system An information system is composed of computer hardware, software and people, and processes data into information.

Information technology Digital technology that is used to develop information systems.

Internet The term is short for 'inter-networking' or an interconnected set of networks. It is the global network of computers, whether the computer is on a LAN in an office or a WAN in an industry extranet or an independent computer in a private home.

Internet service provider An Internet service provider provides communication and hosting services for individuals and companies wanting to access the Internet.

Intranet An Intranet consists of the networked internal connection of computers owned by a company and makes use of Web technology.

Java A programming language originally intended for programming consumer electronic devices like microwave ovens, dishwashers or electronic clocks. Java is interpreted by virtual Java machines that are independent of operating systems, a feature which makes it ideal for Internet programming.

JavaScript JavaScript is used to process data captured via forms on the Internet and to create interactive Web sites. Both the server and the client side use it. JavaScript is embedded in HTML and is interpreted by a browser.

Local area network A computer network that is confined to a limited geographical area like an office or a company is called a local area network (LAN).

Protocol The set of rules for moving information over the Internet.

Semantic Web The Semantic Web enables contextual information to be captured in Web applications.

61

Uniform resource locator The uniform resource locator (URL) is the address of a particular Web site on the Internet. It consists of domain names and a pathway that locates a particular host computer that is connected to the Internet. An example URL is www.yahoo.com or www.dell.com.

Web browser A graphical interface for searching, accessing and viewing hypertext and multimedia files on the Web.

Wide area network A computer network that is spread over a wide geographical area like a region or between companies is called a wide area network (WAN).

World Wide Web The World Wide Web, also known as the 'Web' or 'WWW', consists of pages of information depicted as text, graphics, sound, or video clips, and they contain Java applets – Java programs that are downloaded from the server and run on the local computer.

FURTHER READING

Afuah, A. and Tucci, C. L. (2001) *Internet Business Models and Strategies,* London: McGraw-Hill.

Timmers, P. (1999) *Electronic Commerce: Strategies and Models for Business to Business Trading,* Chichester: Wiley.

Treese, G. W. and Stewart, L. C. (1998) *Designing Systems for Internet Commerce,* London: Addison Wesley.

BIBLIOGRAPHY

Abrams, M. (ed.) (1998) *World Wide Web beyond the Basics,* Upper Saddle River NJ: Prentice Hall.

Chaffey, D., Mayer, R. *et al.* (2000) *Internet Marketing,* Harlow: Prentice Hall.

Knuckles, C. D. (2001) *Introduction to Interactive Programming on the Internet using HTML and JavaScript,* New York: Wiley.

Treese, G. W. and Stewart, L. C. (1988) *Desigining Systems for Internet Commerce,* Upper Saddle River NJ: Addison-Wesley.

 WEB LINKS

www.w3c.org
For the latest developments in the World Wide Web. Tim Berners-Lee heads this consortium, established to promote and develop the Web. It includes links to his personal history of the Web.

www.ieee.org
The Institute of Electrical and Electronics Engineers co-ordinates computing and communications standards.

www.sun.com
For details of Java, applets, JavaScript and the latest developments in Java technology. Sun Microsystems, of Santa Clara CA, introduced Java technology in 1995.

www.cisco.com
The site where you can learn about the business of networks. Cisco Inc., of San Jose CA, is a leading company in computer network technology.

www.ibm.com
Surf 'Security' on this site for details of Internet security products and services. Once the leading computer manufacturer, IBM is a US company that now supplies technological solutions for e-Commerce.

www.dell.com, www.amazon.com
Surf these sites for commercially viable examples of e-Commerce.

www.oracle.com
For examples of database uses in business generally and in e-Commerce.

www.nationwide.com
Assess how Nationwide authenticates its clients.

Part III

The difference e-Business tools can make

Chapter 4

Organizational considerations for e-Business

LISA HARRIS AND NELARINE CORNELIUS

KEY LEARNING POINTS

After completing this chapter you will have an understanding of:

- How managing staff, customers and business partners can lead to common benefits and synergies
- The basic principles of human resource management and marketing
- How e-Business has led to 'e-HRM' and 'relationship marketing'

ORDERED LIST OF SUB TOPICS

- Introduction to HRM
  - Strategic HRM
  - A new HRM?
- Introduction to marketing
- Employees as stakeholders
  - Internal marketing
  - Involvement and participation
  - The value-added of e-HRM
- Customers as stakeholders
- Partners as stakeholders
- Managing change

This chapter introduces the basic principles of human resource management and marketing that are of particular importance to established organizations looking to move into e-Business for the first time. Although they are often regarded as quite separate business disciplines, it will be demonstrated here that a number of synergies can be generated by effectively integrating the management of people (HRM) and the management of customers (marketing) and other key stakeholders such as business partners. We will use the context of new ways of working facilitated by Internet developments to demonstrate the central principle that satisfied employees can lead to satisfied customers, and this in turn translates into value for shareholders. Furthermore, we will demonstrate that the synergies generated by integrating internal and external stakeholder relationships represent an organization's only source of sustainable competitive advantage. The key components of this central theme of interdependent *stakeholder relationships* can be illustrated diagrammatically, as in Figure 4.1.

It would be tempting to suggest that e-Business is just about technological change, but there are greater difficulties in implementing the intellectual, cultural and structural shifts necessary to succeed in a much more interactive business environment. Firms set up specifically to operate through the Internet (the so-called 'dotcoms') are ideally placed to recruit staff and deal with customers in the most effective way, although many are struggling with current economic conditions. Established firms, however, may have a whole history of embedded working practices and customer relationships that require significant change if e-Business is to be implemented successfully. Becoming an e-Business is an enormous undertaking requiring a diverse range of skills. As Kalakota and Robinson note, 'In the e-Business world, companies must anticipate the need for transformation and be ready to re-examine their organizations to the core' (2001: 300). As e-Business tools are encouraging the dissemination of information, reducing (and in some cases eliminating) the need for 'privileged points of contacts or gatekeepers in organisations', they are also contributing to the move away

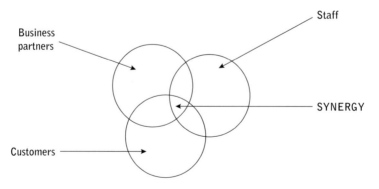

Figure 4.1 *Interdependent stakeholder relationships*

from centralized, hierarchical approaches and transforming traditional relationships within and between organizations (Timmers 1999). Firms that are embracing the Internet in this way have become known as 'clicks and mortar' organizations. The term represents the combination of 'old' and 'new' business practices and is derived from the expression 'bricks and mortar' that symbolizes a wholly physical presence.

INTRODUCTION TO HRM

Strategic HRM

Much of what we know about general human resource management (HRM) – the management of people through formal policy, structures, systems and procedures within a clear strategic framework – has largely been developed for 'bricks and mortar' companies. Typically, one might consider a number of HRM sub-systems, such as recruitment and selection, reward management, performance management. Further considerations would also be the impact on organizational efficiency and effectiveness, and also the realization of strategic goals.

There is no single or simple account of HRM. There are many models that exist, and that have been developed in the United Kingdom and the United States in particular. John Storey's (1992) account of human resource management is particularly helpful, as it highlights two important characteristics of HRM in particular. The first is the shift towards more strategic HRM from the more 'traditional' *personnel management* activities, which were a model of people management that was far more 'supportive' in nature and operated in tandem in unionized firms with *industrial relations* (concerned with the relationship between managers, trade unions and the labour market). Lundy and Cowling (1996) have developed a more detailed model of *strategic HRM* in which they make more explicit the *key functional activities* that support any strategic position. These include:

- Selection
- Performance assessment
- Training and development
- Rewards
- Employee relations

What is also important within the Lundy and Cowling model is the importance of a proactive approach to strategic HRM issues, which they argued might be pursued by:

- Paying attention to developments in the external environment and how stable or dynamic conditions are.

- The identification of what an organization is really good at, its core capabilities.
- The link between an organization's general strategic plan and the 'people management' aspects of this: in other words, strategic human resource management.

What was the pressure for this shift? Storey suggests that greater competition has forced those organizations that wish to respond more strategically to move their people management activities from more 'handmaiden', reactive, support roles to those that are more strategic, change-initiating and proactive.

Put simply, strategic HRM itself can be thought of as the marshalling of human resources in order to afford sustainable competitive advantage. This can be done through a variety of formal HRM systems, such as recruitment and selection, or through more informal systems, such as culture change. To be effective, SHRM needs to be an integral and proactive part of a company's strategic planning processes. The essence of SHRM can be set down in the company's mission, as well as strategic and related operational objectives. However, we should remember that most of these models have been developed for large bricks-and-mortar organizations. What we know about HRM in smaller companies is far more limited, and we certainly know that our understanding of how best to manage such companies is poorer. Furthermore, there is precious little which relates to 'hybrid' organizational structures within which we might place most 'clicks and mortar' operations. The information becomes even more 'thin on the ground' when 'dotcoms' are considered.

None the less, not even a dotcom is technology alone: people are an important and integral part of such organizations. However, the danger with any kind of e-Business is if the technology is regarded as both the primary ends and the means. This would not be the first time that technologically led change has resulted in the people management aspects being left behind. Business process re-engineering, Total Quality Management and cellular manufacturing are all examples of significant technological redesign of organizational processes where many companies have underestimated the impact of the 'people factor' (see Oram 1998 on business process re-engineering and HRM), and where subsequently the interventions have underperformed or failed outright. Many e-Businesses appear to be also rather slow in addressing HRM issues. Carter (2001) conducted a number of interviews with key informants in the HRM and e-Business fields, and there appeared to be a consensus that many businesses were simply not putting the right HRM infrastructure in as the company grew. As a result, many employees in such businesses were dissatisfied, felt undervalued and suffered from high turnover as disgruntled employees knew that there were often work opportunities elsewhere.

Case study:
EGG

At the Internet banking wing of the Prudential, Egg, attempts have been made to establish a distinct e-Business rather than a bricks-and-mortar culture. The head of HR operations, Chris Stephenson, argued that 'It soon became apparent that while most tools we would be using were the same as in the main Prudential operations, how we would apply them (the pace, method and their use) would differ.' Cultural differences are crucially important. Stephenson notes that at Egg 'You must make fast decisions, be prepared to take a risk and be entrepreneurial. All this spills into how you approach and manage your human resources ... e-Culture is about entrepreneurs, individuals being empowered.' Training at Egg consists of both face-to-face and e-Training. Staff can make use of *Egg Learn*, an integrated learning package available via the company Intranet, or *Egg Start*, an online induction package. A third program, *Touch*, provides off-site training in understanding Egg culture.

Source: Adapted from Carter (2001: 28–36).

A new HRM?

Although the understanding of HRM in e-Businesses is embryonic, there are some scholars like David Ulrich and practitioners such as Albert Vicere who are starting to suggest new configurations for HRM, which may better match the new organizational configurations of e-Businesses. Ulrich (1989) has suggested that those with responsibility for HRM will need to focus on:

- Understanding HRM practices
- The structure of the overall organization
- The competition faced by the organization
- Finance principles
- Computer information systems

Vicere (2001) suggests that the drivers of globalization and information technology also require a new approach to HRM. In particular, those managing HR will need to focus on selection, development, appraisal and rewards. Specifically, these are as follows:

Selection

Although interpersonal effectiveness, personal drive and results-orientation remain important, companies will also need to pay far more attention to:

- e-Skills.
- The ability to establish and work with partners in networks (see 'Partners as stakeholders' later in the chapter).
- Risk-taking, and ability to cope with rapid changes in business practice.
- Excellent communication skills (across *all* media).
- Brand image as employer. Management will need to pay more attention to the brand character of their companies as a means of attracting the brightest and best candidates. (See the section on employer branding later in the chapter.)

Development

The importance of knowledge workers in knowledge management companies is self-evident. But for e-Businesses there are additional demands:

- Employees should have the desire and expectation that they will continuously acquire new skills and learn.
- Learning must be at the core of line managers' competence map, for themselves and employees: they should be able to provide feedback, teach, coach and provide access to the latest thinking and tools that will enable employees to upgrade their skills and knowledge systematically.
- The nature of the work itself should provide the basis for development also. Special projects, job shadowing and special placements can help employees learn more than just routine 'classroom' learning.

Appraisal

Appraisal systems will need to be well developed and delivered in order to ensure that the best and fullest feedback is provided for staff. This is likely to require a major training input for managers and good briefing sessions for staff. The associated skills that the line manager will need to deliver these more sophisticated systems include:

- Coaching
- Mentoring
- Effective two-way communication

Rewards

Vicere argues that, in knowledge worker-dominated companies in particular, employees will have a keener sense of their intrinsic worth, and the value of their expertise in the labour market. Their demands in terms of remuneration and reward will need to be addressed carefully in particular in relation to:

- Creating employee commitment to the company. Vicere suggests that share options for staff are one of the most powerful ways of creating real ownership, and in turn increasing shareholder value.
- Better work/life balance. Employees in e-Businesses can and do work very hard, but they also expect the time to be able to play hard. e-Connections and more flexible working arrangements such as telecommuting may well appeal to many employees.

So what are the key areas that we would suggest companies need to pay attention to?

- The need to match the approach to HRM with the age and size of the company. Small to medium-size e-Businesses often do not use the Internet-based HRM support services that are now widely available. Further, there are many ways in which companies are now using their intranet services as a way of managing people. These new e-Human Resource Management (e-HRM) systems have been developed by companies such as Compaq and Cisco Systems, and enable stakeholders – including managers, HRM specialists and employees – to engage more proactively with HRM issues and decisions (Trapp 2001). e-Businesses are like any other business and need to review their 'people management' approaches as the needs of the business and of employees change.
- HRM can and ought to be a central lever and driver of change and, in particular, culture change. There needs to be an appreciation of this link, and it should be used proactively and positively.
- HRM policies and practices need to be able to deliver a diverse menu of flexible, formal and informal terms and conditions of employment as appropriate compensation for the long hours and intense nature of much e-Business work. Further, the HRM approach developed needs to match and facilitate the kind of job structure and working practice that are in place. If individual working is the dominant way of working, can contracts be 'personalized' to reflect different needs? If team working is to be encouraged, is this reflected by opportunities for team training and development and, more important, rewards for team performance?
- Although getting the policy right matters, the key for many e-Businesses to getting an approach to HRM that works is by not sidelining the HRM

function to a specialist activity divorced from 'front line' activities. Increasingly, organizations are moving towards line management delivery of HRM. This is not only more likely to get HRM ideas into action, but also means there is a shorter feedback loop between the impact of the policy or practice and the way that line managers and subordinates respond positively or negatively to it. Importantly, it also keeps the 'people management' side of the business as a main focus of the line manager's day-to-day responsibilities. This is more likely to happen if reinforced through the formal assessment of line managers for their people management skills, involving mechanisms such as annual performance appraisals.

- One of the keys to HRM in businesses in general, but likely to be imperative to shape-shifting e-Businesses in particular, is the proactive use of HRM approaches for the management of organizational knowledge and learning. There is a large literature on organizational learning and learning organizations – which is more concerned with learning how to do things differently, often to improve the strategic capability of a company. The importance of training, the identification and management of formal, informal and tacit knowledge also have a significant literature but, once again, typically divorced from the HRM literature. This is unfortunate, as good HRM can enable organizational knowledge and learning to become more of a reality than approaches divorced from HRM, given the latter's potential role in shaping culture and facilitating learning and knowledge sharing through, for example, training and development.

- In many economies, there is a shortage of people with the skills needed to work in the 'knowledge economy' in general and e-Businesses in particular. This 'war for talent' means that, in order to attract the best candidates, e-Businesses need to pay attention to the effectiveness with which they recruit, select, induct and attract candidates, especially where potential candidates are scarce. Many companies have gone for twenty-four-hour, global e-Service provision (e.g. online and telephone ticket purchase services for the major airlines such as British Airways) as one way of dealing with such shortages and providing a round-the-clock service, aided by Internet technology. However, though the demands of managing a local work force can be great, they are likely to be much greater for a global work force, though the potential rewards of capitalizing on the range of expertise of a global work force are high.

- Getting closer to the customer is often proclaimed as one of the key objectives of e-Business, be it through telephonic or electronic contacts. HRM approaches need to help to facilitate knowledge sharing and good internal employee relations, as well informed, well trained, competent and satisfied employees are more likely to deliver 'authentic' service.

74

The last point is particularly important. The work of 'emotional labourers', those for whom changing the mood of others is central to the primary task, has been well documented for flight attendants in the airline industry, and for nurses also (Smith 1992). Within this work, there are implicit bi-polar labour processes, one of which includes authentic and inauthentic behaviour. Universally, customers warm to and value more authentic behaviour from service providers. Traditionally, many service industries have relied heavily on 'scripts', and staff are often monitored in order to assess how tightly they comply with them. However, these scripts are usually perceived to be inauthentic, just going through the motions, by customers. So, for example, in the call centre the script reigns supreme. This offers the advantage of consistency of service, but at a low and inauthentic level. Even within the call centre, more opportunity for authentic, individualized responses to customer demands is likely to afford competitive advantage, but can be delivered only if the employee is trained, feels committed and has an appropriate degree of autonomy about how the work is undertaken.

The time is right for considering what we know about HRM in e-Businesses, and also, what those responsible for HRM in organizations will need to consider, and then make choices about. One important way in which the best decisions can be made is through deciding what aspects of HRM are absolutely core to a company. We need to think of those factors that, if removed, would cause the business to underperform or be harmed in some way and, in particular, reduce competitiveness. In other words, some of the important choices that need to be made are:

- What are the core HRM competences of the business? These are the aspects of an organization's HRM that would cause the greatest difficulty if impaired and, thus, should be heavily protected.
- What specific functional activities or 'HRM bundles' are the ones that ensure best operational practice for a company?
- How do the choices about HRM operations link with strategic human resource management?
- How is operational and strategic HRM integrated in the overall company strategy?
- What is the direct and indirect connection and overall impact of HRM on important stages of front-line activity, such as product or service quality?
- Is HRM going to be delivered as a line management or a specialist activity?
- How can we use the latest electronic HRM systems (e-HRM systems) to help us deliver people management?
- Is e-HRM going to be core or peripheral to the company's management?

75

THINK POINT

What are the things that might need to be considered when deciding on the HRM needs of an e-Business and why?

Feedback. There is no single answer, but factors such as strategic objectives and the size and shape of the organization matter. There is a need to be careful to avoid being too driven by the technology and, as a consequence, neglect the 'people factors' that help to make the e-Business a reality.

INTRODUCTION TO MARKETING

> Because the purpose of business is to create and keep customers, it has only two central functions – marketing and innovation. The basic function of marketing is to attract and retain customers at a profit.
>
> (Drucker 1999: 1)

Marketing has traditionally been regarded as a specialist business function covering such customer-related topics as:

- Public relations: managing interactions with the public.
- Advertising: promoting products or services.
- Customer service: delivering value to customers.
- Market research: analysing market trends or customer behaviour.
- Brand management: developing the 'image' of products or services.

These tasks can be summarized under the general heading of the 'marketing mix' that encompasses the 'four Ps': Product, Price, Promotion and Place. Marketers need to manage each of these areas effectively if they are to meet the needs of their customers better than their competitors do. In addition, regular analysis of the internal and external business environment by tracking changing customer needs and the activities of competitors is essential in order to maintain – and hopefully enhance – the firm's position in the market.

A more modern viewpoint regards marketing as a guiding management philosophy or 'attitude of mind' throughout the organization that puts the customer first, commonly described as a *'marketing orientation'*. This is a much broader view of the role of marketing than was previously envisaged, and it cuts across a wide range of organizational functions. Successful adaptation of a marketing orientation requires effective management of other stakeholder groups such as staff, business partners, shareholders and suppliers, and this is the viewpoint adopted in this chapter. As Chaffey (2000: 3) notes: 'The marketing concept should lie at the heart of the organization, and the actions of directors, managers and employees should be guided by its philosophy.'

The Internet supports the concept of the marketing orientation because it provides a powerful interactive communications medium both within the organization (through the use of an intranet) and externally with other key stakeholder groups (through the use of an extranet). It also facilitates the gathering and management of data necessary to formulate and implement marketing strategies. BT, for example, is using its intranet to develop a competences database of employee IT skills, thereby opening up a pool of potential labour for jobs and highlighting training needs.

THINK POINT

Why might some employees not welcome the open exchange of information through intranets?

Feedback. A cynic might claim that 'information is power' and individuals in possession of certain important information have a vested interest in keeping such data to themselves. Senior management may be reluctant to disclose details of strategy in the belief that it is a mark of status to have access to privileged information. Fortunately, attitudes like this appear to be less common these days as traditional hierarchies of management are broken down.

EMPLOYEES AS STAKEHOLDERS

Internal marketing

The basic premise behind *internal marketing* is that a company's communications with its customers and other external stakeholders are unlikely to be effective unless employees within the firm are aware of (and prepared to buy into) the message that the firm is trying to put across. It is fashionable to refer to employees as 'internal customers'. If all employees are clear about the company's mission, objectives and strategy then there is a much better chance that customers will get the same message. Research has shown that firms where employees understand organizational goals had considerably higher returns on capital than those where employees felt excluded or uninformed. It has been estimated that more than 20 per cent of a firm's communications are actually with itself rather than with external stakeholders. Yet internal communications are rarely accorded the same degree of attention and resources as external communications. Sometimes very basic errors are made. For example, if the person responsible for mailing out corporate brochures is not told that a facility for customers to e-mail such requests to the firm has been implemented, incoming messages may well be ignored by that person in the mistaken assumption that someone else is dealing with them. It should now be evident that the principles of internal marketing mirror those of human resource management, discussed earlier in the chapter.

Organizational structure was once the way in which companies could control the flow of information within the firm. Clear hierarchies of responsibility meant that information flowed slowly up and down functional areas, but was often not made available to other parts of the organization, or could be excluded from certain individuals. Individuals' position in the management hierarchy could be ascertained by the degree of access they had to important information. Powerful fiefdoms could be established by individuals who controlled access to such information. With the development of internal company intranets, it is possible (in theory at least) for such information access barriers to be transcended. Real-time access to information can be available to any employee with Internet access, and the activities of diverse functional areas may become transparent to employees at all hierarchical levels. In practice, of course, decision makers can still choose to restrict access through passwords or firewalls. There are obvious benefits here to a marketer analysing market conditions or customer behaviour, but the sheer volume of information now available to organizations can create problems of its own.

For established firms looking to add online channels to their existing marketing activities, many of the marketing challenges are internal. Significant organizational change may be involved and effective communication within the firm of the need for change and the role of each employee in effecting it is essential to ensure staff commitment. Internal customers can be segmented into supporters, neutrals and opponents of change and communications with each group phrased appropriately. It is particularly vital to ensure 'buy-in' from key decision makers with the authority to enforce change, as well as from potential *champions* (sometimes referred to as 'rainmakers') who will drive the project forwards and communicate their enthusiasm to others.

THINK POINT

How might a project manager's communication with 'supporters', 'neutrals' and 'opponents' of a proposed change in marketing strategy differ in style and approach?

Feedback. Supporters do not need to be convinced of the value of a project, but instead encouraged to communicate their commitment to others. Neutrals need to be persuaded of the merits of a project in order to convert them into supporters, and the concerns of opponents need to be listened to and addressed, or further explanations of the need for change given and the potential benefits of supporting the change highlighted.

It is often suggested that internal communications can be enhanced through induction programmes, training courses, benefits, the use of intranets or through working in cross-functional teams. However, things are rarely that simple. Payne regards a supportive organizational culture as a key ingredient in the success of internal marketing:

> Internal marketing involves creating, developing and maintaining an organizational service culture that will lead to the right service personnel performing the service in the right way. It tells employees how to respond to new, unforeseen and even awkward situations. Service culture has a vital impact on how service-oriented employees act and thus how well they perform their tasks as 'part-time marketers'.
>
> (Payne 1995: 48–9)

Inappropriate cultural norms can militate against successful relationship building. Too often, customer care programmes are instigated as a 'quick fix', without making any changes in management behaviour, or attempts to evaluate the success of the programme. While press attention has focused on the achievements (and, more recently, the struggles) of Internet entrepreneurs, little mention has been made of the service workers who make up the bulk of the demand for labour in new technology industries. Many work in call centres that have been dubbed 'the new sweatshops'. In service-intensive organizations the power is in the hands of lower-level, front-line employees, upon whose handling of service encounters managers must depend for the achievement of organizational objectives. As Piercy (2000: 261) notes: 'Too many employees who deal directly with customers are damaging the product, service or corporate brand every time they open their mouths.' For example, the technique of 'mystery shopping', where researchers anonymously check out the quality of service provided by staff, may well be feared and resented. Dissatisfied or demotivated staff can try to sabotage enforced 'smiling' policies or even wear their name badges upside down. One major UK DIY retailer implemented a customer care programme that required shop floor staff to be much more proactive in serving customers and suggesting suitable products. What management failed to note was the limited extent of employee commitment and willingness to accept the extra pressures associated with such responsibility. Instead of feeling empowered and motivated by the 'upgrading' of their jobs, many staff resented the interference and preferred the security and predictability of sitting at the till all day.

Although 'clicks and mortar' organizations might be expected to struggle with integrating online relationship building, it is interesting that the 'dotcom' brigade does not seem to be immune to the problem. Leibovich, in an article appropriately entitled 'Service workers without a smile', provides an interesting account of employment conditions at Amazon, world-famous for its ground-breaking policies of online customer relationship building. Staff are pressured to work as quickly as possible in order to achieve customer satisfaction targets, particularly those who earn low wages packing books at the firm's distribution centres or answering e-mails from customers. The author notes: 'Customer service employees work in a patchwork of cubicles scattered over three downtown Seattle buildings. The quarters have an old industrial feel, with gritty exteriors that belie the company's sleek online identity' (Leibovich 1999: 3).

As mentioned earlier, the principles of internal marketing can also be extended to prospective employees with the notion of *employer branding*, in recognition that employees are a significant source of competitive advantage in a market place where products and services are easily copied. Employer branding involves treating staff and potential staff as internal customers. The aim is to acquire a reputation as a good firm to work for, thereby attracting and retaining the brightest and most dedicated employees, enabling the firm to stand out from its competitors. In an age where people expect to work for a number of firms (or indeed for themselves) during the course of their career, retaining key staff is becoming more and more difficult. Some firms are experimenting with paternity leave, flexible work arrangements and empowerment of staff or open communications through simplified management hierarchies in order to be seen as a 'good employer'. 'Forward-looking companies are working on the assumption that they have to do a continuous selling job on the employee' (Grimes 2000: 13).

THINK POINT

Can you think of any firms that have a reputation as a good employer? What particular features or benefits make them stand out in this way?

The 'four Ps' of marketing can also be applied to the internal market:

- *Product* to be sold to staff is the values, attitudes and behaviours that are required if the plan is to work effectively.
- *Price* is what employees have to pay in terms of changing their behaviour, learning new skills and stepping outside comfort zones.
- *Promotion* is the media and message used to advise of changes required and the reasons for implementing them. It may take the form of written documents, verbal presentations, road shows or videos. It also includes paying attention to feedback from employees and responding to problems experienced.
- *Place* is the distribution channel through which the communication messages are delivered, for example meetings, committees, training sessions and social occasions.

Piercy (2000) summarizes the relationship between internal marketing and relationship marketing in Figure 4.2, below.

In what may be regarded as the ultimate integration of internal marketing and customer relationship marketing, Ulrich (1989) advises giving customers a major role in staff recruitment, promotion and development, appraisal and reward systems. While this policy may be too radical for many organizations, it can be seen from this discussion that a suitable internal climate is a necessary first step in the development of a customer orientation, rarely a simple task for an established organization. In much of the human resources literature, relationships between employees have received far less attention than relationships between employees and managers. Even discussions of team working often focus on what the team can deliver for the manager, the company or the customer. This is a pity. Employee–employee relationships are extremely important for organizations for many reasons, as they can:

● Help to create a positive and constructive company climate and culture.
● Provide an important source of allegiance to the company through commitment to colleagues.
● Create channels for knowledge exchange, particularly informal or tacit knowledge, vital for product and service delivery and quality.

External customer satisfaction

	High	Low
Internal customer satisfaction (High)	**Synergy (a)** Happy customers and happy employees	**Internal euphoria (c)** Never mind the customer, what about the squash ladder?
(Low)	**Coercion (b)** You will be committed to customers ... or else	**Alienation (d)** Unhappy customers and unhappy employees

Figure 4.2 *External and internal customer satisfaction.* (a) Synergy *is the state to which many firms aspire but few achieve in practice.* (b) Coercion *means that control systems are implemented effectively to force employees to meet satisfaction targets, for example by linking wages directly with output.* (c) Internal euphoria *means that employees are so well treated that the culture becomes inward-looking and the needs of customers are overlooked.* (d) Alienation *means high staff turnover and customers lost to competitors through the creation of a vicious circle*

- Provide a vital basis for internal marketing, particularly through building 'internal customers' and internal customer relations, for example, between departments. Although formal internal service-level agreements can help, it is often informal personal relations and agreements that get the job done more efficiently and effectively, and improve a company's service quality overall.

Perhaps one of the most over-hyped assertions made by organizations is the desire to have motivated staff committed to the company. In reality, there are numerous examples of organizations in which such statements are mere rhetoric not backed up by action. What are the sources of employee commitment? In practice, this can be achieved through a variety of means that have to be very carefully tailored to specific types of work and whether or not employees are working individually or within groups. Very broadly, we can think of the ways in which motivation – making employees more willing to undertake their work for the good of themselves and the company as a result of personal drive and commitment, making them identify more strongly with, and be more loyal to, their work, their work teams and the company – is generated as follows:

'Hard' reward strategies

These might include:

- Reward for performance above the standards or targets set, such as financial bonuses, or forms of remuneration over and above the basic wage, which can be offered on a regular basis (e.g. daily, monthly or yearly).
- One-off rewards such as all-expenses-paid holidays, meals, shopping vouchers, etc., for good performance. Such rewards are often used for staff performance that is well regarded by customers as a signal of what kind of care is valued by customers and, in turn, by the organization.
- Share options are an excellent way of getting employees literally to 'buy into' the company's business performance. It also helps to draw employees' attention to aspects of a company's performance that lie outside their immediate job (e.g. changes and opportunities in the competitive environment).

'Soft' formal reward strategies

These might include deciding on and then publicizing 'Employee of the Month/ Year' winners, where the winners are made known to the organization in newsletters, posters or on the company intranet. A 'hard' reward may be given, but a primary objective is to publicize good performance and to share knowledge about how that good performance was achieved with both employees and, of course, customers.

'Soft' informal reward strategies

- *Team meetings*. Time for reflection is difficult in a busy environment, but 'time out' not only to seek improvements but also to share success can provide positive and constructive feedback on individual and team performance.
- *Regular positive feedback*. How can employees know if they are doing a good job or not? The good colleague, supervisor or manager will not just wait until the annual appraisal but can provide such feedback as frequently as they wish. Informal feedback and praise for a job well done are a primary source of maintaining motivation among staff, often referred to as the *organizational climate*. A strong motivational climate is very important at any time, but can be vital at times of crisis and change, in order to maintain focus when things may become uncertain or difficult.

Involvement and participation

Again, it would be easy to be cynical about gaining employee commitment. It could be argued that commitment is often thought about as a one-way street where the employee is expected to commit heavily to the company but the company expects to put in the minimum of effort. Some of the rewards listed earlier can provide commitment, but more can also be done. The most effective mechanisms operate through involvement and participation processes. Blackburn and Cornelius (2001) have suggested that involvement and participation can add value to workplace organizations, certainly by generating employee commitment but also by encouraging workplace learning. So, for example, problem-solving meetings can help information exchange about actual and potential problems and their solutions. The key is really how 'participative' are participation processes?

In unionized firms there may be joint consultation between management and unions on matters such as pay and conditions. In non-unionized firms, involvement and participation are often achieved through the following:

- *Team briefings* where managers brief employees on actual or possible changes, and feedback and suggestions are sought.
- *Problem-solving and quality circles* in which front-line issues are discussed and suggestions for improvement and change made.
- *Empowerment interventions* where employees are given the autonomy to make decisions about specific aspects of their work without having to consult with their supervisors or managers.

83

The company culture and organizational climate play a vital role in determining the willingness of both managers and employees to pursue these approaches. Further, the more exploitative the culture and demotivating the climate, the less likely such approaches will be taken seriously or succeed.

The value-added of e-HRM

Perhaps one of the most exciting developments that all organizations can exploit is e-HRM. e-HRM concerns the use of electronic means for managing key aspects of HRM. Once again, a note of caution: the technology may be the means but it is not the end: the value of e-HRM is highly dependent upon a number of factors, including:

- The basic quality and relevance of the e-HRM systems in use.
- Whether employees, managers and HR professionals are adequately trained to use e-HRM systems.
- How effectively e-HRM is integrated with other more conventional systems of HRM, including strategic HRM.
- Identification of the most appropriate Internet and intranet systems that meet the organization's needs.

Case study:
e-HR: GETTING IT TO WORK FOR YOU

The big selling point of e-HR is that it can liberate HRM from administrative chores and allow a stronger focus on more strategic matters. But are the early adopters of Web technology achieving this benefit, and at what cost? Roger Trapp interviewed a number of users of e-HR, and on the whole their responses were positive but cautious. For example, Katherine Cotter at Cisco Systems said that it is important not to use technology slavishly, but in a manner that reflects an organization's culture. 'The way we use it reflects our culture,' she said. 'Culture, not technology, is the driver. A lot of companies can benefit from it but use it differently.' Cisco manages by exception. Routine tasks such as checking expenses claims are normally handled automatically and employees can have direct links with health care providers so that they do not have to involve HR specialists. At the sandwich/café chain Prêt à Manger, employees can log on to a central system from wherever they are working and book an absence request or check their personal details. The shipping company P&O NedLloyd Europe's shore staff in the United Kingdom are able to access the company's Internet-based HRM package, either from their PCs or via kiosks at depots. At its most basic, e-HR enables a company and its employees to address HR issues via the intranet. The system works in pretty much the same way for managers as it does for employees, though they have passwords allowing more access privileges.

Source: Adapted from Trapp (2001: 24–32).

Case study:
HR AT IBM

At IBM, employees in seventeen countries have HR information at their fingertips. The Director of HR in the UK and Ireland, Paul Rodgers, says, 'With e-HR the employee has more ownership. For the company, the up side comes from having more accurate information about your work force.' IBM managers are able to search globally for specific skills. Using employee databases, IBM's HR managers can track individual careers and offer opportunities for high-flyers. And there is a self-assessment area where staff can go online and check whether their skills fit their current job description.

Source: Adapted from Hoare (2001).

HR information systems have been around for some time, but there are two more recent developments in particular that are worth noting:

- Internet-based HRM knowledge systems, which provide dedicated expert advice, particularly for companies that may not have a full-time personnel profession, and may lack some basic or the most-up-to-date HRM knowledge.
- Intranet-based systems that allow employee and manager access to employee information and, in turn, find out about jobs for, and the skills profiles of, employees available across a corporation. Fundamentally, the majority of intranet-based systems are information files which, if well designed, can form the basis of powerful management information systems and, importantly, empower the employee to know what opportunities are available, such as job and training opportunities.

Such developments are important because they provide the potential for greater flexibility of managing human resources and, importantly, greater opportunity for:

- Specialist delivery of HRM.
- Line management delivery of HRM.

85

- Employee self-management of aspects of HRM, such as seeking job opportunities in the internal labour market.

Case study:
MANAGING CHANGE AND CALL CENTRES

According to Datamonitor, around 2.1 per cent of the UK population will be involved in call centre work in 2001. An emerging reliance on twenty-four-hour availability of teleservices is now being complemented and surpassed by e-centres. However, what are the difficulties involved in staffing call centres? In one case study a company had been blighted by problems of high staff turnover, but was also in the process of expanding, making identification of the 'right people' a key concern. The traditional, informal, telesales 'profile' – sociable, dynamic, flexible and autonomous – failed in the e-centre context. These features were suitable for 'field sales', but created problems in the e-centres, where work was far more controlled. As many of the communications in the new e-centres were global and e-mail-based, written communication skills and accuracy in returning information to clients became more important than verbal eloquence. Line managers and HR staff were made more aware of this shift, and it is anticipated that turnover of the new e-operators is likely to fall.

Source: Adapted from Grieg (2001: 16–17).

CUSTOMERS AS STAKEHOLDERS

Relationship marketing is a highly topical area, with the prolific use of 'relationship' terminology in company literature, corporate announcements, advertisements and even job titles. It can be defined as 'a business strategy that proactively builds a bias or preference with its individual employees, channels and customers resulting in increased retention and increased performance' (Newell 2000: 14). In theory, any short-term losses accrued by gathering and analysing the necessary data to build relationships are mitigated over time by the return on investment from lasting customer relationships and their ensuing profitability. Gummesson (1997) prescribes RM as a 'universal panacea' that is applicable to all organization types. Some theorists argue that 'traditional' marketing is defunct and relationship marketing represents a dramatic change in marketing focus over the past two decades. The key factors that lead them to this conclusion are:

- Higher returns from repeat sales over time.
- Increasing levels of competition mean service quality may be the only differentiator.

- Higher costs associated with recruiting new customers than managing existing ones.
- Scope for cross-selling increased.
- It creates possibilities for strategic partnerships.
- Loyal customers will recommend the company to others.

In order to develop a relationship marketing programme within an organization, the following actions are necessary:

- Identify key customers (i.e. the sources of highest potential profit over the long term).
- Examine the expectations of both sides.
- Identify ways in which you can work more closely with these customers.
- Think about how operating procedures may need to be changed in order to facilitate closer communication.
- Appoint a relationship manager as a natural focal point.
- Be satisfied with small gains in the early stages – build over time.
- Recognize from the outset that different customers have different needs and this should be reflected in the way the relationship is developed.

The differences between transactional marketing and relationship marketing are highlighted in Table 4.1. Relationship marketing proponents criticize 'traditional' marketing as a 'narrow, transactional, one-sale-at-a-time view of

Table 4.1 *Transaction marketing and relationship marketing compared*

Transaction marketing	Relationship marketing
Focus on single sales	Focus on customer retention and building loyalty
Short time scale	Long time scale, recognizing that short-term costs will be higher, but so will long-term profitability
Emphasis on product features	Emphasis on product benefits that are meaningful to the customer
Limited customer commitment	High customer commitment
Little emphasis on customer retention	Emphasis on higher levels of service tailored to individual customers
Quality is a production concern	Quality is the concern of all, and failure to recognize it stores up problems for the future
Moderate customer contact	High customer contact, with each contact being used to gain information and build the relationship

marketing' (Payne 1995: 17). Thus an overly short-term orientation towards marketing activity is taken and 'the unit of analysis is a single market transaction' with 'profits expected to follow from today's exchanges, although sometimes some long-term image development occurs' (Gronroos 1997: 323).

In recent years, speculation about the potential of the Internet to facilitate relationship marketing through communication with customers on an individual basis has ensured that the debate remains prominent in both theoretical and practitioner circles (see, for example, Parker 2000; Newell 2000). Personalized e-mail messages can be distributed to highly targeted groups of customers at very low cost. Personalization software allows the name of the user to be incorporated into the Web pages, any previous transaction details to be displayed and related areas of interest to be flagged. Research by Cyber Atlas (www.cyberatlas.com) in 1999 found that Web users who configure, personalize or register on Web sites are more than twice as likely to buy online as those that do not.

ACTIVITY

Read the personalization case studies and try the demonstrations on www.broadvision.com. How do these techniques allow value to be added to customers?

Peppers and Rogers (1997) highlight the importance of the following relationship marketing issues, which are greatly facilitated by the Internet:

- Using the technology to achieve mass customization of the marketing message – and even of the product itself. Mass customization can range from minor cosmetic choices (for example the choice of car colour, trim and specification online) to a collaborative process facilitated by ongoing dialogue (for example, Motorola can manufacture pagers to 11 million different specifications).
- The learning relationship, by which they mean a continuous two-way dialogue that allows the offering to be adapted to meet specific needs. This can be achieved by means of online feedback forms, analysis of queries to customer service facilities, or through use of increasingly sophisticated software that analyses customer site searching behaviour before purchase.
- An incentive for the customer to engage in the dialogue. It must also be easy and convenient for the customer to engage with the company, so lengthy registration forms are often counterproductive. The best incentive is good, free, up-to-date content.

- Acknowledging the privacy of the customer and the other demands upon their time. This means communicating only with customers who have requested information, and making it easy for customers to 'opt out' if they wish. It also means guaranteeing not to pass on customer details to other companies in the form of online mailing lists.

However, despite the obvious value that the Internet adds to relationship marketing, there are a number of challenges for 'clicks and mortar' firms that are still also committed to customer interaction either face-to-face or by telephone:

- How to integrate 'online' and 'offline' relationship marketing strategies to ensure commonality of message and create synergies. A simple example of such integration concerns the use of 'callback' buttons where a customer can request, through the Web site, a telephone call from a salesperson in order to discuss the purchase request in more detail. See www.facetime. com for a demonstration! There are also implications for the way in which marketing departments are staffed in terms of the allocation of 'online' and 'offline' duties and the additional training requirements necessary.
- There can be a significant additional cost burden associated with providing an extra channel to market. Many firms fear 'cannibalization', whereby, instead of attracting new business, Internet channels merely provide additional choice to existing customers, adding to costs but not revenue. The danger is that competitors will offer customers the choice, making anything less look inadequate in comparison.
- Marketing departments are traditionally organized by geography (which of course is limited in importance on the Web) or by product. In the latter case it is difficult to implement strategies of personalization when the customer relationship crosses product line boundaries. Organization by customer group makes the most sense in terms of personalizing interactions and assessing lifetime customer value, regardless of the customer's physical location or specific product choices. However, this is not a simple undertaking because it may require significant re-engineering of business processes and organizational structures.
- While 'dotcoms' such as Amazon can track wide-ranging purchases back to a single customer account and customize future promotional campaigns and cross-selling opportunities accordingly, 'clicks and mortar' firms often lack the necessary sophisticated and integrated computer systems. These developments require a feel for the whole product range and geographical spread of the business that is beyond the scope of an individual marketer. They also imply a need for cross-functional team working to improve the organization's internal communication effectiveness. To address these difficulties, the sharing of information through intranets and extranets

can help staff acquire, update and develop the customer profiles necessary for relationship building campaigns to work.

- Customer expectations are rising; many now expect an immediate response to queries at any time of the day or night, and are unimpressed if the Web site does not display the most up-to-date product information and availability. This puts pressure on firms to ensure customer service centres are adequately staffed and that their sites are easy to navigate and contain the information that the customer seeks.

Furthermore, even such radical restructuring cannot be regarded as just a one-off activity. Firms looking to remain competitive in the e-Business arena have to be prepared to reorganize and restructure themselves more or less continuously. If the restructuring of traditional businesses really is so central to their development of successful e-Business strategies, it is essential to understand how to manage change effectively in order to sustain competitive advantage. As described earlier in the chapter, this is because it is easier for a newly formed organization to operate in 'virtual' or 'networked' ways than it is to impose massive organizational change upon a long established, hierarchical and inflexible organization. As Siegel warns:

The customer-led company has a broad interface across which all employees can get to know their customers. Employees invite customers in to collaborate on new products, support systems, and methodologies . . . Facilitating those interactions will take new communication skills, new tools, and the ability to move people in and out of product teams easily.

(Siegel 2000: 35)

THINK POINT

Can you think of examples of firms that have successfully developed relationships with their customers?

Feedback. Amazon now has a 'relationship' with millions of customers – if such a thing is truly possible. By monitoring and analysing the buying habits of its customers, customizing products and information to meet those habits, and responding quickly to queries, loyal relationships can be built as customers will be less inclined to try out a competitor. Other companies have tried to develop relationships with their customers by cultivating an exclusive image. American Express used the following expression to good effect: 'Quite frankly, the American Express card is not for everyone.' The idea is that, by limiting the numbers, the value of each relationship increases. By inference, being accepted by American Express makes you special, and the apparent scarcity increases demand.

We will return to the key issue of change management later in this chapter. The next section extends the discussion of interacting stakeholder relationships by examining the human resource and marketing issues involved in the development of inter-organizational networks.

PARTNERS AS STAKEHOLDERS

Kalakota and Robinson believe that the dominant business design of the future will consist of a flexible network of relationships between firms, customers and suppliers, creating 'a unique business organism' (Kalakota and Robinson 2001: 18). Such structures enable resources to be pooled and hence generate economies of scale, with each network member contributing its particular expertise. It might be argued that these strategies are not new, and represent little more than the outsourcing of non-core activities to reduce costs. Kalakota and Robinson, however, argue that enthusiastic protagonists are going much further: changing corporate cultures, accessing key skills and implementing sophisticated technological systems in a manner that no individual firm could achieve alone. As an example of how networking strategies are transforming organizational structures, Anders (2000) describes how Wells Fargo Bank is creating synergies by teaming with a number of small Internet firms. The bank prefers to learn from the new mind sets and high energy levels of such enterprises, rather than trying to foster innovation within its own bureaucratic structures that smother creativity through their slow decision-making systems. From an Internet firm's perspective, valuable credibility can be obtained through association with a trusted brand in the banking world.

While there are undoubtedly many firms that have an established tradition of successful inter-organizational networking, Internet developments have made such initiatives increasingly central to e-Business strategy. At an early stage of the Internet era, Tapscott (1995) predicted the creation of competitive advantage in a digital world through collaboration as networks of enterprises generate efficiencies for the benefit of all parties. In his most recent work he is unequivocal about the value of such networks, which he terms 'business Webs' or 'b-Webs':

> Business webs are inventing new value propositions, transforming the rules of competition, and mobilising people and resources to unprecedented levels of performance. Managers must master a new agenda for b-Web strategy if they intend to win in the new economy.
>
> (Tapscott *et al.* 2000: 17)

Turner (2000) also emphasises how the development of the information economy (in particular the transition from 'market places' to 'market spaces' without the need for physical contact) is pushing firms towards organizational structures based on networks. Clear communication of the way things are done, respective responsibilities and project objectives take on even more importance. Common HR policies and practices to equalize employment conditions may be necessary, or a common skills and competences database, so that effective teams can be put together at short notice and employee skills thus become a common resource across the network. According to a special report on business and the Internet in *The Economist*:

> The first and most crucial shift in thinking is to get away from the idea that any business is more or less a free-standing entity. The objective for large companies must be to become e-Business hubs and for smaller ones to ensure they are vital spokes. The companies involved must be willing to bring suppliers and customers deep into their processes and to develop a similar understanding of their business partners' processes. That implies a degree of openness and transparency which is new to most commercial organizations.
>
> (*Economist* 1999: 95)

This warning is endorsed in the same publication by Symonds:

> The ability to collaborate with others may be just as much of a competitive advantage as the ability to deploy the technology. Certainly the technology matters, but getting the business strategy right matters even more. And that may mean not just re-engineering your company, but reinventing it.
>
> (Symonds 1999: 223)

At the operational level, there are a number of challenges for marketers:

- Web-based inter-organizational networks mean that customer communications do not necessarily involve just one customer talking to one enterprise. To provide the kind of service that improves the chance of customer loyalty, companies need to co-ordinate their partners and vendors and customers through extranets that facilitate the sharing of information across company boundaries.
- The practical organization of marketing functions and activities within an inter-firm network may be complex. Decisions need to be taken on where responsibility lies for particular tasks, to avoid duplication and customer confusion. Kalakota and Robinson (2001) suggest considering partners and vendors to be part of the firm's extended enterprise, and this means sharing customer communication issues with everyone in contact with the customer through integrated applications such as customer service, field service, sales and marketing. Such integration can be regarded as the most critical issue currently facing 'clicks and mortar' firms in developing a successful e-Business strategy.

- Open policies of information sharing mean a whole host of issues have to be addressed concerning the 'ownership' of customer data, notwithstanding the technical difficulties inherent in integrating computer systems belonging to different organizations.
- The notion of developing and sustaining advantage over competitors is deeply entrenched for marketers. However, Hamel, Doz and Prahalad in an influential article advocated strategic alliances and networking between firms with their proposal that collaboration rather than competition is a winning strategy. They concluded that firms benefiting from competitive collaboration see it as competition in a different form, regarding 'harmony as the most important measure of success, co-operation as limited and learning from partners as paramount' (Hamel *et al.* 1989: 67). Key challenges for marketers now include defining the boundary between competition and collaboration, in other words being able to ascertain where the 'internal environment' becomes the 'external environment'.

MANAGING CHANGE

If a firm is able to manage all these stakeholders effectively, the management of change is a key issue because e-Business opportunities can give rise to a seismic shift in the way a firm does business. The changing business environment is creating both challenges and opportunities, but facing the challenges and taking advantage of the opportunities requires change.

One of the first challenges companies face when attempting to embrace e-Business and its corresponding technologies is how to move from being a physical or 'bricks and mortar' organization to being a digital or 'virtual' organization. It is here that a company encounters its first problem, which is one of technology. The particular difficulty relates to the attempt to evolve their 'legacy' systems (i.e. the technical infrastructure they have accumulated over time) to an infrastructure that will support e-Business. Few businesses find themselves in the position where they can 'throw away' the old and introduce new, customized computer systems. Legacy systems often perform essential activities upon which daily business processes depend.

THINK POINT

Can you think of any examples of businesses that are heavily dependent on legacy systems?

Feedback. Banks, for example, rely on systems that have been compiled and integrated from diverse sources over many years, but are still in daily use for processing transactions. There are many other examples!

Reactions to change can vary greatly. Some workers readily embrace new technologies, some can be hostile, and the reason for this hostility can often be attributed to poor communication and shifts in organizational power. Nadler and Tushman (1997) explain that implementation of change involves the disruptive transition from a current state to a future state, and as a result individuals or groups can resist change. They claim that there are three types of problems encountered when an organization goes through a significant change – power, uncertainty and control. Change can be viewed as a threat to existing power structures and it creates uncertainties, so the struggle for power escalates as individuals and groups attempt to control their environment by resisting change. The uncertainty of change also creates anxiety as individuals are not sure where they stand and whether at the end of the change process they will have still have a role within the organization. As a result individuals can act irrationally as they find it difficult to understand and interpret information related to the change. Nadler and Tushman also highlight the fact that within large organizations individuals do not usually openly resist change; instead they 'subtly or passively' resist. During the change period it becomes difficult to maintain control because goals are changing, as are structures and roles, and certain control systems become irrelevant.

What can be done about this? Employee involvement and participation can also affect the success of change. Markus claims that people's reaction to change is also dependent on:

> Whether they have had a say in selecting the technology or the way it is introduced and used, how the new technology is communicated, how much training and support are provided, and how carefully the roll out is planned and executed.
>
> (Markus 1999: 34)

Involving employees in the change process through internal marketing means that they become responsible for the success of the change, becoming 'owners' of the change process. This policy is endorsed by IBM Global Services, who recommend that in order to build a successful e-Business organizations need to challenge their employees to:

> Identify the cultural changes that will also be needed and to shape the processes, the linked education, learning and competency development that will be required to deliver real value in the new ways of doing business that they are proposing.
>
> (IBM 1999: 16)

One way in which an organization's HRM can be thought about is as a system within which the elements interact. Importantly, an impact on one part of the system may well have an impact on another part. So for example, training may be important to help with the change, but what about job redesign? Further, this is likely to require changes in the job description and person specification needed for recruitment. Indeed, you may need to change the method of recruitment (e.g. adverts may need to be placed in different publications so that you target the right potential candidates). So organizations need to think carefully: what are the HRM aspects that need to be addressed specifically within the context of the broader change? Another critical point to make is that organizations are bound to encounter complications in asking individuals to make changes that they are incapable of implementing, so adequate investment in training and development programmes is essential. If individuals do not possess the skills and capability necessary to introduce planned changes, the likelihood of success is significantly reduced.

THINK POINT

Can you think of any examples of 'clicks and mortar' organizations that have separated their 'online' and 'offline' businesses?

Feedback. British Airways is another high-profile organization that set up a separate e-Business division in order to mimic the speedy decision making and organizational flexibility of an Internet start-up company.

To conclude this section, it is worth reporting the findings of Rosabeth Moss Kanter (2001), who undertook a survey of 785 companies to investigate the barriers to e-Business change. The results are listed below in overall descending order of importance from most important to least important. It is worth reminding you here that companies more than twenty years old face fewer market place and technology barriers than younger ones do, but they face many more internal barriers – from decision-making uncertainty to divisional rivalries.

- The unit has no staff with adequate technical or Web-specific skills.
- Customers and key markets do not want to change their behaviour.
- There are more important projects that require existing resources and time.
- Technology and tools are inadequate, unavailable or unreliable.
- It is hard to find the right partners to work with.
- Suppliers are not co-operative or not ready for e-Business.
- Employees are not comfortable with change.
- Leaders are not sure where to begin: they don't understand how to make the right choices.

- Top executives do not personally use computers and are not personally familiar with the Internet.
- Rivalries or conflicts between internal divisions get in the way.
- It is hard to find the capital for new investment.
- Managers fear a loss of status or privileged position.
- Employees fear loss of jobs or unions and employee groups fear loss of membership.
- Government rules and regulations get in the way.
- The company is successful as it is: leaders see no need for change.
- The company had a bad previous experience with new technology.
- It is a waste of time or money: it is not relevant to the business.

CHAPTER SUMMARY

In this chapter we have emphasized the importance of integrating both HR and marketing perspectives in order for the management of stakeholder relations to be effective. The basic premise of this concerns the development of good internal employee relations as an essential prerequisite for effective relationships with external clients to be built. We have also noted the increasing importance of effective employee and organizational knowledge management as a potential source of sustainable competitive advantage, particularly in a more transparent e-Business environment in which information is easily obtainable, but at the same time business strategy is readily copied. Finally, we have acknowledged the change management problems faced by established organizations in developing an e-Business presence and considered how this issue can be effectively managed.

GLOSSARY

Cannibalization The notion that sales will be compromised by offering an Internet channel to market, as existing customers simply alternate between a greater choice of delivery channel.

Clicks and mortar A 'traditional' organization moving towards the inclusion of electronic trading operations to complement its core business.

Dotcom An organization formed specifically to operate on the Internet, with no street presence.

Employer branding Application of attributes as per traditional product brands to the company as a whole, in order to attract and retain top-quality staff. In a nutshell, it means being known as 'a good place to work'.

Extranet Intranet facilities which are extended to include suppliers, distributors, customers or business partners and allow relevant data to be shared beyond the usual boundaries of the firm.

Intranet Intranets are internal company networks for the use of employees only which are based on the same technology as the global Internet. They are cordoned off from public access by software known as 'firewalls', permitting enhanced communications across management hierarchies and the boundaries of business functions.

Marketing mix The traditional framework for managing a firm's relationships with customers, namely product, price, promotion and place (the four Ps).

Marketing orientation A focus upon achieving organizational objectives through meeting customer needs more effectively than the competition.

Project champion (rainmaker) A role as a key internal driver and enthusiast of project progress, often in the face of inertia or resistance if change is being instigated.

Stakeholders The primary groups which have an interest in the activities of a firm and to which it has a moral obligation, i.e. employees, customers, business partners, suppliers and shareholders.

FURTHER READING

Harris, L. and Dennis, C. (2002) *Marketing the e-Business*, London: Routledge. Develops in more detail the principles outlined in this chapter, with particular reference to the e-Business challenges facing established organizations.

Jobber, D. (2001) *Principles and Practice of Marketing*, 3rd edn, London: McGraw-Hill. Chapter 1 provides a useful overview and case examples of the basic principles of marketing.

Cornelius, N (ed.) 2001 *Human Resource Management: a Managerial Perspective*, Padstow: Thomson. Chapter 1 provides a useful summary of the development of HRM and some of the key principles. The book also contains specialist chapters on HRM and small business, HRM change and strategy and HRM and commitment. This is a basic text for those who do not have an academic or practitioner background in HRM.

BIBLIOGRAPHY

Anders, G. (2000) 'Power partners', *Fast Company*, September.

Blackburn, A. and Cornelius, N. (2001) 'Gaining commitment through involvement and participation processes' in N. Cornelius, *Human Resource Management: a Managerial Perspective*, Padstow: Thomson.

Carter, P. (2001) 'Cyber house rules', *People Management,* June: 28–36.

Chaffey, D. *et al.* (2000) *Internet Marketing*, London: FT Prentice Hall.

Drucker, P. F. (1999) *The Practice of Management*, London: Heinemann.

Economist (1999) 'You'll never walk alone', *Survey Business and the Internet,* 26 June.

Grieg, E. (2001) 'From call centres to "e-Centres": managing change in the new technology centres', *British Journal of Administrative Management,* 16–17.

Grimes, C. (2000) 'Software giant strives to stem exodus of staff', *Financial Times,* 13 June.

Gronroos, C. (1997) 'From marketing mix to relationship marketing: towards a paradigm shift in marketing', *Management Decision,* 35, 3–4: 322–39.

Gummesson, E. (1997) 'Relationship marketing as a paradigm shift: some conclusions from the 30R approach', *Management Decision,* 35, 3–4: 267–72.

Hamel, G., Doz, Y. and Prahalad, C. K. (1989) 'Collaborate with your competitors – and win', *Harvard Business Review,* 67, 1: 133–9.

Hoare, S. (2001) 'e-HR: the way forward', *Times,* 30 August.

IBM (1999) internal company document, London: IBM Global Services.

Kalakota, R. and Robinson, M. (2001) *e-Business Roadmap for Success,* 2nd edn, Harlow: Addison Wesley.

Kanter, R. M. (2001) 'The ten deadly mistakes of wanna-dots', *Harvard Business Review,* 79, 1: 91–100.

Leibovitch, M. (1999) 'Service workers without a smile', *Washington Post,* 22nd November.

Lundy, O. and Cowling, A. (1996) *Strategic Human Resource Management,* Padstow: Thomson.

Nadler, D. and Tushman, M. L. (1997) 'Implementing new designs: managing organizational change' in M. L. Tushman and P. Anderson (eds) *Managing Strategic Innovation and Change,* Oxford: Oxford University Press.

Newell, F. (2000) *Loyalty.com: Customer Relationship Management in the New Era of Internet Marketing,* New York: McGraw-Hill.

Oram, M. (1998) 'Re-engineering's fragile promise: HRM prospects for delivery?' in P. Sparrow and M. Marchington (eds) *Human Resource Management: The New Agenda,* St Ives: Financial Times Pitman.

Parker, R. (2000) *Relationship Marketing on the Internet,* Holbrook: Adams Media.

Payne, R. (1995) *Advances in Relationship Marketing,* London: Kogan Page.

Peppers, T. and Rogers, M. (1997) *Enterprise One to One,* London: Piatkus.

Piercy, N. (2000) *Market-led Strategic Change,* 2nd edn, London: Butterworth Heinemann.

Siegel, D. (2000) *Futurize your Enterprise: Business Strategy in the Age of the e-Customer,* New York: Wiley.

Smith, P. (1992) *The Emotional Labour of Nursing,* Basingstoke: Macmillan.

Storey, J. (1992) *Developments in the Management of Human Resources,* Oxford: Blackwell.

Storey, J. (ed.) (2000) *Human Resource Management: a Critical Text,* Padstow: Thomson.

Symonds, M. (1999) 'The net imperative: survey business and the Internet', *Economist,* 26 June.

Tapscott, D. (1995) *The Digital Economy,* New York: McGraw-Hill.

Tapscott, D., Ticoll, D. and Lowry, A. (2000) *Digital Capital,* New York: Brealey.

Timmers, P. (1999) *Electronic Commerce: Strategies and Models for Business-to-business Trading,* New York: Wiley.

Trapp, R. (2001) 'Of mice and men', *People Management,* 7, 13: 24–33.

Turner, C. (2000) *The Information E-conomy,* London: Kogan Page.

Ulrich, D. (1989) 'Tie the corporate knot: gaining complete customer commitment', *Sloan Management Review,* 19–27.

Vicere, A. A. (2001) 'New economy, new HR', *Vicere Associates.* Online. Available HTTP: www.vicere.com/newhr.htm (accessed 21 July 2002).

 WEB LINKS

www.tcm.com
Training and Development Resource Centre (TCM). Excellent starting point, with links to over sixty non-commercial sites, mailing lists and a business showcase.

www.hr-guide.com
HR Internet guide. A good source of general HRM information.

www.inst-mgt.org.uk
Institute of Management. A range of management topics including HRM and Marketing are listed here.

www.peoplemanagement.co.uk
Chartered Institute of Personnel and Development. The lead body on personnel issues in the United Kingdom, with a number of case examples.

www.bps.org.uk
British Psychological Society. This Web site contains information relating to a range of topics, including work and organizational psychology, work design, etc.

www.amazon.co.uk
Keep up to date with the latest e-Marketing books.

www.marketing.haynet.com
Online version of *Marketing Magazine*. Keep up to date with the latest news.

www.e-envoy.gov.uk
Regular monthly updates detailing progress in the government's efforts to make the United Kingdom 'the best place in the world for e-Commerce'.

www.forrester.com
Provides free summaries of the latest research reports on the growth of e-Commerce.

www.theecademy.com
UK-based daily e-mail news service on the latest e-Business developments and local networking events.

www.wilsonweb.com
An exhaustively detailed reference on the full range of Internet marketing issues, available as a free monthly newsletter. American in origin, but still a valuable resource and often light years ahead of UK developments.

www.ecommercetimes.com
Another useful and comprehensive daily e-mail news service on the latest e-Business developments. Again, a US perspective.

www.busreslab.com
Useful specimen online questionnaires to measure customer satisfaction levels and tips on effective Internet marketing research.

www.marketresearch.org.uk
The Market Research Society. Contains useful material on the nature of research, choosing an agency, ethical standards and codes of conduct for research practice.

www.statistics.gov.uk
Detailed information on a variety of consumer demographics from the government statistics office.

www.hotcoupons.com
Site visitors can key in their postcode to receive local promotions, and advertisers can post their offers on the site, using a specially designed software package.

www.nielson-netratings.com
Details the current levels of banner advertising activity, including the creative content of the ten most popular banners each week.

www.doubleclick.net
Offers advertisers the ability to target their advertisements on the Web through sourcing of specific interest groups, and display only at certain times of the day, or at particular geographical locations, or on certain types of hardware.

www.broadvision.com
Specializes in customer 'personalization' software. The site contains many useful case studies showing how communicating through the Internet allows you to find out more about your customers.

www.streamwave.co.uk
Online demonstrations of the latest technological developments which will form the basis of the next generation of Internet marketing communication applications.

www.marketingportal.cim.co.uk
The Chartered Institute of Marketing site, providing extensive links to online resources on all aspects of marketing.

www.mad.co.uk/mw/
The online version of *Marketing Week* magazine, allowing access to data services, archives and a discussion forum (registration required).

www.marcommwise.com
Useful articles on all aspects of marketing communications.

www.facetime.com
Good example of a site that overcomes the impersonal nature of the Internet by allowing the establishment of real-time links with a customer service representative. Try the free demonstration!

Chapter 5

Using marketing databases in e-Business

MICHAEL COLLINS

KEY LEARNING POINTS

After completing this chapter you will have an understanding of:

- How data can be acquired
- How to maintain the quality and integrity of your data
- Various methods of holding and managing data
- The tools available for data analysis in the marketing environment
- How to apply the information and knowledge to be derived from the data

ORDERED LIST OF SUB TOPICS

- The role of the marketing database
- Working with data
- Sources of data
  - Leveraging current business processes
  - Tactical activity
  - Purchase or rent lists
  - Marketing partners
  - Data enhancement from external sources
  - Business information vendors
  - Adding research data
  - Other data elements
- Data quality
  - Key issues to manage
  - Decay
  - Data appraisal

- Data storage and management
  - Data warehouses
  - Data marts
  - Marketing universes
- Tools and techniques for data manipulation and analysis
  - Data counts and visualization
  - Online analytical processing
  - Data mining
- Campaign management
- Dynamics of data-led marketing

THE ROLE OF THE MARKETING DATABASE

A database may be defined as a comprehensive collection of interrelated data, which can be accurately manipulated or retrieved. A marketing database will typically contain details of customers and the transactional or behavioural histories associated with those customers and can benefit all the elements of the marketing mix, whether in broadcast or direct communications or in sales promotion or PR.

There is a role for the database in supporting advertising, market research, product development, sales force management and motivation and sales promotion. Hence the concept of Database Marketing should not be confused with Direct Marketing, nor should it be considered a medium in itself, competing with others in the marketing mix, but rather as a tool to improve performance, efficiency and effectiveness in marketing communications.

The marketing database helps develop a clear, *actionable* understanding of customers and develop a dialogue that ideally should always be relevant, timely and focused on qualified opportunities.

Database Marketing of the 1980s and 1990s strove for *one-to-one* relationships and its success has been commendable *within the context of the available techniques.* New concepts, tools and expertise will now help deliver an outcome that is closer to the vision. The increased awareness and availability of data within organizations has coincided with the appearance of new, intuitive data analysis tools. This combination allows the derivation of information and interpretation of trends within time frames conducive to achieving the required dynamics.

As companies seek to integrate their suppliers, their customers and their marketing partners in complex relationship structures, new quantities of data are becoming accessible for exchange and sharing and the value of the data as a corporate asset is increasing.

The existence and growth of the World Wide Web and the increasing exponents of the medium have implications on both sides of the data-driven communications equation. On the one hand, the Web provides a novel, exciting and convenient medium for delivering a message to customers and prospective customers. On the other, it presents a channel for data collection that makes possible concepts that were only hypothetical in the past.

WORKING WITH DATA

Data are things that are given, facts that when combined with other facts can constitute information. Jenkinson (1995) identified four types of explicit data, referred to as Primary Research, Secondary, Performance and External. Whilst these types remain valid, some broadening of the definitions is required to gain a better understanding of how they link and are complementary:

- *Basic data.* Rather than being just primary research data received directly from the customer, basic data may be viewed generically as the most fundamental elements, acquired usually as part of a standard business process. These will include a customer's name and address, e-mail address, definitions of the company's products or services, its URL, pricing, campaign definitions, branches and channels of distribution, sales force or dealer network.
- *Qualifying data.* Qualifying data are data from any source that in any way add description to the basic data. For example, a company may wish to collect the demographics of its customers (age, sex, income, occupation), their lifestyle information or geographical profiles.
- *Behavioural or transactional data.* These are data that record how customers have reacted, what they have bought or enquired about and all the transactional information a company may hold.
- *Externally sourced data.* External data cover everything that augments, qualifies or enhances the basic data that are acquired from outside the business and outside the relationship with customers or suppliers. For example, companies may rent or buy lists of prospects to add to their database or may acquire additional data to enhance their existing records such as correcting the postcode or adding qualifying data elements.

There is a fifth type of data. It is not explicit but is known as *tacit* data. These are data that are normally held in the minds of the people using the database. The data represent their understanding of their relationship with their customers or suppliers; they are the low-level view acquired through experience or local knowledge and are intuitive, intimate and topical. Their inclusion enables the explicit data to be put into context and interpreted and helps convert information into manageable knowledge, itself a combination of data and information-processing technology with human creativity and innovation (Malhotra 1998).

SOURCES OF DATA

There are a variety of methods for acquiring data into the business. Some are a function of the business processes such as completing a sale or taking an enquiry. Others may be contrived tactics with the main objective of collecting a particular item of data for the database. Essentially, data can be acquired from six types of source: (1) leveraging current business processes, (2) tactical activity, (3) purchase lists, (4) marketing partners, (5) enhancement from external sources, (6) business information vendors.

Leveraging current business processes

Business processes can be amended so that new information is acquired as part of regular activities; for example, adding questions to an application form, having a telesales agent ask additional questions or having a sales person qualify a prospect prior to making a sales call. Companies must satisfy themselves that they are acquiring all the data they can from the encounter with the customer or prospect (or even supplier). Most common data sources are:

- *Sales.* Does the company collect details for each sale? Is the basis of the customer database to be found in the accounts department?
- *Web site registrations.* Customer registrations are a reliable source of information so long as the precautions for data quality have been applied (see explanation later in this chapter). Companies often take this opportunity to ask some additional questions to acquire qualifying information for the database.
- *Enquiries/help line.* When customers and prospects call in or complete an enquiry screen on the Web site there is an opportunity for the company to acquire additional information or qualify or verify data already held.
- *Complaints.* This may be the first occasion a company has to acquire even primary data about this customer – perhaps also take the opportunity to acquire some additional information. Record the complaint on the database; classify it and its outcome so that this can be used in later relationship management. A properly handled complaint can mean a more satisfied customer. Often a customer whose major complaint was handled well becomes a better customer than one who experienced a number of minor complaints.
- *Redemptions.* Sales promotion campaigns or consumer competitions can yield valuable data if one or two relevant questions are added to the entry form.
- *Marketing research and surveys.* Such surveys can provide high-level data that can be extrapolated across the database.

- *Accounts.* Ascertain spend levels, returns and credit control issues, all of which may be used as segmentation or selection criteria for marketing initiatives.
- *Third parties and marketing partners.* Companies may identify non-competitive marketers whose target markets are similar to their own; there may be opportunities for piggy-back activities or cross-marketing or joint venture initiatives.
- *Branches and channels.* Companies with front-line contact with their customer base will identify opportunities for data gathering.
- *Servicing.* Do customers have to come back to have their product serviced? This provides an opportunity both for data gathering and timely verification.

Tactical activity

Companies may launch specific tactical promotional campaigns, the object of which is to augment the database or acquire additional data. They could include:

- *Sales promotions, prize draws and competitions.* These all provide the opportunity to collect entrants' details. The techniques can be used tactically to gather primary information (e.g. prospecting or customer identification) or for data enhancement, by requiring entrants to proffer new information about themselves or their household.
- *PR events.* Those who attend company events, product launches, etc., demonstrate an affinity with the brand. Primary and qualifying data can be captured as qualification of entry or through sales promotion or prize draw techniques at the event.

The increasing use of the Internet for customer data acquisition has introduced a key benefit to database marketers. The wide acceptance of customers to use registration or query form screens obviates the cost of data capture and potentially increases the accuracy of input. With all other media the hard copy captured data have to be punched in, either by a company employee or more usually by a data entry bureau that may be on the other side of the world, and this can impose a considerable cost on the exercise.

Purchase or rent lists

Companies can acquire lists from external sources to augment their database, expanding the volume of prospects or qualifying or updating existing records. Some will be available for purchase, others on a lease basis, allowing a pre-defined number of uses or unlimited use within a specified time period. Most lists are available on a one-use rental basis.

Leased and rented lists will be seeded with names of contacts to guard against illicit use of the data. Reputable list managers or brokers should be able to furnish this detail and will provide a data mandate confirming the origin and ownership of the data and any data protection implications. The British List Brokers' Association or the Institute of Direct Marketing can give advice on choosing a list supplier.

Box 5.1:
CHECKLIST FOR BUYING OR RENTING LISTS OF DATA

When considering the purchase or rental a four-point checklist should be applied:

- What is the original source of the data?
- Why was the list compiled? Often a good indication of what the list will really contain.
- How often has it been used? Has it been over-exploited in recent times?
- What response rates have been achieved in the past?

When selecting a list for rental or purchase it is essential for the user to compile a robust brief that cannot be misinterpreted. Learn from the experience of the case study below.

Case study:
MISTAKEN IDENTITIES

An estate agent dealing in very expensive properties wished to acquire a list of house-holders in the smartest areas of England. It went to the trouble of selecting those neighbourhoods with the highest Council Tax bandings and translating them into the specific postcodes it felt defined the geographical areas it desired. The agent then merely requested names and addresses in those areas from a list broker supplying data from the electoral roll. By requesting data purely by postcode, and with no other qualifying data, the selection it received comprised a list of people living in those areas which included chauffeurs, cooks and household staff. Given the type of house-holders in those areas, many were not on the electoral roll, since they were overseas nationals, or people for whom these properties were second or third homes.

Marketing partners

Data can also be acquired through data swaps with other organizations with which there is an affinity. There are some industries that have formally created data pools used by members who may even be competing (e.g. charities). Formal marketing partnerships can also yield data from a number of contributors and partners will have predetermined access and use. All these must of course comply with data protection best practice and legislation.

Data enhancement from external sources

Address enhancement

Additional qualification data can be sourced externally. Postcodes and postal address structuring can be applied either by specialist bureaux or by using software that has as its reference the postal address files of the countries in which the company is marketing. There are around 200 national postal administrations around the world providing this data.

This rapid addressing concept has been widely adopted by call centres that need to ensure swift and accurate address entry; entering the postcode drives the automatic population of most of the address. Web site registration is being made easier and more accurate by providing a similar function using the postal address files. The site visitor merely has to enter his postcode for the majority of the address to be populated in the appropriate fields.

It should be noted, however, that this process provides such results only in territories where the postcode can be linked to a discrete selection of addresses, as in the United Kingdom. The move towards the 5+4 format in the United States will help to some degree, but those countries using the standard European four- or five-digit code or clones of the US-originated 5-digit zip code can proceed only as far as confirmation of city. Some countries, for example the Republic of Ireland, have no postal codes at all.

Adding qualifying data

Companies that specialize in qualified databases can match a subject company's data to theirs and provide the missing information. Companies such as Claritas, Consumer Surveys, Consodata and Experian have established databases of millions of households in the United Kingdom and continental Europe. Each record is qualified by an extensive array of research factors that can provide demographic and lifestyle information for consumer databases, and social value grouping information can be acquired and added in, thereby adding both explicit and aspirational/attitudinal (psychographic) elements for profiling. Some data companies can also provide purchase intention for specific types of products or services.

107

The psychographic aspect can be a major influence on segmentation. Psychographics is not, as some believe, synonymous with lifestyles. Two households may have identical demographics and be differentiated by their lifestyle preferences, but further differentiation may be achieved by understanding their aspirations and attitudes towards the product, the brand or their own profile.

Case Study:
ROVER

Rover, the motor manufacturer, needed to identify prospects for a new mid-range car. Having used demographic and lifestyle questionnaires across its new car owner database, it had a robust profile of the prospects it sought. Mailing lists were recommended that met this profile, and one particular list seemed especially apt. To be certain, a selection of names was tested by telephone research. Whilst the demographics and lifestyles were accurate, the psychographics were not. These people were so concerned with their personal image that they preferred to have a pre-owned, larger prestige car with perhaps a personalized licence plate on their driveway rather than a brand-new but smaller car. The list was a list of second-hand car snobs and not of any great use to Rover's new car sales task, and hence Rover's proposition would be irrelevant to a prospect on that list.

For business-to-business, similarly, business demographic criteria (turnover, number of employees, type of premises, sector, etc.) can be added, as can the job titles of business contacts and the names of people in specific job functions. Arrangements can be put in place for changes of important elements, like key personnel, to be provided on a proactive basis so that the quality of the data can be readily maintained.

Business information vendors

Business information vendors can also provide information on sectors or performance within certain markets, specific company information, competitor activities and even information on weather, travel and currency fluctuations can be provided on a 'constant awareness' basis and can be integrated into the data strategy.

Adding research data

Research data can be both discrete and general. If research is discrete then it can be matched back to the subject, providing specific qualification criteria for those who respond. Information can then be extrapolated across other similar subjects to provide selection criteria, expanded profiles or segmentation.

Other data elements

Some data elements may be 'organically generated' within the database. Such data are referred to as *derived* data and may be acquired as a result of analysis or applying specific calculations. A simple example may be the automatic calculation of customers' age from their date of birth or the creation of banded values such as age groups (twenty-one to thirty-five, fifty-plus, etc.) from discrete personal data. More complex algorithms can be applied to generate scores or propensity quotients that can be used as additional selection or segmentation criteria.

There is overhead attached to holding data in terms of storage, disk space and the implication on hardware and software. There is also a management overhead – the greater the amount of data held, the more management time will be required in data checking, handling data problems and administering the database. There is also a data protection implication: are you acquiring and holding data that really you have no use for and should not be collecting as it is irrelevant to your business?

THINK POINT

Why is it important to qualify demographics with other qualification data in the development of a consumer profile?

Two customers may have identical demographics but totally different lifestyles and/or psychographics; in order that the message is as relevant as possible these variations are essential information for the marketer.

DATA QUALITY

The value of the data in the database will relate directly to its quality and integrity. It is possible to achieve meaningful results without sophisticated modelling, so long as you have high-quality, robust and reliable data. The better the quality of the data, the more reliable the answers will be to queries run against the database.

Validation processes help with quality and integrity, making sure that the data being added to the database is valid. Business rules manage the validation process, and reference tables ensure conformity and adherence to standards and should be applied in all aspects of data acquisition and use. When designing a data capture device, like an entry form or application screen on a Web site, or when capturing data either using in-house data entry resources or an external data punching bureau, the brief should be the same, with all referring to the same set of rules.

The analytical or selectivity applications of the database rely on conformity; hence the table of references ensures that only values within the predetermined set may be entered into the database. For example, a Web site registration form may request details of how the customer first accessed the site. Normally termed the source code, or media code, this is an important piece of data, since not only does it provide feedback on marketing response but it also establishes a criterion on which customers could be selected for future contact.

If left to their own devices to complete a free text field, customers may enter, as in Figure 5.1, a free text string complete with typographical errors. Using a reference table of acceptable responses, conformity is assured and the quality of the data is maintained (Figure 5.2). Bear in mind also the data storage overhead: the free text string has to be held verbatim, whilst the selected value in a table need only be held as a code reference.

Key issues to manage

Data acquisition – are all marketing initiatives sharing the same data goals, are the needs of other departments being taken into consideration?

Decay

Data will decay over time. Business data tend to decay at a greater rate, since people move jobs, companies move premises or reorganize, acquire or are acquired by other companies or go out of business more often than individuals move house. Estimates suggest that 30 per cent of management and professional staff change positions annually.

Where did you first come across our site?	Freind told me about it

Figure 5.1 *Free text string complete with spelling error*

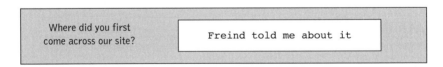

Figure 5.2 *Conformity ensured and the quality of the data maintained*

Box 5.2:
KEY ISSUES TO MANAGE

- Does activity in one area conflict with a communication strategy of another?
- What controls can be put in place?
- Adherence to the business rules of the database and the data validity criteria.
- Data protection – best practices.
- Use of the data – is it being overused? Are you risking the relationship by too many communications bombarding the customer?

With regard to individuals, during the last UK property boom attrition rates of up to 12 per cent a year were experienced, meaning that in just four years about half the volume of any consumer database would be out of date. About 8–10 per cent of the population currently move house or die per year.

Depending on the provenance of the data and how often it has been mailed in the past, companies will embark on cleansing, using such tools as NCOA – the National Change of Address File (Royal Mail), the Mortality File and, in order to maintain data protection best practice, the Mailing Preference Service. NCOA can also provide the new address of the gone-aways on your file, since the source of the data is Royal Mail's postal redirection service for home movers.

Most reputable data-processing bureaux will be able to provide a service whereby a company's data are washed against these external data sources in order to suppress those who have died, moved or have an objection to receiving direct communications.

People change their names too; remember that in some countries most married women will change both title and surname.

Decay can also be the result of natural progression, when the customer is no longer in the market for the product or service. For example, once a person turns thirty-one years old they are out of the market for a Club 18–30 holiday; similarly once a baby becomes potty-trained the parents no longer buy nappies.

Data appraisal

In order to assess the quality of the data, an audit should be carried out. View the data on screen or in hard copy – most databases will allow the user to export data into a more familiar environment, like Microsoft® Excel, where you can either view the data or print out the spreadsheets if more convenient, checking for key indicators regarding the reliability of the data.

Box 5.3:
CHECKLIST FOR APPRAISING DATA QUALITY

- *Do fields hold what they claim to hold?* The column header may define the field, but past users may have decided to use the column for something else, just because there was no field for their purpose.
- *Is it in a usable format?* Are the data free text format or have rules or reference codes been applied? Codes are obviously much easier to analyse than free text, e.g. if the age of the customer is held, is it in years or is it the date of birth? Obviously, date of birth is preferable, as the age in years changes.
- *How extensively populated are the fields?* Are there fields on the database that are sparsely populated? For example, does every customer have a title (Mr, Mrs, etc.) and are the addresses postcoded? The fact that there is a field in existence does not mean that the data are there.
- *Ascertain the age of the data.* Have they passed their 'Use by date'? Remember the levels of decay. Is the file even worth looking at?
- *What needs to be done to make the data usable/valuable?* What needs to be done to improve the quality of the data? How can the integrity be protected? Can the empty fields be populated?

The cost implications associated with holding data have already been considered. Similarly any investment in enhancement of the data must also be driven by commercial benefit. If the greater part of the database is of adequate quality it is sometimes not worth processing to enhance only a marginal element. Rather consider what could be achieved most easily and reliably. The quick wins.

Acquiring data from a number of sources could 'infect' the database through variations in format or unreliable or invalid information within the data set and also through the processes that are in place for loading such data.

It is therefore imperative for business rules to be devised that address both data validity and format, whilst ensuring that the load process maintains the integrity of the database, with specific parameters to govern data overwrites, data deletion, amalgamation and change controls. This would also comprise back-up and archiving policies and disaster recovery.

THINK POINT

How can the quality of the data being added to the database be protected so that they remain reliable?

Establish and apply in all cases a set of business rules that govern the input of data to each field of the database; wherever possible restrict input values to a table of predetermined values that will ensure conformity and more reliable selections and reporting. Carry these rules and input values across to any briefings for data capture to be carried out by an external resource.

DATA STORAGE AND MANAGEMENT

Essentially the database environment comprises three elements – the central database or data repository, the tools for data maintenance and the tools for reporting and data analysis (see Figure 5.3). The central database is independent of the tools.

The structure of the central database will depend on the application of the system. Often, where the central database has been constructed for key commercial transactional purposes (the 'lifeblood processes', such as order processing or financial activities), this may not be conducive to returning swift responses to querying or reporting.

Extensive querying and analytical activity can place a demand for processing on the central database and this additional demand may limit the resources available for transactional processing. Hence the marketing database, normally constructed in a relational structure with varying degrees of normalization to ensure optimization for analysis, increasingly resides outside the transactional systems of the business, integrating data from various sources, both internal and external, that help build the information.

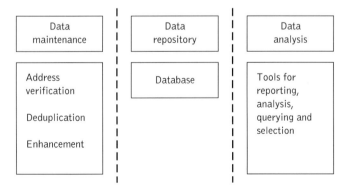

Figure 5.3 *The database environment*

113

Data warehouses

The technological advances demonstrated by data warehouses, data marts and marketing universes have facilitated the management decision processes that benefit from the integration of data from across the business. All these are concerned with extracting data from large corporate legacy systems and delivering either selected attributes or data merged from disparate systems into manageable chunks that can then be used for management decision, analysis or to automate operational or communications processes.

Kimball (1996) defined a data warehouse as a copy of transaction data specifically structured for querying and reporting. Gupta (1997) suggests that simply a data warehouse is managed data situated after and outside the operational systems. However, the concept of data warehousing in marketing has broadened beyond being solely transaction data, providing an optimized structure for the integration of disparate data sources from both within the business and external sources.

Data warehousing essentially removes the processing of data querying and analysis away from the lifeblood systems of the enterprise, which could become overloaded with query traffic from users and interrupt the essential business process flow. It also permits the relationship between data from different systems by acting as a central data repository with a common data structure and data dictionary to facilitate selection and analysis.

'Data warehouse' and 'data mart' are frequently misunderstood terms, with many having strong beliefs regarding their use and benefits. From a technology standpoint there really is no difference in that both are databases tasked with processing, combining and structuring data in order that its use will benefit the business.

Probably the most distinctive attribute of a data warehouse or mart is its architecture and design, and these are heavily influenced by the business requirements. A balance must therefore be struck between an infinite ability to load any data with little or no recourse to technical rework versus an adaptable 'business-focused' design that reflects the corporate structures and processes and, most importantly, is recognizable by the people who will use it.

A data warehouse typically contains a wide variety of data that present a consistent view of the business, to support the management decision process across the enterprise. It may combine databases across an entire corporation and will address a strategic requirement and is likely to contain a high volume of data to a greater level of detail than a data mart.

Data marts

Demarest (1994) suggests that data marting deals almost exclusively with servicing a distinct community of users, focusing on their need for information from diverse systems, reflecting the user's understanding of the business.

Thus a data mart is usually subject-oriented, smaller, likely to contain more summarized data (i.e. less detail) and will be applied tactically within a single business unit or department. Hence it is not unusual to find the accounts department with its own data mart, HR with theirs and Marketing with theirs, but each will reflect the requirements of the specific department as regards data attributes, level of history held and channels of access and analysis.

Data marts take account of the PC user or the desktop analyst, presenting only the data that interest him in a way that is appropriate to the business processes and culture of the department or business unit.

Not all data marts need be physical. Data can be brought together into a universe for analysis or into an aggregated and summarized multi-dimensional structure referred to as an OLAP (online analytical processing) cube. Both these are established so that end users can 'drill down' into the data to refine their analysis with a specific set of analytical tools. Being virtual structures they can be created to serve a tactical purpose and then destroyed, with new universes or cubes being created containing different data attributes or alternative summarizations or aggregations.

However, data marts could be sub-sets of a data warehouse, providing subject-specific access for different users' reporting and decision support requirements.

Marketing universes

Any of these structures could be termed a marketing universe, i.e. a data repository, existing separately from the central transactional system that contains all the required data, incorporates the feeds from external sources and is subjected to the analysis tools.

Both data warehouses and data marts are predominantly static (although those applied to support e-Commerce are increasingly near real-time), reflecting the business as it was at the time of last update or creation, respectively. However, it must be noted that modern data warehouses and marts are not just replicas of the data in other systems: the data are enriched, enhanced and, in the case of the marts, specially aggregated or summarized in line with the user's requirements. The data mart or data warehouse may often be viewed within the organization as a 'marketing database'.

Box 5.4:
GENERIC DEVELOPMENT PROCESSES FOR DATA MARTS

- *Source systems identified.* Review the transactional system(s), sources of qualifying data and external data feeds from which tables and attributes might be migrated for integration into the data mart.
- *Source tables and attributes.* Assess the tables and attributes within those systems and identify those to be migrated for integration into the data mart. Attributes should be considered in terms of their likely importance and not by the level of population, for example.
- *Construct target database.* Construct a target database for each market sector or business unit (e.g. Marketing) containing relevant source tables from the source system(s), with Primary Keys and Foreign Keys. Referential integrity should be applied and enforced, and each table and attribute assigned a meaningful name where applicable, bearing in mind users' needs. Often the descriptions within a legacy or *lifeblood* system will be coded and a translation to a more instantly recognizable description means greater user-friendliness within the target database. From this a list of the data attributes can be compiled and the relationships between them defined.
- *Extraction, Transformation and Load (ETL).* Create processes to map data from source to target and to contribute to an audit trail facility. These processes will have to be repeatable, for implementation whenever a refresh of the data mart is required, normally on a regular scheduled basis.
- *Training.* Users will require training in the use of the data mart and in the business intelligence tools to be applied and understanding the implications of data analysis. A super-expert user should be appointed and specially trained to be able to handle *ad hoc* issues within the business environment.
- *Piloting and testing.* The system should be piloted across a fixed period and the users provided with a process for advising the development team of queries or problems encountered. These issues could range from system functionality to data queries. A series of follow-up meetings would normally support the process. Following the initial process, the query process and possibly regular meetings should be maintained to deal with any further issues and questions on a scheduled, regular basis.

THINK POINT

Why might a data mart be better suited to marketing applications than a data warehouse in a business with large, disparate transactional data sources?

One or more data marts can be constructed to the requirements of the marketers, containing only the data they need and reflecting their departmental requirements, rather than having to deal with a repository of vast amounts of largely irrelevant data.

TOOLS AND TECHNIQUES FOR DATA MANIPULATION AND ANALYSIS

As marketers over recent years have gained access to greater volumes of data from both within and outside the organization, so the technology has kept pace if not exceeded the requirement for analysis and data manipulation. This technology is not addressing raw data access, such as SQL, but delivering business intelligence and a greater level of automation directly to the marketer's desktop.

Box 5.5:
TYPES OF TOOLS REQUIRED FOR DATA MANIPULATION AND ANALYSIS

- Infrastructure (basic IT platform) and (ETL)
- Pure statistical
- Data warehousing and data marts
- Intelligent and neural agents
- Data querying, visualization and counts
- OLAP/Reporting
- Data mining
- Campaign management

The techniques and the software that supports them can be mapped according to their 'marketer friendliness'. Some applications belong unquestionably in the IT department, others with the statisticians and mathematicians. Each can be plotted against a departmental (IT or in the business) axis and a functional (statistician or marketer) axis (Figure 5.4).

117

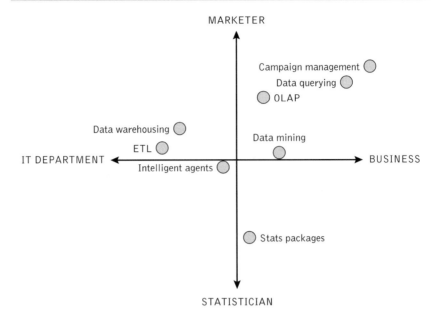

Figure 5.4 *Where data tools are useful within organizations*

The remainder of this section will be concerned with the tools in the top right quadrant – the Marketer/Business area of the map. There are fuzzy borders between applications, often fuelled by the ambitious claims of the developers, revisions of the tools to address additional functionality and different understanding of the terms being used. So this is not a review of products, but rather an appreciation of techniques and how ideally the software should support them.

Data counts and visualization

These tools will enable a user to construct queries against the data to deliver volumes of records that meet the specified criteria, often as a means of campaign planning. These will often be multiple criteria, such as purchasers of a particular product, from a certain geographical region, between certain dates. Once run, the application will present a volume, which can then be reviewed and amended if required by changing the query parameters and the data viewed, either graphically or in tabular format.

A data visualization and counting tool may operate online, that is, working directly against the central data repository, or offline, relating to a summarized data universe or data mart. The offline scenario reduces the query traffic to the database and so can avoid bottlenecks on transactional systems, but relies on summarization or data aggregation that is usually carried out by middleware as part of the loading process.

The user will establish the data attributes to be included and can then create the query using the data attributes, values and full Boolean logic (the ability to select using the operators 'and', 'or' and 'not'). For example, the user might request all customers who have bought product A *and* bought *or* enquired about product B and have *not* made a purchase in the last twelve months. Queries can normally be saved to be reused with different selection values (for example, select customers who have bought product C *and* bought *or* enquired about product D and have *not* made a purchase in the last eighteen months).

This function also allows derived data to be saved back to the database or to augment the data mart; for example, the outcome of the query may identify a robust selection criterion (for example, regular customers) and so a new attribute may be created on the database to denote this against all appropriate records so that these may be selected easily in future queries.

Products in this category that marketers may encounter are FastStats, Viper, Alterian, Visual Miner or ZipCounts.

Online analytical processing

Online analytical processing (OLAP) is technology for understanding data through access to views of the database that reflect the dimensionality of the enterprise as understood by the user (OLAP Council 1997). It is characterized by the ability to undertake multi-dimensional analysis.

The data are transformed into a 'cube' or analysis universe (data mart), which contains dimensions that represent attributes of the database (for example, time, place, product and customer data) and measures (value, volume, etc.). These will have been determined in advance so that the analysis universe can be created, but it does mean that only those dimensions and measures included can be used for analysis; should the train of thought during the analysis turn to other elements, a new 'cube' will have to be created.

Some applications use a physical cube whereby data is extracted out of the database and into a separate physical structure to which the business intelligence tools then are applied. So whilst there is online access to the database, the actual analysis can be offline, within the physical cube. Some create a view of the data in cube or universe format, so to all intents and purposes it appears that there is a separate structure but in fact it is a visualization of the database and puts the same query traffic encumbrances on the database as discussed before with commensurate impact on other database users.

The multi-dimensional structure of the 'cube' provides hierarchical levels that can be drilled through and most tools will permit the user to 'slice and dice' (Codd 1993), enabling the user to slice through the data structure and reorientate the analysis against a specific dimension and then drill down to the lower levels. This drilling down should not be confused with data mining (see p. 120).

119

OLAP tools are designed for flexible analysis and reporting, rapid development and fast query performance against large volumes of data. The down side, possibly, is the resource required for the development and maintenance of the 'cube' and the indices required to meet the performance expectations.

Products in this category that marketers may encounter are Business Objects, Cognos or Essbase.

Data mining

Data mining relates to the use of automated process in the discovery of patterns buried within a large data set. There are two approaches, one where the analyst has a hypothesis and wishes to identify the extent to which it is prevalent within the data, and the other where the analyst has no preconceptions and requires the revelation of latent significant patterns within the data.

In the first instance, where there is a hypothesis to test, the analyst would be working with predetermined key indicators defined by the business as a known pattern of behaviour or combination of behaviour with customer profile attributes. For example, taking an insurance company, a particular profile of customer may have a propensity for making spurious claims. The attributes defining this profile and behaviour would be applied to the database of customers and their transactions and responses, and a model of customer type and behaviour built, to predict future behaviour.

Once constructed, the outcome would normally be validated using an OLAP or querying tool. The analyst would then continue to mine the data to check the peripheries (who do not match the model exactly but are close by) and the extremes (those so distant from the model outcome to be of interest).

In the second instance the business cannot define key indicators or does not know its data adequately. In this case parameters of statistical significance are set to govern the patterns that are returned to the analyst, the software having mined through the database of, for example, customers and their transactions and responses. Again, an OLAP or query tool would validate the outcome, permitting some train of thought analysis to add a lateral dimension to the process.

Data mining requires breadth (numbers of columns, data sets) and depth (volume of data) and, as can be seen, an introduction of tacit data in the form of the analyst's interpretations and subsequent validation querying.

Products in this category that marketers may encounter are Synera, White Cross, Clementine or Data Miner.

CAMPAIGN MANAGEMENT

Campaign management tools enable the marketer to establish the content and execution of direct marketing initiatives. They can be used both tactically (one-off or to address short-term objectives) and strategically (longer-term, multi-level communication strategies).

The software will enable the marketer to apply the segmentation developed using a querying or OLAP tool, to specify the interaction between the segments and create the association between different cells with a specific offer or proposition and an appropriate medium of delivery (mail, phone, e-mail, etc.).

It will also permit the establishment of test structures (specific cells that may be used for testing the effectiveness of an alternative offer or creative treatment) and control files, used to assess the effectiveness of the campaign or elements of it. Most modern campaign management systems permit the marketer to plan the campaigns in a visual way, creating campaign maps similar to the one in Figure 5.5.

In this case five types of customers have been identified and are in mutually exclusive segments; in addition there is a segment of objectors, people who have requested that they are not contacted, and these are used to suppress names and addresses from the selected audience. The records are then de-duplicated; in this case the marketer wants only one communication per household rather than one per person.

The net file will then be divided into campaign cells depending, for example, on offer or timing and then, in this case, a fixed percentage from each is attributed to a different creative treatment. The control file is a 1-in-n trawl through

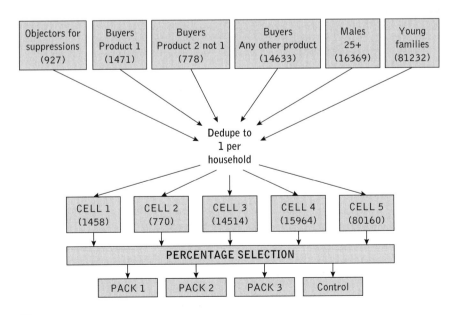

Figure 5.5 *Notional tactical campaign design*

the overall audience. Contacts in the control file will either receive a control pack (i.e. a creative treatment that has a known response expectation) or will receive nothing, to assist in the calculation of incremental sales achievement.

For strategic campaigns, the multiple stages of the communication schedule will be based on response and external criteria, creating a series of triggers for specific actions. The campaign management tool will help automate this complex process, covering all types of response media and communication channels and maintaining any testing requirements.

The use of suppressions, as used simply in the tactical scenario to remove objectors, can be extended to prevent over-communication or the delivery of a proposition that may cross with a previous or planned communication.

The strategic model shown in Figure 5.6 takes account of responders and non-responders to each element and allocates them accordingly into a pre-planned follow-up phase. This process can continue with many phases, each taking account of the one before, to create a logical process of conversion or retention.

Products in this category that marketers may encounter are Campaigner, E.piphany, Xchange, Vantage, Intrinsic, Quadstone or Cascade.

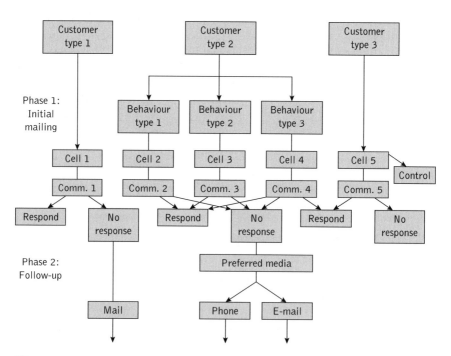

Figure 5.6 *Notional strategic campaign design (up to second phase)*

DYNAMICS OF DATA-LED MARKETING

Commercial intelligence and knowledge management are being addressed on varying levels of sophistication, often usually emanating from IT departments. Instead they need to be a key process in the definition, implementation and ongoing measurement of the commercial strategy.

Information gathering has emerged as a natural activity of the sales force, research and development, purchasing and marketing functions by nature of their regular external contacts. Until now this has been a disparate activity suffering from, on the one hand, the natural tendency to contain information within departmental boundaries or, on the other, exhibiting reluctance to share information within the business.

e-Commerce has imposed new, reduced time scales in direct marketing activity. Previously the direct marketer could anticipate when a mailing or phone call was effected and, within some degree of control, when a response would be generated. Access to the Web has reduced this element of control. A marketer can no longer engineer when a contact may wish to encounter his message, proposition or brand, or, indeed, come across it.

As companies move seamlessly across borders, this process will become increasingly involved. A complex struggle will take place. Enlightened multinational corporations may gain advantage over leaner and fitter small and medium-size enterprises (SMEs) through the tactical use of information, whilst empowered SMEs may outsmart those larger competitors that remain with the traditional methods.

There is a need to establish valid methods of acquiring data from customers and visitors to e-Commerce Web sites and applying the resultant information and knowledge to drive variations in Web site content and appearance and to determine commercial propositions and further data acquisition.

Customers and prospects presented with the same Web pages on each visit and being expected to reactively search for relevant products and offers will soon tire of e-Commerce and the marketer will lose the opportunity to develop a true relationship with the customer. Similarly, a visitor to a site presented with a vast array of qualification questions would be equally turned off. Tailoring the view of the site to the visitor will mean that qualification questions can be posed on an incremental basis, to populate the database using a hierarchy of importance to drive the questionnaire.

The development of the Web has coincided with the appearance of new, intuitive data analysis tools employing techniques that provide for the delivery of information and the definition and interpretation of patterns within that information, within time frames conducive to achieving the required dynamics.

123

Case study:
FINANCIAL SERVICES COMPANY, ENGLAND

The company had a large corporate account-based database on an IBM AS400 platform (addressing different transactional or customer service needs), plus a number of small department-owned databases run on PCs that included a Marketing database that was held externally and a system for managing events and conferences.

The problem

No links existed between the Marketing and Events databases or between the Events database and the AS400 systems. This meant that there were duplicate records but nowhere could the company achieve a total view of the contacts. Nor were there any business intelligence (BI) tools; the Marketing Department was relying on pre-set reports. Each time a marketing campaign was planned, selections had to be made from each of the databases and discrete extracts run; these were then provided to the mailing house, which undertook a de-duplication process subject to predetermined selection hierarchies, to provide the final mailing file.

The objective was to provide:

- A single, comprehensive view of a customer's dealings.
- Improvement in the quality of management information.
- A means to acquire and retain useful client information in a database.

The CRM issues demanded a central data repository. The recommendations were for the company to audit its data and pass it through a cleansing and enhancement process, prior to matching the duplicate records and merging data according to pre-set business rules.

The solution (see Figure 5.7)

The central AS400 system was augmented, with all additional data and each contact flagged by status (e.g. customer, prospect, enquirer, etc.). Regularly refreshed extracts were exported into a data mart (analysis universe), which was further augmented with qualifying data that the central system could not hold or for which development on the AS400 system was not economic and summarized or aggregated transactional histories. Business intelligence tools were introduced alongside the universe to facilitate querying, *ad hoc* analyses and campaign planning and management.

In this way the company was able to leverage the investment in the transactional system, could close down the satellite databases in the departments and introduce additional purpose-specific data without the need for costly redevelopment of the central system. For the first time the company would have a total customer view and could begin to maximize the opportunities from customer-centric CRM.

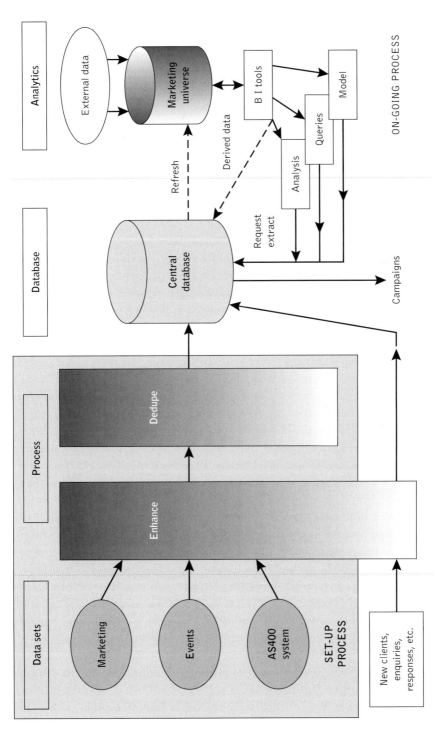

Figure 5.7 Notional solution

As the knowledge culture grows, so the interest in data throughout the enterprise also grows. The benefits of combining information from different departments, from different regions, even from different businesses, are being realized. Software tools such as intelligent agents search for meaningful additions to the knowledge base and data marts with business intelligence software facilitate the analysis of extensive data sets from disparate sources right on the desktops, within hours rather than months and without the mammoth budgets normally associated with corporate data warehouses.

This overall concept, taking the basic principles of data-driven marketing so successfully implemented in direct mail and telemarketing, aims to establish a process for creating the 'back back-end' of e-Commerce, its link to both internal and external marketing data and knowledge bases and the implementation of customer relationship management (Collins *et al.* 2000).

The existence and growth of the Web and the increasing exponents of the medium have implications on both sides of the data-driven communications equation. On the one hand, the Web provides a novel, exciting and convenient medium for delivering a message to customers and prospective customers. On the other, it presents a channel for data collection that makes possible concepts that were only hypothetical in the past.

The beginning of the 1990s saw the introduction of data driving a variety of media beyond the traditional direct mail. For instance, computers were interfaced with telecommunications equipment to derive applications to assist in the management of customer relationships, enabling call centre agents to prepare themselves for calls, access customers' records and have repeat calls from a customer always channelled through to one agent. Or data being used to drive variations in customer magazines and newsletters, with such notable examples as Rover's internationally acclaimed *Catalyst* magazine (Leiderman 1989) bringing lifestyle versionalization and reader personalization to the realm of contract publishing.

However, in all these cases the systems that drove them relied upon pre-selection and qualification of the data. The industry even talked about unqualified contacts as being *suspects* rather than prospects. The sheer wealth of information available on the Web, the ability to identify and acquire it and the tools now available to manage it in all its varying formats and structures all mean that disparate data, wherever they may reside, could be made available to add qualification, enhancement or verification to a marketer's database. The natural corollary to that is a keener degree of customer profiling and targeting and a greater level of personalization of message, proposition and presentation.

Previously the data process was often presented as a funnel to depict a channel for information that is open to as much as possible at the top, but which needs a process of filtering and selection to be applied to that information so that the best is allowed to pass through into the business process (Figure 5.8). The down

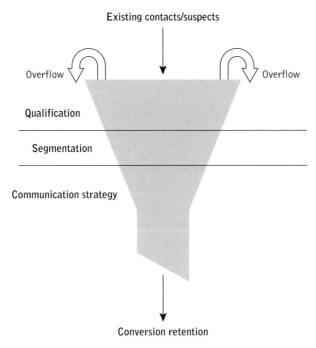

Existing contacts/suspects

Overflow

Overflow

Qualification

Segmentation

Communication strategy

Conversion retention

Figure 5.8 *Model of old-style data processing*

side was that controls had to be in place at the top to guard against overflow, which could mean the loss of both bad and good potential information.

The new information channel is less of a funnel and more of a wide conduit (Figure 5.9). It still allows as much as possible in at the top, but there is less need for those controls since the value of the data cannot be predetermined. Valid, but unstructured, data can be fed in from a multitude of sources, both internal and external, and their value determined once any links are identified. The information can then be attributed to the records on the database and parameters to drive the relationship established.

These new concepts also have implications for clustering and segmentation. Combinations of demographic and behavioural criteria have traditionally defined clusters. Once defined, these have been used to drive product development and marketing activity. Cluster sets change their content and their direction; individuals join and leave as new information is learned about them and as the importance of the business rules inherent in the data relationships is recognized. This means that the clusters are volatile and dynamic. Their dynamism must be tracked and the changes identified in order to keep the marketing strategy and communications schedule on track.

Marketers can find that markets for their products are dwindling, readership for their magazines is flagging and response to their once attractive offers reduced.

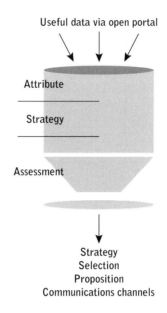

Useful data via open portal

Attribute

Strategy

Assessment

Strategy
Selection
Proposition
Communications channels

Figure 5.9 *Model of new-style data processing*

This may not be because the product is any lower in quality or the price has leapt; it can be that the customer profile once associated with that product or marker has changed shape and has moved out of the target zone for that marketer. As considered above, has the customer turned thirty-one and so is no longer eligible for a Club 18–30 vacation? Has the child reached an age where his parents are no longer interested in nappies?

These changes and new viable targets must be recognized to effect and maintain product and communications strategies. Early warning of changes in customer profiles can be provided from constant data feeds with triggers identified to drive proposition, communication channel and delivery.

CHAPTER SUMMARY

This chapter has explained the important role that data and databases play in creating and maintaining relationships with customers and prospects. With the combination of greater availability of data within enterprises, the trend towards automation of complex processes and the advances in technology that make it all possible, the twenty-first-century marketer sees the database as a vital element of the marketing armoury, a fundamental element in the overall marketing mix and an appreciating asset of the business.

The increasing accessibility of data in real time and the ability to manage the resultant dynamics within the database will be key to the achievement of true one-to-one marketing. The complementary operation of tools for data acquisition, manipulation, analysis and campaign management will provide a chain of triggers and actions that will enable marketers to be more predictive in the potential outcome of their initiatives, but also provide greater confidence in their execution and address more closely the shift towards demand-led business fuelled by e-Commerce.

FURTHER READING

Berry, M. J. A. and Linoff, G. S. (2000) *Mastering Data Mining*, New York: Wiley.
Shaw, R. and Stone, M. (1998) *Database Marketing*, Aldershot: Gower.

REFERENCES

Codd, E. F. & Associates (1993) 'Providing OLAP (Online Analytical Processing) to user-analysts: an IT mandate', White Paper commissioned by Arbor Software, Ann Arbor MI.

Collins, M. I., Jackson, P. and Peters, M. (2000) 'Competitive Intelligence and Knowledge Management,' Society of Competitive Intelligence Professionals conference, London.

Demarest, M. (1994) 'Building the data mart', *DBMS Magazine,* 7, 8: 44.

Gupta, V. R. (1997) 'An Introduction to Data Warehousing', White Paper, Service System Corporation, Chicago.

Jenkinson, A. (1995) *Valuing your Customers*, London: McGraw-Hill.

Kimball, R. (1996) *The Data Warehouse Toolkit: Practical Techniques for Building Dimensional Data Warehouses*, New York: Wiley.

Leiderman, R. (1989) *The Telephone Book*, London: McGraw-Hill.

Malhotra, Y. (1998) 'Tools@Work: deciphering the knowledge management hype', *Journal for Quality and Participation,* 21, 4: 58–60.

OLAP Council (1997) *OLAP and OLAP Server Definitions*. Online. Available HTTP: www.olapcouncil.org/research/glossaryly.htm (accessed September 2002).

 ## WEB LINKS

Sites all visited during August/September 2002

www.compinfo-center.com/ai/intelligent_agents.htm
Intelligent agent software.

www.jimnovo.com
Data mining.

www.olapreport.com
OLAP tools and application.

www.olapcouncil.org
OLAP tools and application.

www.crm-forum.com
Customer relationship management.

www.intelligententerprise.com
Intelligent agent software.

Part IV

The boundaries of e-Business

Chapter 6

The ethics environment for e-Business

LAURA J. SPENCE

KEY LEARNING POINTS

After completing this chapter you will have an understanding of:

- What we mean by ethics
- Specific ethical approaches and models
- Ethical issues that are distinctive to e-Business
- The need for e-Business practitioners to formulate agreed ethical standards

ORDERED LIST OF SUB TOPICS

- The concept of business ethics
    - Definition
    - Are there distinct ethical issues in e-Business?
- Computers in the workplace
    - Advantages and changes
    - Disadvantages
- Computer-mediated communication
    - The changing nature of human relationships
    - Fragility and ownership of electronic data
    - Use, dual use and abuse
    - Monitoring and privacy
- Ethics in cyberspace
- The digital divide?
- Professional behaviour

THE CONCEPT OF BUSINESS ETHICS

Ethics is about understanding right and wrong. Business ethics is an increasingly acknowledged part of business life, and this is no less true for e-Business. This chapter introduces the concept of business ethics and looks particularly at how they relate to e-Business. It will discuss the extent to which ethical e-Business issues are distinctive, how they result in particularly challenging dilemmas because of the need to rely on computers and evolving debates about ethics in cyberspace. The final part of the chapter will include a discussion of how professionalism among e-Business practitioners is one way of encouraging high standards of integrity.

Definition

In theoretical perspectives on business decision making, the dominant discourse is often focused on maximizing profit for company shareholders alone. This perspective is increasingly proving to be inadequate. In practice, profit maximization in the long term may best be achieved by making sustainable decisions that take the consequences for trust between stakeholders (including employees, competitors, suppliers, customers, the local community and shareholders) into account. This is called 'enlightened self-interest' – where business managers take 'ethical' decisions because of the positive impact on the financial bottom line. It is far from being the only reason for the increasing acknowledgement of business ethics. Some business people see the primary role of business as being other than profit maximization. Owner-managers of small firms, for example, have been found to be particularly concerned about the financial and personal welfare of their employees (Spence 2000). Business and managers have increasing power as a result of their activities, and with it comes responsibility for their actions.

While there are common understandings of right and wrong in business life which we use every day and see in newspaper headlines, a detailed consideration of ethics in business cannot rely on shallow statements of how we ought to behave. It is necessary to draw on well established theories of ethics. Here the briefest of introductions will be given to some of the key ethical perspectives. Further reading on ethics is strongly recommended.

Ethical theories offer frameworks by which individuals can reflect on the acceptability of actions taken and evaluate moral judgements and moral character. The theories are normative, and outline ways of assessing good and bad behaviour, usually on the basis that decisions about moral practices can be cognitively arrived at. The purpose of the application of ethical theory is *not* to make blanket judgements about the rights or wrongs of the actions observed. The theory enables a systematic analysis using established structures for analysing behaviour from the perspective of moral philosophy. In this chapter the following theories will be considered: ethical egoism, utilitarianism, Kantianism, discourse ethics theory and virtue theory.

Ethical egoism and utilitarianism are consequentialist theories. This means that, when considering whether an act is right or wrong, the actor considers the likely outcome of that act. Both theories suffer from the fact that outcomes can be difficult to predict and they also ignore the individual rights of others.

The ethical egoist acts in a way which furthers his or her own self-interest (although it may be 'enlightened' self-interest). Faced with the possibility, for example, of copying a competitor's Web page design, the ethical egoist will weigh up what the likely outcomes will be if he or she does so. If caught out and labelled with a bad reputation by employers, possibly even facing legal charges of violating copyright, the ethical egoist will not copy other people's work. If the egoist will not be found out and will save him or herself time and trouble while still fulfilling work obligations, then the outcome is positive for the egoist and he or she should act in order to further their own self-interest. The theory suffers from inconsistency, since the egoist simultaneously must expect that everyone else will further their own self-interests too, which may well conflict with their own advancement.

Utilitarianism promotes the notion of achieving maximum happiness for society (or avoidance of pain and pursuit of pleasure). The person acting ethically according to utilitarianism will weigh up carefully which act will result in the most positive outcomes for those individuals who will be affected by it, a kind of cost–benefit analysis for happiness. When deciding, for example, whether to undercut the prices of high-street booksellers, an Internet-based business that bases the ethics of its activities on utilitarianism would consider all the positive and negative impacts on individuals of not making their books cheaper, and all the positive and negative impacts on individuals of undercutting. In such an example, although a price cut might result in some job losses and reduced dividends for shareholders, the weight of advantage for many customers is likely to be widespread, hence utilitarianism might see price undercutting on the Web as ethical.

Kantianism is a very important ethical theory. Kant argued that every individual must seek to do his or her duty. He defined 'duty' very precisely as obedience to the 'categorical imperative', which is what an individual would consider to be the rational, universal, ethical action. The act is the focus of attention in Kantian ethics and an ethical act is one which complies with the categorical imperative, i.e.:

- It is universalizable – if it is right in one situation for one person, it must be right in every situation for everyone.
- It respects other people and never uses them as a means to the actor's end.

This approach is clearly quite different from the consequentialist perspectives. For Kant the consequences of an act do not matter. It follows that it is our ethical duty not to lie, cheat or steal, to keep promises and not to use others.

Discourse ethics theory focuses on the process by which a decision is reached. Ethical actions are those which are reached by full, open discussion including all those who are connected in any way with a decision. For a business this means including all stakeholders actively in decision making. This is impracticable in some instances, and is not always culturally readily achievable, since some groups are more disposed to work towards consensus than others. The Chinese government, for example, seeks to block access by its citizens to Web sites containing material deemed inimical to the Chinese Communist Party. They do so by blocking access to two Californian search engines, Google and Altavista, via Chinese internet service providers. This action, while no doubt well intentioned, also blocks the autonomy and free choice of the citizens. They have no opportunity to voice their preference, negotiate or discuss the issue. Power is held by one party, unless individuals have the technical ability to overcome the restrictions, for example by using a numerical address.

Virtue theory considers the character of the individual who acts. A virtuous person is one who classically possesses characteristics of justice, wisdom, temperance and courage. Modern-day virtues include co-operation, loyalty, friendliness and trustworthiness. However, there is no definitive list of virtues, and they may be culturally distinctive. The ethical theories are summarized in Table 6.1.

Illegal activities can be ethical, and unethical activities legal. In the realms of e-Business, many of the issues are still finding legal precedent (see Chapter 7 on the legal environment for e-Business). Most of the ethical theories incorporate reference to legal perspectives, for example Kantians will on the whole follow

Table 6.1 Summary of ethical theories

Theory	Basis	Characteristics
Ethical egoism	Consequence-based: maximize own self-interest	Promote own well-being above everyone else's
Utilitarianism	Consequence-based: maximize utility	Greatest good of the greatest number
Kantianism	Act-based	Act in a way which is universalizable Treat people as ends in themselves, never means to ends
Discourse ethics theory	Process-based	Consensus by full, open discussion
Virtue theory	Character-based	What sort of person should I be?

the law, as will ethical egoists, since it is likely to be in their own self-interest so to do. In the global context of e-Commerce, the law simply does not provide sufficient, worldwide guidance on how e-Business managers should behave. Ethics can help fill that gap.

THINK POINT

Microsoft has been criticized in the past for unethical and even illegal competitor activities but what do you think about the character of Bill Gates? He is well known for donating personally large sums of money to good causes. Note that what you are trying to identify is whether the individual is a 'good person' who is seeking to set a good example and flourish.

Are there distinct ethical issues in e-Business?

e-Business enthusiasts will be well aware of the technical and financial advantages of e-Commerce. There are also ethical benefits. These include the potential to remove prejudice and barriers, as transactions are carried out via disembodied computer screens. The lack of need for a physical presence in a particular place, as long as computer access is available, opens up all kinds of possibilities for freedom of mobility and inclusion of those with physical needs which make working in an office environment difficult (ranging from physical disability to a distinct preference for working on a beach!).

Internet-based business activities are opening up markets, improving information provision about different products, including non-corporate information. (For example, typing 'Nike' into a search engine finds company pages as well as sites about Nike products alleging human rights abuses by the company.) The Internet allows consumers much greater access to information, opening up the market and undermining monopolies. Such impacts are highly ethical according to a utilitarian perspective.

Freedom of speech is often cited as one of the benefits of cyberspace (see Hamelink 2000: 139–64). Freedom of speech is a fundamental human right, yet it is not enjoyed by all. The Internet can be a means of increasing freedom of speech. Technology and law have been unsuccessful as a means of controlling what is on the Web. This means, at one extreme, that abhorrent pornography is available and that inaccurate claims made in relation to e-Business products or services are equally difficult to control.

We generally become aware of ethical issues through dilemmas, conflicts and discomfort with situations, behaviours and acts. The remainder of this chapter will focus mainly on the more challenging aspects of e-Business, particularly the implications for workplaces reliant on ICTs and the new issues prevalent to cyberspace.

137

COMPUTERS IN THE WORKPLACE

The expansion of e-Business goes hand in hand with reliance on computers in the workplace. Organizations have become information technology-intensive in their operations, and this in itself has significant implications for employees.

Advantages and changes

Anyone who works in an office will have noticed some of the great advantages of workplace computerization. Among other advantages, the new communication medium eases the sharing of information. For instance, UK customers of www.Amazon.co.uk will find that they are 'known' to the German www.Amazon.de Web site when they log on there for the first time. There is no need to re-register even though a new retail Web site has been accessed. Customer records kept on an electronic database mean that more and more data can be gathered and marketing targeted at individuals. The computerization of many activities results in at least the potential for reducing paper files and archives. In fact the 'paperless office' turns out to be mythical, as some aspects of computerization result in an increase of paper production (for example, the ease of producing several edited versions of a report rather than one completed one), and individuals do not have sufficient confidence that an electronic file can be held with the same security as a paper one. Despite the evident advantages of computers, the fallibility of computers and computer systems and the fragility of electronic data do not lend credibility to reliance on strictly electronic records.

THINK POINT

Like many retail chains, Tesco (Club Card) and Boots (Advantage Card) use loyalty cards to encourage customers to visit again and to gather detailed information about their shopping habits. This enables the store to engage in targeted relationship marketing, where individual needs are known from records of previous purchases, and special offers and new products of interest to the customer are sent directly to them. Marketers argue that this is ethical in terms of providing the customer with precisely the information they want and need. Some customers and consumer groups consider the collection of information through loyalty cards, and subsequent use to generate sales, to be a misuse of data and an abuse of customer loyalty. When signing up for a loyalty card, customers are not told that companies use them to collect this information, and they do not give their 'informed consent' to allow shops to use the data about their purchasing habits. What do you think about the ethics of loyalty cards?

Clearly computers offer some significant opportunities for improving the efficiency and speed of operations. Software for bookkeeping, desktop publishing packages and database management systems, for example, turn previously specialized tasks into jobs for people who are computer-literate enough to use the software. This may allow reduced salary costs and even fewer employees to run the same business. On the other hand, there is a great need for more computer specialists to produce, maintain and support increased computer use in the workplace. Information systems specialists are in many ways the new power base of organizations, and there are clear requirements on their professionalism in maintaining reliable systems with integrity. This redistribution of employment is one of the outcomes of increasing reliance on computers in the workplace.

Disadvantages

Prolonged computer use without a break can result in eyestrain and serious problems from repetitive strain injury (RSI), for example from constant use of the same muscles in manipulating the mouse. Back problems are increasingly common in the workplace as individuals maintain constant, inappropriate positions while sitting at a desk to use a computer. Ergonomic solutions to these problems are available but not widely used. Damage to the environment as a result of computer use is unknown, but the speed of technological updates results in a very short life cycle of computers as two- or three-year-old' machines are discarded as being out of date. In addition of course, computers require constant electricity supply.

Some suggest that teleworking and the reduced need for face-to-face interaction may have negative psychological effects on individuals, who experience isolation and the loss of 'social glue'. Others argue that computerization enables social freedom for the shy and the removal of potential prejudice, as race, age and disability cannot be seen through a computer screen of text. These issues are discussed in further detail in the next section.

COMPUTER-MEDIATED COMMUNICATION

One of the key questions confronted by business ethicists is whether computer-mediated communication (CMC) requires fundamentally different ethical considerations than have gone before. Those who argue that there is a difference cite areas such as the following for their reasoning: the changed relationship between humans, the fragility and ownership of electronic data, use and abuse of workplace facilities, and monitoring and privacy. While none of these factors is in itself unique, the combination of new perspectives, and the rapidity with which new technologies are becoming the norm in the workplace, do establish a heightening of certain issues in a unique combination in relation to ethical use. Here the focus is particularly on electronic mail and Internet technology and use.

139

The changing nature of human relationships

A key characteristic of the computerized workplace is the changing nature of relationships between humans that ICTs have enabled. There can be a lack of 'social glue' in a highly computerized world, where there is no natural space for casual conversation.

THINK POINT

Ex-chief of Matalan, Angus Monro, banned internal e-mails within Matalan! He regarded them as insidious, saying: 'People have got to talk to each other!'

The extent to which e-mails are really different from previous technologies such as communication by fax machine or disembodied telephone is unclear. There *is* a difference: we say things in e-mail that we might never say in hard copy or verbally, and different rules of grammar, punctuation, and even honest representation and use of crude language, seem to apply.

In a UK context, personal relationships are an important bond in managing business and organizations. This is achieved even where communication technologies enable increased personal distance between those communicating. Just as a 'business' telephone call may begin with some social conversation, an e-mail too can combine the social and strictly functional business for which it is composed. Electronic communication may even support 'social glue' by enabling naturally shy people to take part in communication fully without the psychological pressure of face-to-face contact.

The removal of the immediate proximity of sender and receiver of messages may have Equal Opportunity implications. While telephone helps prevent some prejudicial judgements such as those based on skin colour, age or dress, dialect and manner of speaking may still be discerned. The typewritten script of an e-mail, although not guaranteeing grammatical accuracy, offers everyone the opportunity of an equally professional status. Interestingly some interpret this as 'coldness' and use symbols to convey emotions such as happiness (☺), thereby personalizing their message. CMC also allows the leaving of messages for respondents to pick up as and when is convenient for the respondent, and potentially avoids the need for individuals to waste time chasing up absent colleagues. Telephone answer machines can operate on the same principle, but an e-mail can cope with a rather more complex message. This sophistication does not prevent individuals ignoring their messages, but that is a human rather than electronic frailty! CMC commonly allows asynchronous 'discussion', where there

140

is a time gap between normally text-based messages being sent and responses received.

Finally, a key point here must be the combination of communication media. Where a sensitive point is being made about which the response of the receiver cannot be predicted, the messenger may choose face-to-face or telephone communication in order that the response can be read *as the message is delivered*, and the tone of delivery adjusted simultaneously. In fact, just as with other communications methods, there is still a need for 'interpersonal skills' in choosing the medium and the mode of delivery. CMC can be seen as a liberating social force, offering an additional means of communication, and empowering those who are less comfortable with other methods. While it might be a mistake to consider it as a replacement for other means of communication, it can certainly act as a complement and, used sensibly, enables communication rather than disabling it.

Fragility and ownership of electronic data

The apparent fragility of electronic data, for example the fact that important data tables can be altered with almost no trace, adds additional responsibility to the conveyors of electronic information. Issues of responsibility for accuracy and the protection of information become paramount. This, it could be argued, is one of the distinctive features of electronic communication, since systems of protection for intellectual works (such as patenting and copyright) were designed for tangible products. As Chapter 7 of this volume points out, at the moment there is neither clear protection for electronic data nor understanding of the limits of ownership and responsibility for accuracy. Such issues are compounded by the potential for mass dissemination via the Internet and by means of electronic mail. Given that even accidental inaccuracy by experienced keyboard operators occurs at a rate of one inaccurate keystroke per 100, the potential for incorrect information dissemination is great. Similarly the ownership of electronic data, accurate or otherwise, is unclear and could have critical implications for the user and subject of information.

Even if we accept that employers own the data that is sent on their systems (that is, e-mail content sent by employees), interpretation of the data may be incorrectly handled by employers, particularly since e-mails are commonly written in shorthand and abbreviated form.

Use, dual use and abuse

The increasing prevalence of computer-mediated communication in the workplace has focused the minds of employers on the use of organizational equipment for non-organizational tasks. This is not of course a new phenomenon. The blurred lines between work and personal life are to be found in the use of work stationery for personal tasks, the use of private telephones for 'work' calls, the use of work telephones for 'private' calls, the reading of newspapers in work time, unpaid overtime, and so on. Such issues are particularly relevant in office environments. Some occupations, such as factory production line work and call centre operators, are indeed more strictly controlled and delineated in the timing of their activities. There are no clear lines to be drawn in any of these cases. The introduction of widely available ICTs has again broadened the spectrum of possibilities by offering a powerful tool of information access and distribution to many employees.

A distinction can be made here between use, dual use and abuse of ICTs in the workplace. Brown (1996) distinguishes between the realms of business necessity and of individual personhood and suggests that their intersection covers the domain of workplace privacy. In Figure 6.1, a link has been made between Brown's notions of 'business necessity', 'workplace privacy' and 'individual personhood' and the employment of ICTs for 'business use', 'dual use' and 'abuse'. The associations in the diagram are not absolute but they may provide a useful framework for considering the issues of the use of workplace CMC, such as e-mail and Internet access, common to any e-business.

Using the available CMC resources for business necessity is the easiest to identify. Where e-mail or the Internet are employed for purposes directly related to the functional role of the individual in the organization, there is no immediate problem.

Where e-mail or the Internet is used for purposes which have nothing whatsoever to do with the organizational business, or the well-being of the individual in doing his or her task, it might be said that there has been an abuse of the access to CMC facilities. 'Abuse' of a firm's resources can be defined as the use of e-mail by the employee to further personal rather than organizational

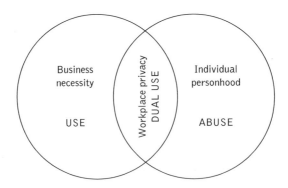

Figure 6.1 *Locating the use and abuse of ICTs in the workplace*

Source: developed from Brown (1996)

objectives. This might include illegal activities such as hacking into national security databases, but is not restricted to them. Examples might be the circulation of offensive materials, the setting up of a personal private business on work equipment or the accessing of indecent Web sites. With few exceptions such actions amount to abuse of the organization's resources.

The most difficult area to discern is the intersection between use and abuse, the area where personal use may have some positive workplace implications, and work use may benefit the individual personally. Internet surfing for hobby interests will hone the IT skills of employees who use those same skills for work tasks. Non-work friends may enable problem solving that would otherwise cost time and resources in-house, whether they be through the resolving of ICT queries or personal counselling. The ability of employees to resolve individual issues such as the renewal of car insurance over the Internet allows them to concentrate on work tasks. Furthermore it is natural, even desirable, that employees become friendly with colleagues, and the combining of social and work discussions within e-mails is a clear example of 'dual use'. Individuals do not leave their personal lives at home entirely, and employers should not expect them to do so. Employers might keep in mind that employees will often take work home with them, either literally or mentally. It seems a fair reciprocal exchange to be tolerant of home life making an appearance in the workplace. Accepting employees as whole human beings, with all the benefits and some of the drawbacks this may bring, is likely to be beneficial to all in the longer term.

No differentiation has been made in the discussion so far between use of workplace CMC and use of work time. This, again, is a difficult distinction. On the one hand utilization of organizational software and hardware may not in itself be considered problematic by employers. The equipment has been purchased for work reasons and once installed the incremental costs of its use are likely to be negligible. However, the work time which employees use in the pursuit of personal goals may well be an issue. Surfing the Internet proves to be a surprisingly time-consuming activity, and responding to personal e-mails may well distract individuals from their work tasks. The relevance of time lost must to some extent depend on the type of work done. Where individuals are doing tasks strictly limited to particular hours, or even paid by the hour, time lost during the working day will be of significance. On the other hand, for professionals who are measured by their output rather than their (intellectual or actual) presence nine to five, time lost might be considered as merely a reallocation of time use. The management of household matters in work time is inevitable in a social environment in which workdays are longer and household management responsibilities are shared between multiple earners with careers.

Important in the consideration of the use and abuse of work time is the fact that the technology is readily available to monitor Internet and e-mail use of networked employees remotely.

Monitoring and privacy

In the context of ICT development, electronic monitoring of employees – in and outside the workplace – has enormous potential for infringing the privacy of employees and customers. ICT archiving and particularly computer-mediated communication mean that employees in the workplace can be monitored to unprecedented levels. Electronic monitoring can be defined as the capture and analysis of 'data' to measure the work (not) performed by employees. These data may show Web sites accessed, e-mail traffic, e-mail content or the use of video and audio facilities.

ACTIVITY

Think about your daily life, including your work life. List occasions and situations where you know you are being electronically monitored, for example by close circuit television in the supermarket car park, or a print-out on your work telephone use.

Electronic monitoring is sometimes seen as a sinister 'Big Brother is watching you' perspective on our lives. Reasons put forward to defend the use of electronic monitoring in the workplace include the following:

- *Security*. Closed Circuit Television (CCTV) can protect against theft and violence.
- Employers pay employees to do a particular job. It could be argued that employers have a *contractual right* to check that employees are doing what they are paid to do.
- Monitoring of employees stops abuse of work time and *increases productivity*.
- Electronic monitoring is simply an electronic version of '*managing by walking about*', which saves management time.
- Electronic means of measurement mean that performance appraisal of employees is backed up by precise statistics and is *unbiased*.
- Electronic monitoring provides data *quickly and frequently*.
- It ensures *realistic targets* are set.

Electronic monitoring may be used as a deterrent to stop inappropriate workplace behaviour, rather than being used to penalize those caught not working 100 per cent of the time. This can be likened to Jeremy Bentham's Panopticon. The Panopticon was a circular prison with no bars. All the cells were arranged around a tower with a single guard in it. From the tower the guard could see into all the cells. However, the prisoners could not see whether they were being observed. Their behaviour was thus controlled by the fact that they *might* be being monitored. In the same way that a speed camera without a film in it can still influence motorists to keep to the legal speed limit, the fact that employees or customers know that they may be being watched means that they act as they would if they *were* being watched.

On the other hand, like watching rats in a cage, constant monitoring can have uneasy effects on individuals. Those against electronic monitoring argue that:

- It constitutes an *invasion of privacy*. Being paid by an organization does not mean that it owns you.
- Monitoring implies suspicion of misbehaviour. This *undermines the trust, goodwill and loyalty* of employees toward the employer.
- Monitoring results in the setting of *unrealistic targets*, because employees cannot keep up the fastest rate constantly. The result is increasing stress, absenteeism and ultimately employee turnover.
- In a climate of increasing empowerment, monitoring erodes the independence of the individual to work in a way which suits him or her (e.g. chat to a friend between 9:30 and 10:00 but work over lunchtime) and *disempowers* the individual's control.
- Electronic monitoring is more suited to *measuring quantitative* factors than qualitative ones, hence number of phone calls rather than relationship building with potential clients is most likely to be measured in a call centre.

In most countries, legally there is generally no reason why employers should not monitor employee e-mails, yet it is unlikely to be in the employer's self-interest to exercise the right. Monitoring employees to check whether they are abusing company resources may be justified if the system is being overloaded, although setting limits would achieve the same ends. Being an employer does not mean having the right to monitor private conversations.

THINK POINT

What do you think the impact of introducing widespread electronic monitoring into a workplace might be? Consider the possible impact on employee behaviour. How might workplace settings, employee types and industries make a difference?

Case study:
DOUBLECLICK

This case looks at some of the difficulties faced by companies which use technical tracking facilities of the Internet as marketing tools. The common response is the imposition of legal constraints. Companies like DoubleClick adopt voluntary practices to defend their approach and guard against legal problems. After reading this case, see the company's Web site for its current privacy approach, www.doubleclick.net/uk.

DoubleClick, the US online advertising firm which was embroiled in a privacy dispute in 2001, is attempting to make sure there is no repeat in its European operations. The firm was investigated by US watchdogs following allegations that it was tracking customers' surfing habits and logging the information in a marketing database. DoubleClick in the United Kingdom has appointed online privacy expert Amanda Chandler as director of data protection, and she admitted that EU privacy laws were chaotic.

'The European directive on data protection is being distributed in different countries at different times,' she said. 'We are living in a state of flux, so it is very difficult to be certain whether the one interpretation is definitive. My role will be to keep abreast of these developments for our clients.'

Ms Chandler, who worked at the Office of the Data Protection Commissioner, will also ensure that DoubleClick follows the UK Data Protection Act.

'The Internet is a very complex thing and it is early days for the industry. There is still a lot of work to be done as the law develops,' she added.

In order to settle the dispute in 2000, DoubleClick appointed lawyer Jules Polonetsky as chief privacy officer and established privacy guidelines. He is determined that the company, which runs and tracks online adverts for clients, will lead the way in Internet privacy. 'We take great pains to ensure that we follow data protection laws, and we are leading the privacy issue in terms of best practice,' he said.

Source: Milmo (2001).

ETHICS IN CYBERSPACE

Hamelink (2000: 9) defines cyberspace as comprising all forms of computer-mediated communication which take place in a 'geographically unlimited, non-physical space, in which – independent of time, distance and location – transactions take place between people, between computers and between people and computers'. In the workplace, common journeys into cyberspace would include sending an e-mail, looking at a Web site, using a search engine and making bookings or purchases over the Internet.

Cyberspace communications have some distinctive characteristics that are important in relation to ethics. These include:

- The ease of communicating to many *anonymous* people simultaneously. For example, by sending an e-mail to a group. Communication can be *spontaneous*.
- The *disembodied* nature of electronic communication – communication is in text, and hence does not convey tone of voice or other non-textual clues, although 'symbols' are increasingly used to convey for example a joke or happiness :) = ☺, or sadness : (= ☹.
- Where a common language is understood, images, documents and *complex ideas* can be communicated across the world as long as the technology is available.
- Cyberspace is *not secure*. This means that transactions on the Web can be accessed by those not party to the transaction. Security is improving, however (see Chapter 3 of this volume), and of course terrestrial transactions are not 100 per cent secure either.
- The *borderless* nature of the Internet makes control extremely difficult. Attempts at national controls, such as prohibiting the purchase of Adolf Hitler's *Mein Kampf* over the Internet in Germany, have failed.
- Communication in cyberspace has extraordinary *archiving* capabilities. Internet sites accessed are recorded (hence Gary Glitter's conviction for accessing child pornography). Companies can also track the cyberspace activities of those who have visited their Web site, if they have the right technology.
- Those who control the technology become very *powerful*, for example Microsoft Corporation and Netscape.

All these factors open up a whole range of possibilities for communicating quickly and easily to people across the world. A new resulting phenomenon of some of these factors is the advent of 'flaming', a kind of electronic road rage in which individuals send rude or offensive, even libellous messages to individuals or sometimes groups, often with no clear understanding of who has access to reading it (for example to a bulletin board or chat room).

THINK POINT

Have you ever sent or received a message that contained something that you think would not have been conveyed by telephone or letter? What makes it possible to send more colourful messages through electronic media than you would present face-to-face?

THE DIGITAL DIVIDE?

As the reach of the information superhighway extends, assumptions about equal access to its benefits are increasingly made. These range from the expectation that all those reading this text will have used e-mail and surfed the Internet to claims that the Internet overcomes global disparities between more and less economically developed countries. Companies from all over the world can compete for the same business via the Internet, with Web pages that don't necessarily convey company size, longevity or financial success.

In fact, at a local as well as a global level, access to the Internet is far from universal. In 1999 it was estimated that 170 million people had Internet access. This is a minute 4 per cent of the world's population. The figure is more meaningful still when it is considered that over 80 per cent of those with Internet access are in North America and Europe (Hamelink 2000: 81). So, rather than being a social leveller, the Internet is yet another divide between rich and poor, the haves and have-nots, the networked and the non-networked.

PROFESSIONAL BEHAVIOUR

The increasing power of information systems professionals, and correspondingly e-Business professionals, requires a high degree of integrity. Codes of conduct, such as that of the British Computer Society, begin to acknowledge some of the difficult decisions faced by computer professionals. Such codes are, however, often too broad to give meaningful advice. Some take a more focused approach. Rosenberg (1999) reports on the 1996 Computer Professionals for Social Responsibility 'Electronic Privacy Principles' which suggest that 'Each employer should provide and act on clear policies regarding the privacy implications of the computing resources used in the workplace.' The policies should explicitly describe:

- Acceptable use of electronic mail and computer resources, including personal use.
- Practices that may be used to enforce these policies, such as the interception and reading of electronic mail or scanning of hard disks.
- Penalties for non-compliance with these policies.

Many argue that employees should at least be informed of any electronic monitoring systems that might be used on workplace computers. These principles suggest a basic position of transparency of any monitoring policy.

Codes of conduct are widely criticized for many reasons, for example that they are only for public relations purposes and just add to bureaucracy, that they ignore context and deny individual responsibility and moral diversity. Codes do have the advantage of offering some guidance, however, and this is desperately needed in an e-Environment which so far lacks any common understanding of appropriate use.

Recommended features of a useful code of conduct are as follows. A good code of conduct:

- Is negotiated with stakeholders and acceptable to them.
- Consists of clear and well founded ethical rules.
- Is internally consistent and coherent with other policies and strategies.
- Should balance: (1) rights and duties, (2) the interests of internal and external stakeholders.
- Allows for exceptions (and shows how to deal with them).
- Anticipates conflicts (and shows how to deal with them).
- Respects individual freedom.
- Would not be used to indoctrinate.
- Is easy and inexpensive to apply.
- Is part of a process with regular review.

ACTIVITY

Why not develop a code of conduct for your company or class? Remember to follow the recommended aspects as closely as possible – in particular, it can't be a solo project!

In conclusion, e-Business managers of the future should take seriously their responsibilities in developing a professional approach to the new opportunities which the e-Commerce environment affords. As a professional body develops, no doubt a specific ethical code will emerge. In the meantime, the socially responsible e-Business professional would do well to aim to act with integrity for the good of others, in a way which is fair, honest, trustworthy, reliable, objective and competent.

CHAPTER SUMMARY

In this chapter some of the key issues relating to e-Business have been discussed. While there are many advantages to operating in a computer-intensive environment, some of the potential ethical dilemmas for employees and consumers have been identified. Technology can mistakenly be given the blame for wrongdoing when it is in fact just the conduit through which acts are carried out, with the potential for exacerbating unethical behaviour because of the speed, reach, and anonymity which it facilitates. That same technology could allow increased scrutinizing of employer activities as a form of regulation, but in the end the answer to the abuse of technology is not more technology, it is more responsible use of the technology we have.

FURTHER READING

Akdeniz, Y., Walker, C. and Wall, D. (eds) (2000) *The Internet, Law and Society*, Harlow: Pearson Education.
Hamelink, C. (2000) *Ethics in Cyberspace*, London: Sage.
Langford, D. (1999) *Business Computer Ethics*, Harlow: Addison Wesley.
Langford, D. (ed.) (2000) *Internet Ethics*, Basingstoke: Macmillan.
Spinello, R. A. (1997) *Case Studies in Information and Computer Ethics*, Englewood Cliffs NJ: Prentice Hall.
On ethical theory specifically:
Beauchamp, T. L. and Bowie, N. E. (1997) *Ethical Theory and Business*, 5th edn, London: Prentice Hall.
Park, J. and Roome, N. (eds) (2002) *The Ecology of the New Economy: Sustainable Transformation of Global Information, Communications and Electronic Industries*, Sheffield: Greenleaf Publishing.
Raphael, D. D. (1994) *Moral Philosophy*, 2nd edn, Oxford: Oxford University Press.
Singer, P. (ed.) (1993) *A Companion to Ethics*, Oxford: Blackwell.
Singer, P. (ed.) (1994) *Ethics*, Oxford: Oxford University Press.
Winkler, E. and Coombs, J. (1993) *Applied Ethics: A Reader*, Oxford: Blackwell.

BIBLIOGRAPHY

Akdeniz, Y., Walker, C. and Wall, D. (eds) (2000) *The Internet, Law and Society*, Harlow: Pearson Education.
Beauchamp, T. L. and Bowie, N. E. (1997) *Ethical Theory and Business,* 5th edn, London: Prentice Hall.
Brown, W. (1996) 'Technology, workplace, privacy and personhood', *Journal of Business Ethics* 15, 1237–48.
Halbert, T. and Ingulli, E. (2002) *CyberEthics,* Ohio: Thomson.
Hamelink, C. (2000) *The Ethics of Cyberspace,* London: Sage.
Herschel, R. and Hayes Andrews, P. (1997) 'Ethical implications of technological advances on business communication', *Journal of Business Communication,* special issue 'Ethics of business communication' 34, 2: 160–71.

Langford, D. (1999) *Business Computer Ethics,* Harlow: Addison Wesley.

Langford, D. (ed.) (2000) *Internet Ethics,* Basingstoke: Macmillan.

Milmo, D. (2001) 'DoubleClick hires privacy expert', *Guardian,* 16 January.

Park, J. and Roome, N. (eds) (2002) *The Ecology of the New Economy: Sustainable Transformation of Global Information, Communications and Electronic Industries,* Sheffield: Greenleaf Publishing.

Raphael, D. D. (1994) *Moral Philosophy,* 2nd edn, Oxford: Oxford University Press.

Rosenberg, R. (1999) 'The workplace on the verge of the twenty-first century', *Journal of Business Ethics,* 22: 3–14.

Singer, P. (ed.) (1993) *A Companion to Ethics,* Oxford: Blackwell.

Singer, P. (ed.) (1994) *Ethics,* Oxford: Oxford University Press.

Spence, L. J. (2000) *Practices, Priorities and Ethics in Small Firms,* London: Institute of Business Ethics.

Spinello, R. A. (1997) *Case Studies in Information and Computer Ethics,* Englewood Cliffs NJ: Prentice Hall.

Winkler, E. and Coombs, J. (1993) *Applied Ethics: A Reader,* Oxford: Blackwell.

WEB LINKS

www.ccsr.cse.dmu.ac.uk
Centre for Computing and Social Responsibility. Comprehensive Web page covering a wide range of information relating to computer ethics. Takes the perspective of the responsibilities of information systems professionals.

www.cyber-rights.org
Web site of a not-for-profit civil liberties organization, Cyber-Rights and Cyber Liberties (UK).

www.bcs.org.uk
Web site of the British Computer Society. Includes the BCS code of conduct.

www.ispa.org.uk
The Internet Services Providers' Association. Includes a code of conduct.

www.cpsr.org
Computer Professionals for Social Responsibility: a public-interest alliance of computer scientists and others concerned about the impact of computer technology on society.

www.w3.org
The World Wide Web Consortium (W3C) develops interoperable technologies (specifications, guidelines, software and tools) to lead the Web to its full potential as a forum for information, commerce, communication and collective understanding.

www.epic.org
Electronic Privacy Information Center (US-based).

Chapter 7

e-Business and the law

DAVE WADSWORTH

KEY LEARNING POINTS

After completing this chapter you will have an understanding of:

- The problem of governing the Internet where no state boundaries or legal jurisdictions exist
- The evolving legal framework of e-Business and the Internet
- How some pre-Internet law can be applied to e-Business activity
- The conflict between preserving the anonymity of the Internet and protecting the rights of individuals

ORDERED LIST OF SUB TOPICS

- Civil and criminal law
- Globalization, jurisdiction and enforcement
- Encryption and privacy rights
  - Data protection
  - The Computer Misuse Act 1990
- Advertising on the Net and consumer protection
- Advertising and consumer protection: criminal aspects
  - Advertising
  - Consumer rights
- Intellectual property
  - Copyright
  - Patents
  - Cyber-squatting
- Internet service providers

CIVIL AND CRIMINAL LAW

In order to balance the conflicting interests in any society it is necessary for businesses to operate within a legal framework. The criminal law consists of rules set down by and enforced by the state in respect of conduct which the state sees as being 'uncivilized' and contrary to society's best interests. In the context of business, this will clearly include matters such as theft and fraud in various forms, such as obtaining property/services without paying for them, or obtaining payment for property/services which one intends never to supply. It may be that the particular nature of e-Business – dealing at a distance with persons or organizations that one has never met, perhaps in remote parts of the world from you and giving them electronic access to your funds – is conducive to this sort of activity. Certainly, many individuals cite data insecurity as a reason for not conducting transactions via e-Commerce. Even those happy to shop online with tried and trusted high-street presences such as Tesco or Sainsbury may be far more reticent in buying online from a supplier based in Tashkent or St Louis of whom they have no knowledge or experience.

As a general rule, states prosecute individuals or companies for crimes committed within their jurisdiction (area of judicial competence). Conviction will usually lead to a fine and/or imprisonment for individuals, although other consequences such as disqualification from being a director of a company may also follow.

In addition to the criminal law, all states also have a system of civil law whereby disputes between individuals (a company is an artificial legal person and thus counted as an individual for these purposes) can be resolved. Such disputes may well not involve criminal activity. Issues such as consumer rights will be dealt with by the civil law and are unlikely to be criminal activities. Examples of this include purchased goods that prove not to be of satisfactory quality or fit for the particular purpose made known at the time of the sale, or defective provision of services under a contract. They are examples of breaches of contract where one party to an agreement fails to honour it in full. Civil disputes may also arise outside contractual relationships and are covered in English law by the law of tort (for example, a case of negligent actions causing loss or harm to another, as in a road accident). In the context of e-Commerce, this might well involve matters such as trade marks and copyright in areas such as domain names and Web pages where another's use of a property over which you claim exclusive rights could have devastating effects. For example, you might not be able to use a domain name on the Web corresponding to the name under which you have traded for some time and built up a considerable reputation and goodwill.

The claimant in a civil law case will sue in a court provided by the state for the settlement of such disputes, hoping to get either compensation (known as damages) for loss or harm suffered as a result of the defendant's actions, or a court order instructing the defendant not to act in a particular way (an injunction), or to carry out her/his contractual duties (a decree of specific performance).

153

These latter orders will be granted at the court's discretion only where damages – the court's normal award to a successful claimant – would be insufficient or inappropriate in the circumstances.

Different countries will have different Acts to cover activities within their jurisdiction but the fundamental concepts of civil and criminal law and their purposes remain the same in all countries. It would, of course, be impossible to detail all laws from all countries, and thus this chapter will refer to English law, to which those involved in e-Commerce in the United Kingdom may well be primarily subject and to which they are likely to have easiest access.

Box 7.1:
TYPES OF LAWS AND REMEDIES

Which type of law do the following involve and what remedy is the court most likely to grant for them?

1 Setting up an e-Business retailing goods whilst having no actual stock or capital with which to obtain stock, and accepting orders and credit card payments online without ever obtaining or supplying goods to meet those orders.
2 An e-tailer supplying a pair of trainers which fall apart after one month's normal wear as everyday shoes to university, the shops, the bar, etc.
3 Replicating the fundamental design of an existing Web site and inserting one's own details instead.
4 'Hacking' into a computer and 'improving' your examination grades.

Your answers should have included the following:

1 Probably a criminal offence under the Theft Act 1968 for which the accused would be prosecuted and, if convicted, fined or sent to prison. It might well not be a crime if the accused could show evidence that, at the time she/he took payment, they intended to fulfil the order (e.g. had suppliers lined up, etc., which perhaps then fell through). *Note* The purchaser would still be entitled to the return of their payment under breach of contract in the civil law, irrespective of the outcome of the criminal case.
2 A civil case under the Sale of Goods Act 1979 under which the claimant would be entitled to their money back (damages) – or a replacement pair/free repair if they so elected.
3 A civil case involving breach of copyright and possibly breach of trade mark. The claimant would be entitled to an injunction ordering the defendant to cease such breaches by removing the Web page and damages to compensate for harm suffered as a result of it having been up.
4 A crime under the Computer Misuse Act 1990 for which the accused would be fined or sent to prison if convicted.

GLOBALIZATION, JURISDICTION AND ENFORCEMENT

Traditionally, as a general rule, countries may make laws relating only to activities occurring within their jurisdiction and considerable problems of sovereignty arise in respect of laws involving *extraterritoriality* – having effect within another jurisdiction. District Judge Preska in American Library Assoc. *v.* Pataki [1997] said:

> The Internet is wholly insensitive to geographical distinctions. In almost every case users of the Internet neither know nor care abut the physical location of the resources to the access. Internet protocols were designed to ignore rather than document geographical locations; while computers on the network do have 'addresses' they are logical addresses on the network rather than geographical addresses in real space.

As all law is essentially territorial and the Web, by definition, is extraterritorial, in that activities within a variety of jurisdictions are possible in one e-Commerce transaction, legal regulation faces considerable difficulties. For example, a US-registered company via an Internet service provider in France may well display a Web page to a potential customer in the United Kingdom. That customer might order a flight from the United Kingdom to Spain and the provision of hotel services and accommodation in Spain. It is clear that all four jurisdictions could have some involvement if problems arise from the contract.

It is possible for a country to exercise jurisdiction over an individual resident within it or a company with assets within that country, but what if others refuse to appear for trial or, having done so, refuse to pay the fine/damages or obey the injunction? Problems of extradition and of enforcing judgements against a party outside the jurisdiction are very real.

Essentially a borderless global technology such as the World Wide Web needs supranational regulation but what body has the authority to make international laws and how could it enforce them? Even the United Nations can be seen as a voluntary club of member nations with very little in the way of sanctions against its members (especially the big and powerful ones), other than expulsion from the club. Its rights over companies and individuals may be seen as even more limited.

In 1980 a UN conference in Vienna adopted the UN Convention on the International Sale of Goods (CISG), which came into force in 1988. It has been adopted by over fifty-seven nations and covers over half the world's trade. It is linked with the North American Free Trade Association and a substantial part, but not all of the European Union. The United Kingdom has not adopted CISG, which also does not apply to goods bought for personal, family or household reasons. For more detail on CISG see Schlectriem (1998).

Within the European Union, the Brussels Convention on Jurisdiction and the Enforcement of Judgements in Civil and Commercial Matters 1968 applies. In the United Kingdom the Civil Jurisdiction and Judgements Act 1968 provides

155

that the Brussels Convention shall have the force of law. In consumer sales the consumer can be sued only in her/his own country of domicile but may elect to sue either there or in the seller's country of domicile. In non-consumer sales, a contracting party can be sued only in her/his country of domicile or the country where the transaction/delivery should have taken place, if that differs.

The 1980 Rome Convention covers the subject of applicability of law and is applicable in the United Kingdom under the Contracts (Applicable Law) Act 1990. Essentially, the convention states that the parties may elect the law by which their contract is governed. If no such election is made, the law of the country where the contract was made applies. Frequently in e-Commerce, parties are required to click on an icon to show that they accept the other party's standard terms and conditions, which might well specify the country's law to be applicable. Software is often shrink-wrapped and the packaging states that end-user licence conditions apply and that by opening the packaging one accepts the terms and conditions of that licence. This is not infrequently backed up by a requirement during installation to click indicating acceptance of the end-user licence terms and conditions.

The EU Distance Selling Directive 97/7, which came into force in English law on 1 November 2000, applies if the negotiations and contract are completed by distance means (e.g. through the Internet) by a purchaser buying as a consumer from a seller supplying in the course of a business. The consumer must, before the contract is concluded, be provided with information on the identity of the supplier, her/his address, the main characteristics of the goods/services, price, delivery costs, arrangements for payment, the period for which the price remains valid and the right of withdrawal.

This must all be provided in a downloadable form. The right of withdrawal is for a minimum of seven working days' cooling-off period without need for reason or financial penalty for having done so, but does not apply in relation to personalized goods, audio/video recordings, software/periodicals/magazines, etc., that have been delivered, or where performance in relation to services has started.

Until relatively recently domain name regulation was governed by US government agencies. This arose because the Web was developed in the United States and many large commercial players internationally are US corporations. In the United Kingdom, Nominet UK took over the domain name registration process in 1996. By 1998 it became clear that the Net was fast expanding into an international medium for commerce, education and communication and that a global system of management was desirable.

At the prompting of the US government, the Internet Corporation for Assigned Names and Numbers (ICANN) was established in 1998 as a non-profit-making group of business, academic and technical interests to regulate the allocation of intellectual property address space and to manage the domain name system. It has limited powers and is in effect an attempt at self-regulation by Internet stakeholders.

Currently the Web would seem to be governed, if it is *de facto* governed very much at all, by a mixture of individual national laws, co-ordinated national laws or cross-border conventions and self-regulation from the more powerful stake-holders connected with the Internet. No one model can meet all the requirements. The national law model has jurisdictional and enforceability problems, and national laws may easily be outflanked on the Net by consumers/suppliers simply going elsewhere to get or do what they want. The cross-border model has problems of authority and enforcement and would require a large and efficient bureaucracy. It shares with the self-regulation model the fundamental problems of democracy, accountability and the worries of domination by one/a few powerful groups or countries looking to their own interests rather than those of the wider community. It may also be that the interests of the community at large will be difficult to define, as debates on freedom of speech and protection against pornography and corruption illustrate.

The ingenuity of those seeking to avoid regulation will almost certainly equal that of those seeking to regulate, and each door closing may be matched by another one opening. Methods such as encryption may well make it difficult for those seeking to control even to know who those evading their measures are, let alone to impose constraints upon them. Spinello says there is 'a power struggle between a frustrated state and a newly empowered Internet community' with 'cyberspace at the epicentre of that struggle' (Spinello 2000: 41).

Case study:
PROBLEMS OF EXTRATERRITORIALITY IN PRACTICE

In Germany in 2000 a Holocaust revisionist, Frederick Toben, was convicted of offences under laws against denying the Holocaust and against spreading Nazi propaganda. Toben had denied that millions of Jews had been killed by the Nazis during the Holocaust. The denials had been made both in pamphlets and on Toben's own Web site. The German Federal Court denied Toben's appeal against his conviction, stating that German national law on this topic applied to the Internet even when the content had originated outside Germany and was put there by a non-German national (an Australian), provided that the site was accessible in Germany. It was not clear to what extent the ruling applied to anyone other than individuals – such as ISPs.

There is clearly a moral/ethical problem here over freedom of speech/expression and control of dangerous/offensive propaganda. There is also the problem of extraterritoriality. In France in 2000 the International League against Racism and Antisemitism and the Union of French Jewish students applied to the French courts for an order to prevent Yahoo continuing to display on its auction site advertisements

157

for Nazi memorabilia. Despite Yahoo's claim of no jurisdiction because its site is based in the United States, the French court issued an order requiring Yahoo to take all measures to make impossible the sale of Nazi memorabilia through its Web site to French citizens.

Yahoo has announced that it will take such measures but has asked the US courts to rule in principle on the validity of a French court ruling on a US ISP. The French government and courts clearly have a right and the power to regulate the conduct of its nationals in France and to prohibit offensive activities, but to what extent can any country prevent the effects of the Net when it is provided by a foreign national from outside its boundaries?

Adapted from De Freitas (2001).

ENCRYPTION AND PRIVACY RIGHTS

One stumbling block to greater use of e-Commerce in areas such as e-Banking and e-Shopping is public apprehension about security flaws and the safety and privacy of data necessarily disclosed to your trading partners by trading in this way. To what extent is such data secure – either in transmission or when held by the other party – and to what extent can third parties get access to it?

The dangers of a third party getting unauthorized access to your credit card number are obvious, although worries about disclosing such data online are strangely inconsistent with happily giving waiters, shop assistants and those involved in telephone sales the card, or details of it, as many of us do regularly without a second thought. Having said that, a study revealed that 59 per cent of companies with Web sites that were surveyed had experienced one or more security breakdowns in 1997.

Article 8 (1) of the European Convention on Human Rights and Fundamental Freedoms 1953 – now enshrined in UK law by the Human Rights Act 1998 – includes a right 'to respect for . . . private and family life . . . home and . . . correspondence'. This would seem to give a green light to those who argue for freedom of speech and privacy on the Net. Unless protected by encryption, communication on the Internet is akin to communication on a postcard – open to any who choose casually to read it, including administration staff at any of the servers through which it passes and potential hackers. The defensive measures that are put in place to prevent this may reduce the likelihood of unauthorized disclosure, but not all systems are as secure as they should be and probably no system is totally protected against determined and increasingly sophisticated hackers. A totally secure encryption system does, however, raise problems for governments.

Case study:
BREACH OF PRIVACY THROUGH HACKING

Raphael Gray, a teenager in South Wales, claimed in January 2000 that he was on a mission to expose the dangers of shopping on the Internet. Using a well publicized flaw in Microsoft's Internet Information Server (not having detected a new flaw for himself), Gray wrote a program that flooded the Web site with data, causing a buffer overflow and making the data on the site insecure. This flaw had been publicized in security bulletins on the Internet but many e-Commerce organizations had failed to patch their systems. Gray extracted credit card details from the databases and told Web sites using Microsoft Internet Information Service that they were vulnerable. Many ignored him, so Gray published the numbers, names and expiry dates of 6,000 credit cards on the Internet.

Gray was caught by means of reading the server logs to discover when and from where the hacks were done and then the logs of the ISP Gray had used to see who was logged on at that time. However, the damage had been done, and it cost Mastercard and Visa £2 million to reassure customers and replace their cards, and those 6,000 were considerably inconvenienced in the interim with no credit card available to them. Gray was apparently of low self-esteem and had a medical condition caused from a blow on the head. The court accordingly sentenced him to a three-year probation order linked with treatment for a mental disorder.

Source: Adapted from Arthur (2001).

Many of the advocates of a totally free Internet would regard such hackers as playing a game, their only crime being curiosity, or a prank producing a little e-graffiti. A seventeen-year-old from Hereford hacked into a national rail Web site and that of Lloyd's of London and posted messages saying 'No trains will be running over the millennium due to Y2K problems' and 'The UK caught the Net boom but forgot about security' respectively. In December 2000 he was convicted of two breaches of the Computer Misuse Act and conditionally discharged for twelve months.

Source: *The Times,* 1 December 2000.

In June 2001 Owen Goddard was charged with posting bogus information on an Internet site — Interactive Investor International — which said (falsely) that Mercury Asset Management had sold its shares in Minmet — a mining exploration group. This caused Minmet shares to halve in value and wiped £70 million off the company's value.

Source: *The Times,* 15 June 2001.

159

Article 8 (2) of the European Convention on Human Rights and Fundamental Freedoms allows an exception to the right of privacy 'in the interests of national security, public safety or the economic well-being of the country, for the prevention of disorder or crime, for the protection of health and morals or for the protection of the rights and freedoms of others'. This certainly accords with the widely held view that no freedoms are absolute and that rights carry with them responsibilities.

Akdeniz and Walker say:

It may seem paradoxical that there can arise any expectation of privacy on this most open and unregulated mode of electronic communication [the Internet] but privacy remains a legitimate demand in the Information Age and involves a claim by an individual to control information . . . created or transmitted via the Internet, including immunity from unwarranted usage or intrusiveness by others.

(2000: 318)

The real sticking point is, of course, what intrusion can be warranted?

The FBI in the United States had considerable difficulties in breaking up an international child pornography ring because everything was on encrypted computer files. An uncrackable secret communication system would also seem like heaven for criminals and terrorists and hell for law enforcement agencies and governments.

With the increasing ease of collecting, processing and transferring personal data about anyone comes the fear of invasion of privacy. Developments like these led to laws such as the Data Protection Act 1998, which sets out a framework of law regarding what data may be collected, kept and disclosed or transferred, and gives the data subject rights of viewing and correcting data held on her/him.

Nevertheless, with the use of encryption, an Internet user may well achieve a greater degree of privacy for communications than is available in respect of postal or telephone communication. Barker and Hurst argue that 'cryptography is surely the best of technologies and the worst of technologies. It will stop crimes, and it will create new crimes. It will undermine dictatorships and it will drive them to new excesses. It will make us all anonymous and will track our every transaction' (1998: 15).

Encryption is now an everyday facet of e-Commerce and can provide confidentiality and authenticity of information transmitted and can validate that it has not been subject to intrusion during transmission or disclosure to unauthorized parties. Digital signatures can be created by encryption so as to authenticate the sender of the information. Easily used encryption software is available in all computer shops and even, in the case of PGP (Pretty Good Privacy), free over the Internet for personal use.

160

ACTIVITY

Go to www.ssh.fi/tech/crypto/sites.html. Microsoft's Windows 2000 incorporates 128 bit encryption.

Many would see legitimate uses of encryption and secrecy as including commercially confidential information, military and governmental secrets, confidential advice and counselling to clients and even reports of human rights violations and war crimes.

Different countries have different views about encryption. For some 'the absence of consensus harms not only the growth and development of e-Commerce but also the possibility of providing a stable and trustworthy environment for Netizens' (Akdeniz and Walker 2000: 318). In a 1997 communication paper, *Towards a European Framework for Digital Signatures and Encryption*, the European Commission thought that there were few criminal cases using professional encryption and that it was unlikely that the use of encryption could be effectively controlled by regulation. In 1999 the EU Directive on a Community Framework for Electronic Signatures sought to legitimize the use of electronic signatures within the European Union, and allowed for voluntary but not compulsory certification schemes. The European Union has not yet managed to reach a common proposal, let alone a policy, on the thorny problem of encryption.

In 1996 the UK government in a discussion paper on *Regulatory Intent Concerning use of Encryption on Public Networks* proposed the introduction of licensed Trusted Third Parties to hold copies of all private encryption keys and thus facilitate key recovery and verification. The Labour government elected in 1997 in its own Secure Electronic Commerce Statement in 1998 followed the same idea on a voluntary but not legally compulsory basis, but those who chose not to use Trusted Service Providers would not have a presumption of authenticity. Quite how voluntary such a system is in such circumstances is, to say the least, debatable. However, a House of Commons select committee report on *Building Confidence in Electronic Commerce* said, 'we can see no benefits arising from the government's promotion of key escrow or key recovery technologies' (HMSO 1999).

Eventually the UK government passed the Electronic Communications Act 2000, which replaced the previous idea of compulsory licences with a voluntary approval regime. The industry adopted self-regulatory kite marking and was threatened with an imposed registration scheme if the voluntary system proved ineffective. An industry-devised scheme, the T scheme, has been drawn up. The Act also gives UK legal approval to all electronic signatures.

The Regulation of Investigatory Powers Act 2000 concerns powers of seizing and disclosing communications data. Decryption powers are granted in Part III, although there must be some power under which the original seizure is authorized.

161

Purposes for authorizing seizure include preventing any crime or disorder, but also health and taxation, and can be extended by statutory order (i.e. no need for a new Act to extend them).

If the authorities seize encrypted raw material the Act includes powers to require the possessor to hand over the key but such powers need the written permission of an independent judicial officer in most cases, and regard must be had to both necessity and proportionality before notice is granted. The exercise of the power to grant such notices is kept under review by the Covert Investigations Commissioner. The disclosure of text rather than the key will also be an acceptable response in most cases, unless the handing over of the key has specifically been demanded, and is proportionate in the circumstances. There is a defence to the crime of failure to disclose or facilitate access if it is not reasonably practicable (which must be proved by the accused), e.g. that she/he never had the key or no longer had it at the time of the request.

The Secretary of State used his powers under the Regulation of Investigating Powers Act 2000 to make the Telecommunications (Lawful Business Practice) (Interception of Communications) Regulations 2000, which authorize the interception of telecommunications by, or with the consent of, a person carrying on a business (including government departments and public authorities) for purposes relevant to that business and using that business's own telecoms system. The controller of the system must make all reasonable efforts to inform potential users that interceptions may be made, thereby getting their express or implied consent.

One quite often is played a pre-recorded message to the effect that the conversation may be recorded for monitoring for quality assurance purposes. Such interceptions are authorized for establishing the existence of facts; ascertaining compliance with regulatory practices applicable to the system controller in her/his business; to ascertain the standards which are achieved by those using the systems as part of their duties; monitoring to see if the communications are business or personal; to prevent/detect crime or in the interests of national security.

This will often be done in the form of monitoring employees' e-mails and telephone calls. Monitoring by concealed CCTV or tape recorders will be justified only in very limited circumstances – such as where a crime is suspected and blanket monitoring cannot be justified – said Elizabeth France, when she was Data Protection Commissioner. Provided the employer makes every reasonable effort to inform staff of any intended monitoring and the interception is proportionate and for legitimate business reasons then it probably will not breach the Data Protection Act or the Human Rights Act.

Data protection

The position in the United Kingdom is governed by the Data Protection Act 1998, which was the United Kingdom's response to the EU Data Protection

Directive 95/46/EC. The Act is coming in over a period of time until 2007 and replacing the 1984 Act. All EU member states have fundamentally the same laws regarding data protection. There are eight Data Protection Principles under the Act:

- Personal data shall be processed fairly and lawfully. Schedule 2 says processing may be carried out only where the individual has given her/his consent; where it is necessary to perform a contract with the individual; when it is required under a legal obligation; or when it is necessary in the legitimate interests of the business and not prejudicial to the interests of the individual. Sensitive data – defined by Schedule 3 to include matters on racial/ethnic origin, political opinions/religious beliefs, trade union membership, health, sexuality and criminal convictions – can be processed only with explicit consent (i.e. the individual has positively opted in).
- Personal data shall be obtained only for a specified and lawful purpose(s) and should not be processed in a manner incompatible with that. A data processor must notify the Data Protection Commissioner (formerly the Data Protection Registrar) for inclusion on a publicly available database. There will be exemptions from such notification where processing is 'unlikely to prejudice the rights and freedoms of data subjects'.
- Personal data shall be adequate, relevant and not excessive for the purposes for which they are obtained under principle 2.
- Personal data shall be accurate and, where necessary, kept up to date. The data subject may, on payment of one reasonable fee, request to be given details of all of the data on her/him, the purposes for which it is being kept, the source of and any potential recipients of it. This *must* be supplied within forty days of the request. The data subject can ask the processor to correct/erase/destroy any inaccurate data and this can be enforced by a court order.
- Personal data shall not be kept for longer than is necessary for the notified purpose for which it was collected.
- Personal data shall be processed in accordance with the rights of data subjects including the right to have details of it, to have it corrected, to know its source and likely recipients, and to know the logic behind any decision-making process of which the data is likely to be the sole basis which significantly affects her/him – e.g. allowing her/him credit in a proposed hire-purchase/credit sale transaction. The commissioner may issue an information notice where it is suspected that a principle has been breached, or an enforcement notice where there is evidence that a principle has been breached. The data subject may also prevent the processing of data for the purposes of direct marketing or where such

processing would cause her/him harm or distress – subject to a public interest defence. Catherine Zeta Jones and Michael Douglas tried to use this right to prevent illicitly obtained photographs of their wedding being published when they had sold exclusive rights to take and publish photographs to another rival magazine.

- Appropriate technical and organizational measures must be taken to protect against unauthorized/unlawful processing of data and against accidental loss/destruction/damage to personal data. These measures must ensure, in the light of technical developments and the cost of implementation, a level of security appropriate to the extent and nature of the harm that breach of this principle might cause, i.e. the greater the extent or the nature of such harm the greater the expense and precautions that ought to be taken.

  This will include matters such as reasonable steps to ensure the reliability of any employees, etc., who might have access to the data. If data is processed by another on the data controller's behalf, the controller must order the processor (with evidence in writing of the order) to take all reasonable steps to check the reliability of the processor and of their systems, as well as issuing the order.

  BS 7799 may assist data processors to check the adequacy of their security regimes. This should apply not only to persons with authorized access, but also to others who might gain unauthorized access (e.g. other staff, cleaners and repair persons, where there are insecure passwords or they are left in obvious hiding places).

- Personal data shall not be transferred outside the European Economic Area (essentially the European Union plus Norway, Iceland and Liechtenstein) unless the country ensures an adequate level of protection for the rights and freedoms of data subjects in relation to processing personal data. Many states outside North America and the European Union may not comply with this. Adequacy or otherwise will be judged in the light of the nature of the data, the country of origin and destination, the purposes for which the data is being processed and the levels of protection and international obligations of the destination country.

  Section 55 of the Data Protection Act 1998 makes it a criminal offence 'knowingly or recklessly without the consent of the data controller to obtain or disclose personal data . . . or procure the disclosure to another person'. There are defences in relation to disclosure necessary for the purpose of preventing or detecting crime or where it was required or authorized by law.

The ordinary laws of fraud and theft will also apply to activities carried on over the Internet.

The Computer Misuse Act 1990

This Act deals with hacking and deliberate modification of computer material, e.g. by inserting a virus.

Section 1 makes is a crime knowingly to seek to obtain unauthorized access to computer material. This is a minor (summary) offence triable by magistrates and punishable by up to six months' imprisonment or a fine. The Act needs the computer to have been caused to perform a function. Reading data already displayed on the screen is not a crime but causing the machine to display it and then reading it is. The offence will be committed even if one fails to overcome any security devices or even if there are no such devices, provided one attempts to gain unauthorized access. The offence will also be committed if, as in Bow Street Magistrates *ex parte* government of the United States [2000] the accused has access to some data and exceeds it by seeking to gain access to other data – not just checking the credit of accounts of which she was given details by her employer but accessing 189 other accounts as well.

Section 2 makes it a crime to commit the Section 1 crime with intent to commit or facilitate a further offence. On conviction on indictment (at Crown Court) this offence is punishable by up to five years/a fine, or six months/a fine on magistrates' summary conviction. It is sufficient that there is an intent to commit or facilitate a further offence even if in fact one is not committed. The intent may well be to commit theft or fraud, or to blackmail another with information obtained by such access.

Section 3 creates a crime of causing an unauthorized modification of the contents of a computer with intent to impair the operation of the computer; prevent/hinder access to any data/program held in the computer; or impair the operation of any such program or the reliability of such data. It is immaterial whether the modification is intended to be temporary or permanent and whether it is aimed at a particular machine or not. The penalties on conviction are the same as those in Section 2.

It covers all forms of intentional alteration or deletion of data, or programs to hinder legitimate access or the reliability of the data. The most common case would be the introduction of a virus, on a disk or via an e-mail attachment, with intent. However, the offence can be committed in other ways, e.g. the nurse in R. *v*. Rymer [1993] who memorized a doctor's access code to get unauthorized access to a hospital computer to alter patients' records of treatment and drug dosage.

Similarly the introduction of a worm into a computer to take up space and slow the computer's operations down would be an offence under this section. The speed at which worms can be spread was illustrated by the 'Internet Worm' in 1988. A student released a worm, a self-replicating C program from Cornell University's computer system. It spread because of a flaw in the Unix operating system software on machines and repeatedly replicated itself, taking up large chunks of memory. The worm did not access data or destroy files but caused performance deterioration and crashing of the system. Within twelve hours of its first release a program had been devised to stop the worm but by then 2000 computers had to be taken offline to be cleaned up at a cost of $1 million-plus.

In R. *v.* Carey [2002] a computer engineer had updated a client's system but had done it so badly that it cost the client thousands of pounds to have it put right. When the client refused to pay him the engineer hacked into the system and wiped all the data on it. Carey was convicted under Section 3 and jailed for eighteen months.

Box 7.2:
APPLYING THE COMPUTER MISUSE ACT

Which section of the Computer Misuse Act (if any) would apply in the following circumstances?

1   A teenage hacker 'testing' the data security of Web sites.
2   A student hacking into a university computer to 'modify' his grades and obtain a higher class of degree.
3   The student in the above case having been denied access by the security system and having been traced and identified.
4   A police officer using the police national computer to get details for his brother of a man having an affair with his brother's wife so that the brother could confront the man.
5   John, with a grudge, knowingly gives Susan a disk contaminated with a virus intending to infect her computer. A mugger steals Susan's handbag, uses the disk and infects his own computer.

Your answers might well be:

1   An offence under Section 1, since the hacker is knowingly seeking to obtain unauthorized access to computer material – even if there is no evidence that the hacker intended to make any criminal use of it.
2   An offence under Section 2, since the student is intending to commit a crime under the Theft Act. In a similar example earlier in the chapter (p. 54), we were looking only at the distinction between civil and criminal matters, whereas now we are looking specifically at Section 2. This requires that the action has to be done with intent to commit/facilitate a further offence.

3   Similarly an offence under Section 2, since the intent to commit the offence is still there and he has knowingly attempted to obtain unauthorized access to the data.

4   Probably no offence because, although it is debatable whether the officer's access was unauthorized – since he has authority to interrogate the police national computer even if not on personal matters – there is no Section 2 intent to commit a further offence. It would have been different if the intent was to assault the adulterer; merely to confront him is not a crime.

5   A Section 3 offence, because John intended to impair the operation of a computer (Susan's) and committed an act which caused unauthorized modification of the contents of a computer (the mugger's). The Act does not require the intent to be against a particular computer, and the intention (*mens rea* – guilty intention) and the action of unauthorized modification (*actus reus* – guilty action) are both present.

ADVERTISING ON THE NET AND CONSUMER PROTECTION

In English law a contract is formed after an offer – a definite indication of the terms on which the offeror is prepared to be legally bound – is accepted by the offeree – the person to whom the offer has been made. An offer may be to the world in general – in which case anyone may accept it – or to a particular person – in which case only they can accept it.

Thus in Boulton *v.* Jones [1857] an offer was made by Jones to a particular individual retailer, X, to purchase goods, intending to set off part of the price against a debt owed by X to Jones although not explicitly saying so. Unknown to Jones, X had sold the business to Boulton, who supplied the goods and invoiced Jones for the full price. Jones refused to accept and pay for the goods at full price and was sued for breach of contract. Jones's defence was upheld; the offer had been made specifically to X and only he could accept it and form a contract. Boulton's attempt to do so was a counter-offer to sell at full price and Jones was entitled to reject it, so no contract was formed.

In Carlill *v.* Carbolic Smoke Ball Co. [1893] the wording of an advertisement – '£100 will be paid to anyone contracting influenza having bought a Carbolic Smoke Ball and used it according to the instructions' – and £1,000 having been deposited in a particular branch of a named bank 'to show our sincerity in the matter' – was so clear and definite as to amount to an offer. Mrs Carlill had accepted the offer by buying and using the ball correctly and was entitled to £100 when she got influenza. It was no defence that the Carbolic Smoke Ball Company did not know her and had not intended to make an offer to her. The offer was to the world in general and therefore anyone could accept it.

167

Once an offer has been accepted, a contract has been formed and any attempt not to perform it exactly as per its terms will breach that contract. An offer may be revoked (withdrawn) at any time before it has been accepted, although the revocation needs to be communicated to the offeree to be effective.

Care must be taken to distinguish an offer from an invitation to treat, which is a statement inviting others to make an offer. Price lists, catalogues, menus, newspaper advertisements have all been held to be invitations to treat and the would-be customer's attempt to order is an offer to buy on the stated terms. One of those terms is often 'subject to availability' and thus if a particular item has sold out when an order is placed one can simply reject the offer and one is not in breach of contract. Clearly it would make little commercial sense to reject an offer at the stated price if the item were still available, and indeed would be an offence if done on the grounds of sex or race. Pharmaceutical Society v. Boot's Cash Chemists [1953] decided that goods on supermarket shelves were an invitation to treat, not an offer to sell, and Fisher v. Bell [1960] came to the same conclusion in respect of goods in a shop window with a price ticket on them.

An offeror is legally bound by the terms of the contract once his offer is accepted, while one who makes an invitation to treat is clearly free to accept (and thus form a contract) or to reject any offers that result from it, without any legal consequences. Amazon's UK Web site (www.amazon.co.uk) says 'availability for titles in our catalogue is listed on each item's detail page. Beyond what we say on that page we cannot be more specific about availability. As we process your order, we will inform you by e-mail if any items you order turn out to be unavailable.' This wording seems much more consistent with an invitation to treat than with an offer to sell. Therefore clicking to order an item on the Amazon.co.uk Web page is an offer to buy and not acceptance forming a binding contract.

Amazon's mispricing policy is also interesting 'Despite our best efforts a small number of the more than 1.5 million items in our catalogue are mispriced . . . If an item's correct price is lower than our stated price we charge the lower amount and send you the item. If an item's correct price is higher than our stated price, we will contact you for instructions before despatching.' This would appear to be a mixture of legal accuracy and pragmatic business sense. As the Web site is an invitation to treat, the customer's clicking on an item to order it is an offer to buy – at the price and other details stated on the Web page.

Thus if the correct price is higher than that stated Amazon is legally correct. By despatching the goods at a higher price Amazon would be seeking to 'accept' something other than the offer which was made (at the Web page price). In practice – as in Boulton v. Jones – they would, in fact, be making a counter-offer; which is also what they would do by contacting the customer and informing them of the price increase. The customer is then free to accept or to reject Amazon's counter-offer.

If the price is lower than that on the Web page Amazon is making the assumption, almost certainly correct, that the customer will be more than happy to receive the item at a price lower than anticipated. Legally, by despatching the item, Amazon is making a counter-offer to sell at a price lower than the one in the customer's offer to buy. It is hard to envisage that any customer will, in fact, reject that counter-offer and return the book, refusing to buy at the lower price, but they would be legally within their rights so to do.

Case study:
THE ARGOS WEB PAGE INCIDENT

In 1999 people browsing the Argos online Web page saw television sets – normally costing £300 – displayed at a price of £3. Large numbers clicked on the order button to purchase a television for £3 but Argos refused to honour the orders, claiming a mistake in pricing. The Argos Web site (www.argos.co.uk) states: '*General Information*. All items are subject to availability. Prices are subject to change without notice, VAT is currently 17.5 per cent. Argos reserves the right to alter or change product specification. Alternatives of similar value or specification may be offered.' None of the dissatisfied customers in fact brought a legal action against Argos and it is very unlikely that they would have succeeded had they done so.

The catalogue, shop window and newspaper advertisement precedents would all point to the Web page as being an invitation to treat, with the would-be purchasers offering to buy at £3 when they clicked to order. The 'subject to availability', 'prices subject to change without notice', 'right to alter or change product specifications' and 'alternatives of a similar value or specification may be offered' wordings reinforce that view. If the Web page were an offer, then clicking to order would make a binding contract and Argos would be in breach if it tried to increase the price, change product specification or supply alternatives. If the Web page is an invitation to treat, the customer is offering to buy by her/his order click. Argos is free to accept that offer, reject it (as it did with the £3 offers for televisions) or make one of the counter-offers (of a higher price, different specification goods or alternative goods), detailed in its Web site wording. Certainly the fact that alternatives of a similar value or specification 'may be offered' – note: not 'supplied' – is consistent with a counter-offer. Any customers receiving alternative or higher-priced goods would be well within their legal rights to refuse to accept or to pay for them.

Source: *The Times*, 21 September 1999.

169

ADVERTISING AND CONSUMER PROTECTION: CRIMINAL ASPECTS

Advertising

Advertising can have legal consequences in both the criminal law and the civil law. Since 1968 the United Kingdom has regarded it as important to protect consumers from being misled and has sought to regulate that aspect of the conduct of business via the criminal law. Section 1 of the Trade Descriptions Act 1968 makes it an offence 'in the course of a trade or business' to apply 'a false trade description to any goods', or 'to supply any goods to which a false trade description is applied'.

The falsity of the description must be 'to a material degree', i.e. such as would be sufficiently influential to have a significant impact on a possible purchase. Contrast Donnelly v. Rowlands [1970], where milk from one dairy was supplied in bottles from another but with caps on the bottles clearly indicating the correct dairy of origin, with Routledge v. Ansa Motors [1980], where a car made in 1972 but neither registered nor used in any way until 1975 was described as a 1975 model. The false description on the bottle was held not likely to influence a consumer (particularly with the correct caps) and thus not material and no offence had been committed. Although the description of the car may have been technically correct, what was left unsaid made it materially misleading in an area that would be considerably influential to a purchaser, and so an offence had been committed.

It is important to note that the statement must have been made in the course of trade or business. A car hire business was still acting in the course of its business and could therefore be guilty of an offence when selling off hire cars after they had reached a certain mileage – London Borough of Havering v. Stevenson [1970] – but a self-employed courier trading in his vehicle for a new one was not in the course of his business and had not committed an offence by failing to disclose that the two-year-old vehicle had done over 100,000 miles and that therefore the 18,000 on the odometer (which might have been consistent with a two-year-old vehicle for a low use owner) in fact reflected 118,000 miles.

False trade descriptions are usually made by sellers, but in Fletcher v. Budgen [1974] a car dealer told a private seller that there was no possibility of repairing the car in question and that it was fit only for scrap. The seller accepted £2 for the car, which the dealer subsequently repaired at a cost of £56 and advertised for sale at £315. The dealer was convicted of applying a false trade description to goods in the course of a business. Descriptions covered by the Act include quality, size (e.g. 14 ft × 20 ft) etc.; method of manufacture (e.g. hand-made); composition (e.g. pure new wool); fitness for purpose, performance, etc. (e.g. 50 m.p.g.); other physical characteristics (free television with each sound system).

There is no requirement to prove intention, nor a defence of lack of intent. In MGN *v.* Ritters [1997] a newspaper advertised a £50 watch for £4.99. The prosecution said the advertisements suggested that the watches were generally available at £50 at the time of the advertisement. The defence, that there was no intention to deceive and that the watch was worth £50 even if not on retail sale at that price, failed.

Section 24 provides a defence of due diligence when the statement was made taking reasonable care and when the defendant reasonably believed it to be true (i.e. that due care had been taken in making the statement and the defendant not only believed it to be true but had reasonable grounds for so believing); or that the false statement was applied by a third party and there were no circumstances which should have alerted the defendant to its falsity.

The defendant must either have applied the false trade description her/himself in any manner likely to be taken as referring to the goods (e.g. marking on the goods, on packaging, on advertising) or supplied them after a request which used such a description (even though the *seller* did not actually use such words). In R. *v.* Ford Motor Co. [1974] the customer asked for 'a new Cortina'. The dealer completed the order form, not writing the word 'new', but it was clear to all that that was anticipated. Ford supplied a Cortina that had had minor damage prior to delivery, but had been repaired perfectly and was as new. Ford were held to have applied the description 'new' to the goods but were not guilty since what was delivered was 'as new'.

Section 14 of the Trade Descriptions Act 1968 makes it an offence in the course of a business to make a statement which one knows to be false, or recklessly to make a statement which is false, in respect of services/accommodation/facilities provided or the location or amenities of any accommodation provided. Accommodation covers hotels and holiday accommodation and not the sale/rental of housing generally, which is covered by the Property Misdescriptions Act 1991. In Wings *v.* Ellis [1984] W. supplied E. with a brochure which described an hotel as having air conditioning. After the brochure had been printed and distributed, W. found this was not so and committed an offence by not including an amendment slip detailing the error in E.'s brochure. In Westminster Council *v.* Ray Alan (Manshop) [1982] a Section 14 prosecution for a 'Closing Down Sale' notice on a shop when it was not, in fact, closing down failed because the shop was a supplier of goods and the section refers to the supply of services.

Section 20 of the Consumer Protection Act 1987 makes it an offence in the course of any business to give (by any means whatsoever – clearly including a Web site) consumers a misleading indication as to the price at which any goods, services, accommodation or facilities are available. This would include hidden extras on a price (for example, not indicating that a price did not include VAT where such was chargeable) and false comparisons with prices previously charged. The Secretary of State has issued a code of practice for practical guidance on Section

171

20. Although it is only advisory, rather than mandatory, failure to adhere to it may be evidence of a breach and adherence to it may help to establish a defence.

In 1996 Littlewood's were fined after admitting seven specimen charges when their winter sale catalogue had more than 1,000 items wrongly priced (*Times*, 14 November 1996). BSkyB were fined in 1997 after leaflets had failed to make it clear that watching the Bruno–Tyson boxing match would cost an extra £9.95 after the purchase of the Sky service (*Times*, 11 September 1997). In 1999 a Bristol estate agent was convicted after placing on a Web site photographs of a property for sale taken in such a way as to be misleading as to what was actually being sold (*Times*, 4 November 1999).

Section 25 of the Trade Descriptions Act 1968 provided newspapers and magazines with an 'innocent publication' defence if they were responsible for 'publishing' a statement that they should not reasonably have been aware was false. This would also apply to Internet service providers – until such time as they were made aware of the allegation of falsity in information on any Web sites or the service provided by them. No doubt the provisions of the Trade Descriptions Act and the Consumer Protection Act are just as applicable to statements made in 'e' means of trading as in those by word of mouth, newspaper or other forms of advertising.

Consumer rights

The Consumer Protection Act 1987, Section 10, makes it an offence, in relation to goods sold for consumer use, to sell/supply/agree/offer to supply goods which do not meet the general safety requirements, or to expose or possess such goods with the intention of supplying them. It is therefore an offence to supply, to agree to supply, or to offer to supply, or to have displayed, or have in your possession such goods with an intention to supply. An offence may thus be committed even without an actual sale, since putting them on your Web site or in your shop window with intent to sell will be committing the offence.

Section 3 defines not meeting the general safety standard as where the safety of the product is not as persons generally are entitled to expect 'in all the circumstances'. These will include the purposes for which the product has been marketed; the appearance of the product and its packaging; any marks (BSI kitemark, etc.) used in relation to the product; any instructions or warnings supplied with the goods and what might 'reasonably be expected to be done with or in relation to the product'. An example might be a toy builder's hard hat with no warning attached that it is just a toy and not to be used for protection purposes.

An e-trader will therefore need to require an undertaking of compliance of goods with the general safety standard from her/his suppliers. However, Section 39 provides a defence of due diligence where one could not reasonably have known that the goods did not meet the general safety standard.

Box 7.3:
APPLICATION OF THE CONSUMER PROTECTION ACT

homedecor8.com sells furniture direct to the public online via its Web page. homedecor8.com manufactures much of what it sells but also sells up-market imported fashion furniture. homedecor8.com's contracts with its suppliers state, 'All goods supplied must correspond to any UK furniture, upholstery and fabric safety regulations current at the time of supply.' homedecor8.com requires all invoices to carry a written undertaking that 'the goods supplied in respect of which this invoice is being submitted comply with all current UK safety standards at the date of this invoice'. Trading standards officers make test purchases from homedecor8.com and find that sofas from the Giorgio Carbonne Italiana Supremo range have upholstery filling not meeting UK safety regulations in terms of fire safety. The term had been in Giorgio Carbonne's contract and they had given the written undertaking with the invoice. homedecor8.com are prosecuted under Section 10 of the Consumer Protection Act 1987. What will the likely outcome be?

Your answer should have included:

homedecor8.com will be guilty if it has sold (and a sale has taken place here), agreed to sell or exposed for supply (the Web site is exposing goods for supply) goods which do not correspond to the general safety standard. Clearly that will include meeting all current safety regulations. Section 39 will provide a due diligence defence to homedecor8.com if it can show that the offence was due to the act of the Italian supplier and that it had relied on information given by that supplier and had taken 'all reasonable steps and exercised all due diligence in so relying'. homedecor8.com appears, on the face of things, to have a good defence but may well be guilty unless it can show that it also tested the goods from time to time for compliance, rather than just relying on the seller's word for it.

For example, in Garnett *v.* Boot's Chemists [1980] Boot's were not able to use the Section 39 defence in respect of pencils sold in their shops supplied from overseas that did not comply with the Pencils and Graphic Instruments Regulations 1974. Boot's had relied on contractual compliance and written undertakings but had not tested at all. They were held not to have taken 'all reasonable steps and exercised all due diligence' and were therefore guilty. homedecor8.com may also be criminally guilty on a similar basis.

The Sale of Goods Act 1979 automatically adds implied terms into all contracts for the sale of goods giving buyers rights against the seller – whether the seller is the manufacturer or not. Any attempt to evade these terms in a consumer sale – where a person buys for private use/consumption and not in the course of a business – is void and of no legal effect under the Unfair Contract Terms Act 1977. In non-consumer sales (business-to-business or B2B situations), clauses seeking to avoid or limit the effect of these Sale of Goods Act rights are valid subject to passing a test of reasonableness in all the circumstances. This will include the extent and clarity of the notice given of such a clause, the relative bargaining strengths of the parties and whether the purchaser could have gone elsewhere and not be faced with such terms.

In St Albans City Council v. International Computers [1996], ICL's clause limiting liability to £100,000 failed the reasonableness test in all the circumstances and ICL was liable for the full loss actually suffered. The limitation figure was very small compared with the possible risk and the actual loss suffered; ICL was a multinational with substantial resources and worldwide insurance cover of £50 million, whereas St Albans council was not a profit-making organization and all losses would fall on the ratepayers; their specialist needs meant they were limited to one or two suppliers, each of whom imposed similar clauses on a take-it-or-leave-it basis. Conversely in Green v. Cade [1978] a standard form of contract based on negotiations between the National Seed Merchants' Association and the National Farmers' Union was held to be reasonable and binding in respect of a financial limitation on claims because the parties were of relatively equal bargaining power and such clauses were usual in the trade for the sort of loss suffered.

Section 12 implies a term that the seller shall have the right to sell and passes on full rights of ownership unless otherwise disclosed at the time of contract.

Section 13 implies a term that the goods shall correspond to any description given and that the buyer may reject goods that do not do so: e.g. ½ in. timber staves of which 80 per cent were between ½ in. and ⁹⁄₁₆ in., or cans of fruit packed thirty to the case and delivered packed twenty-five to a case.

Section 14 (2) implies, where goods are sold in the course of a business, that the goods are of satisfactory quality – meeting the standards that a reasonable person would expect in all the circumstances. This would cover fitness for normal use, durability, appearance and finish. Circumstances would include description (e.g. goods in a sale described as 'shopsoiled' or 'seconds'), packaging, get-up, price and the normal use to which such goods would be put. Clearly one cannot expect the same quality from second-hand goods as from new ones. The price will also often have a bearing on quality, durability or finish.

Section 14 (3) implies that goods sold in the course of a business must be fit for any particular purpose made known to the seller, expressly or implicitly, at the time of the sale. Clearly, if nothing is said about purpose then the normal purpose(s) is implied.

The Supply of Goods and Services Act 1982 implies similar terms to goods supplied under a contract of hire (as opposed to sale), and under a contract for the supply of goods and services, where perhaps the major part of the price is paid for the service. This means the Sale of Goods Act is not applicable, despite the fact that goods are included. For example, on paying to have one's portrait painted one does get ownership of the frame, canvas and a quantity of assorted paints but one is paying the vast majority of the price for the artist's skill in applying the paint to the canvas.

Section 13 implies that, in contracts for the supply of services, the work will be performed with reasonable skill and care (probably no more than the common law tort of negligence implies anyway). Section 14 implies that the work will be carried out within a reasonable time. Section 15 that the price charged will be reasonable. What is reasonable in Sections 14 and 15 will have to be determined in the light of what the buyer expressly agreed to.

Liability is strict and irrespective of the seller's fault but the seller will have similar rights against the seller to him so that if she/he is liable to the buyer owing to the actions of a subcontractor she/he can sue the subcontractor to recoup that sum. The Unfair Terms in Consumer Contracts Regulations 1999 implemented EU Directive 91/13 EC and protects consumers who have entered into a contract containing non-negotiable terms imposed by the seller – which will usually be the case with e-Commerce online sales. Clicking to order will usually be expressed to be subject to the seller's terms and conditions expressed elsewhere on the site. The protection covers situations where the regulations deem things unfair to consumers and make such terms voidable at the option of the consumer – i.e. consumers can elect to be bound by the terms or not as they wish. Matters covered include where the seller is entitled to retain a deposit/impose a penalty on the consumer in the event of non-performance; where the seller is entitled unilaterally to alter the terms of the contract or the goods or services to be supplied (e.g. last-minute changes in destination/hotel in holiday contracts); where the buyer is bound without sufficient time to consider the contractual implications before entering into the contract – essentially situations where the term does not fulfil the requirement of good faith and causes a significant imbalance of power between the parties to the detriment of the consumer.

All these laws on consumer rights apply as much to e-Business deals under English law as to contracts made by any other (e.g. oral or written) means.

Case study:
CASES INVOLVING THE SALE OF GOODS ACT

Beale v. Taylor [1967]

A car was advertised and sold as a 1961 1,200 cc model as per its vehicle registration document (log book). It turned out to be a 'cut and shut' job with the rear of a 1,200 cc 1961 model and the front of a 1960 948 cc model which had been in front and rear-end crashes respectively. The seller was liable under Section 13 since the car did not correspond to the description, even though he had acted in good faith, with no knowledge of the inaccuracy of the description and no intention to defraud. Liability is strict, and non-compliance with the implied terms renders one liable. Taylor could sue whoever sold the car to him on the same basis of breach of Section 13.

Griffiths v. Peter Conway [1939]

The sellers were not liable when a customer contracted dermatitis from wearing a Harris tweed coat supplied to her by them. Under Section 14 (2) the coat was of satisfactory quality, since it would not have had this effect on persons who did not have abnormally sensitive skin and could thus have happily been worn by most people. Under 14 (3) the sellers were not liable, since they had not been warned by the customer of her skin condition and thus her implied purpose was for wearing by a person with normal skin – for which it was perfectly fit.

Crowther v. Shannon Motor Co. [1975]

The purchaser bought a second-hand Jaguar car with 80,000 miles on the clock – which the salesperson described as 'barely run in for a Jag'. After being driven for over 2,000 miles in three weeks the engine seized up and the sellers were held liable under Sections 14 (2) and 14 (3), since the vehicle was not of satisfactory quality nor reasonably fit for the purpose for which it was purchased. Even though it was a used vehicle the price and the type of vehicle meant the buyer was entitled to expect more from it. The result might have been different if it had been a smaller-engined and therefore more highly stressed vehicle, sold at substantially less than the book price for a car of its type and age.

Rogers v. Parish [1987]

A top-of-the-range Range Rover bought new was held to be in breach of Sections 14 (2) and 14 (3) and the purchaser could return it after seven months and 5,000 miles because it had numerous minor defects needing repairs (many unsuccessful), had been returned to the dealers for repair (and was thus unavailable to the buyer) on many occasions, and was beginning to show signs of rust and paint blemishes. Satisfactory quality includes appropriate levels of durability and reliability in all the circumstances and, in the case of such a vehicle, appropriate levels of comfort and appearance.

INTELLECTUAL PROPERTY

Most forms of personal property (as opposed to real property, which is land or an interest in land) are tangible and are transferred by delivery with intent, for example, the purchase of a book where the seller transfers ownership of it to the buyer by physically handing it to her/him in return for the purchase price. Possession given without intent (e.g. of a video which one has rented) or taken without consent (e.g. theft of one's handbag) does not give any right of ownership. The old expression that 'possession is nine points of the law' shows that one of the major ways of enforcing ownership is by taking/maintaining possession, but ownership gives the additional right of denying possession to others.

Property can, however, also come in intangible form – such as debts owing to you, which clearly appear on the assets side of a balance sheet, and what is known as intellectual property such as copyright, design rights, trade marks and patents. These are valuable rights of ownership, which however cannot be transferred by physical delivery and cannot be enforced by seizing possession. Usually, rights of ownership have to be enforced by legal action, perhaps to confirm ownership, or to prevent further abuse of one's rights and to get compensation for harm already suffered. For example in 2000 Ludlow Music successfully sued Robbie Williams and EMI because his song 'Jesus in a camper van' substantially copied the lyrics of a Woody Guthrie song, 'I am the way', of which Ludlow owned the copyright. (*Times*, 3 October 2000.) Similarly, in 2001 the AA agreed to pay Ordnance Survey £20 million in an out-of-court settlement for breach of copyright by copying its maps, which the AA had published as its own work. The Ordnance Survey had deliberately put in a number of secret errors into each of its maps which had been exactly reproduced in the AA maps, thus exposing the plagiarism. (*Times*, 6 March 2001.)

Copyright

This is covered by the Copyright, Designs and Patents Act 1988 and exists in original literary, dramatic, musical or artistic work, sound recordings, films, broadcasts or cable programmes and in the typographical arrangement of published editions.

177

Copyright arises automatically with publication in a tangible form and there is no need for registration or to use the © symbol in the United Kingdom. However, its use does confer protection in a number of countries (including the United States) under the Universal Copyright Convention 1952. It also serves as a warning that the material is subject to copyright and raises presumptions about the first date of publication, therefore ownership of copyright, so it does no harm to use it.

Copyright can be enforced in the United Kingdom where there is a reasonable connection between the work and the United Kingdom – for example, the work is first published there, or the author is a UK national or is normally resident there. UK copyright will also give benefits in other states with which the United Kingdom has reciprocal arrangements, i.e. signatory states to the Berne Convention (originally 1886, last revised 1971) and the Universal Copyright Convention 1952. The Civil Jurisdiction and Judgements Acts 1982 and 1991 mean reciprocal arrangements with all EU states and those in the European Economic Area. The Copyright (Application to other Countries) Order of 1993 means that having copyright in one signatory state could mean one would qualify for copyright protection in the others.

The Duration of Copyright and Rights in Performance Regulations 1995 harmonized copyright duration across the European Union to seventy years from the author's death or fifty years from first broadcast or from the end of the year of release for sound recordings. Copyright remains fifty years from the author's death for works originating outside the European Union.

Copyright covers all literary/dramatic/musical/artistic works such as books, letters, pictures, sculptures, photographs, charts, maps and models, musical notation and the words and recordings of performances. It also covers software programs, files and databases under the Copyright (Computer Software) Amendment Act 1985, the Copyright (Computer Programs) Regulations 1992 and the Copyright and Rights in Databases Regulations 1997. Copyright does not vest in ideas but in the expression of them.

Writing is defined in Section 178 to include any form of notation or code, whether by hand or otherwise, and regardless of the method by which, or the medium in or on which, it is recorded. This would clearly cover material written conventionally on paper and musical notation but also in a computer memory or on a disk. Design material for a computer program, such as listings, flow charts and specifications, are also covered.

Copyright vests in the author or her/his employer if the work was done in the course of employment, but can be transferred. If, therefore, one is commissioning work, one needs to negotiate a transfer of the copyright if that is what one wants.

Case study:
INTELLECTUAL PROPERTY CASES

In IBCOS Computers *v.* Barclays Highland Mercantile Finance and others [1994], Barclays' co-defendant, while working for IBCOS, wrote a suite of programs for handling the financial affairs of agricultural machinery dealers. On leaving IBCOS he signed an agreement that the copyright belonged to IBCOS and that he would not write competing software for two years after leaving. Within that time span he did, in fact, write such software for Barclays which contained spelling and punctuation errors in the same places as the IBCOS suite of programs and an identical piece of redundant code. IBCOS sued for breach of copyright and breach of confidence even though the new suite of programs was not marketed until the two-year period was over. IBCOS won – even though the similar functions of the programs would mean some similarity in content. Where such similarities as these indicated copying, the court should assume that there had been copying and not just similarities in writing style, unless evidence to the contrary was produced.

The copyright owner has exclusive right to copy the work; to issue copies to the public; to play/perform/display/broadcast the work publicly or adapt the work. She/he may, of course, license others to do any of these. Breach of copyright must be for the whole of the work or a substantial part of it – substantial, that is, in terms of the quality and essence of the work, not of the quantity, which has been copied.

In Newspaper Licensing Agency *v.* Marks & Spencer [2001], a copy of a newspaper article which gave no indication of how the rest of the page was laid out was not a substantial part of the published edition (the whole newspaper) and was therefore not in breach of copyright in the typographical arrangement belonging to the publishers. NLA under licence had distributed cuttings to M&S, but M&S had then, without a licence, made further copies of the cuttings and distributed them in-house. Reproduction of the whole of a newspaper article, or indeed the germ of the idea behind it, would be in breach of the literary copyright – and of the photographic copyright if there were a photograph in it. Indeed, a newspaper article with photographs which had been written by a team of in-house staff and freelancers might well consist of a basket of copyright ownerships. Copyright in the work of the in-house staff would vest in the employer while that in the freelancers' work would remain with them unless otherwise agreed in the commissioning agreement. The same would be true in respect of the photographs.

The author (even if the copyright vests in someone else) has what are known as moral rights of paternity (to be identified as the author), to prevent false attribution, and integrity (to object to changes which would amount to a serious distortion of the work). The Act allows fair dealing (probably one copy per person of one issue of a journal or a chapter of a book – depending on what has been copied) for the purposes of research/private study; criticism/review/ reporting or instruction by lecturers/teachers/pupils.

The Copyright (Computer Program) Regulations 1992 allow exceptions to copyright infringement. These are decompiling a program for interoperability with an independently created program; making back-up copies as necessary for lawful use (often installation instructions tell you to make a copy, use that as the working copy and keep the original safe as a back-up in case of damage/corruption); error corrections (if not excluded by the licence agreement); in defence of the public interest – e.g. to publish a code used by hackers, to help to prevent hacking.

Design rights

Under Part 3 of the Copyright, Designs and Patents Act 1988 the author of an original design automatically gets a design right giving control over its use for manufacturing purposes. The design must be original and must be recorded in some way (e.g. a drawing or a prototype). Design covers 'any aspect of the external/internal shape or configuration of the whole or part of the article'. This includes designs for a three-dimensional article, but not surface decoration or any must fit/match aspects where appearance is dependent on matching other parts of an integrated item, such as motor vehicle spares. The right lasts for fifteen years (or ten from when first manufactured, whichever is the shorter) but with others having rights to licences in the last five years. The right is in the creator of the design (or the employer, as per copyright).

The Registered Designs Act 1949 and the Registered Design rules 1989 give the owner of a novel two- or three-dimensional design with 'eye appeal' a monopoly over exploiting it for a five-year period (extendible by four more five-year extensions). The design must be registered at the Designs Registry – part of the Patent Office. The 'eye appeal' means it must be visible in use and be such that its aesthetic quality is a material reason for purchase/use. It must also be capable of standing alone in that it does not merely rely on another item for its shape (as, for example, a car door would do).

Trade marks

The Trade Marks Act 1994 defines a trade mark as 'any sign capable of being rep-resented graphically which is capable of distinguishing the goods/services of one undertaking from those of another'. Words, designs, letters, numbers, the shape of the goods or their packaging and moving images and jingles are all capable of being trade marks. A plain colour or standard shape may not be registrable but colour combinations or unusual shapes (such as with drug capsules) may well be.

The mark must be distinctive, so that name alone will not suffice but might do if presented in a distinctive way, such as a signature or particular lettering. Names that are identical or very similar to ones already in use are not distinctive, and therefore not registrable, and neither are generic names – ones that simply relate to the character/origin or intended use of the product.

Names presented distinctively and thus registrable as trade marks would include the signatures in Walt Disney and Clarke's shoes. Distinctive lettering in names includes McDonald's and Marks & Spencer. Non-verbal marks include numbers (4711 cologne), symbols (the Direct Line phone on wheels and its jingle) and the shape of packaging such as Coca-Cola bottles and Jif lemons. In Philips Electronics v. Remington Consumer Products [1998] Philips's drawing of a three-head electric shaver was held to identify function and not to be distinctive enough to identify a particular manufacturer and thus was not registrable as a trade mark.

Registration is via a process of application to the Trade Mark Registry and a checking process. Registration is for a ten-year period, renewable indefinitely for further ten-year periods. Infringement proceedings can be backdated to the original filing of the application and its publication by the Registrar.

The Community Trade Marks Regulations 1993 allow registration of a Community Trade Mark (valid across the whole of the European Union) through one application to the Office for the Harmonization of the Internal Market in Alicante. However, a single notice of objection in any one member state would delay the whole process considerably. The Madrid Agreement and Protocol 1995 allows an application in the owner's home country to be the basis of an international application, nominating other signatory states where protection is also applied for. However, not very many states have thus far ratified the protocol.

Patents

Patents are covered by the Patents Act 1977. The inventor of a new 'inventive step' capable of industrial application may apply for a patent on it and get a twenty-year right to exclusive exploitation of it. The invention must be new. Something which is currently known about or in industrial use, or details of which have been published in a learned journal, is in the public domain and so no longer new and not patentable. It must be an *inventive step*, not one that would have been obvious to a person skilled in the art at the time. It must also be capable of industrial application, meaning that new scientific theories or discoveries are not patentable, but novel industrial applications based on them will be.

The Act excludes from patentability:

● A discovery, scientific theory or mathematical method, as being a description of a phenomenon rather than an invented thing.

- A literary, dramatic, musical or artistic work or other aesthetic creation – these are already covered by copyright.
- A scheme for performing a mental act, playing a game or doing business (not so in the United States, where business methods are patentable, e.g. Amazon's 'one click' registration) or a program for a computer – largely natural human mental acts not inventions.
- The presentation of information – this is already covered by copyright.
- Any invention which would be generally expected to encourage offensive, immoral or antisocial behaviour.
- Any variety of animal or plant or any essentially biological process for the production of animals or plants, not being a microbiological process or the product of such a process.

In Vicom Systems' Patent Application [1987], a distinction was drawn between a computer program and a technical process carried on under the control of a program. The latter was patentable.

Microbiological processes are patentable, such as the technology behind creating a genetically modified mouse with particular characteristics. Similarly the Plant Varieties and Seeds Act 1964 allows thirty-year protection against unauthorized production for standardized, stable and distinct plant varieties.

The EU Directive on the Legal Protection of Biotechnological Inventions 1998 provides that all member states should protect biotechnological inventions. States may still exclude animals and biological processes from patentability, but not biotechnological inventions such as isolated gene sequences which have technical effect. Cloning on gene sequences alone will not be patentable.

An application for a UK patent is made to the Patent Office, which will carry out searches and then, if clear, publish the first filing of the patent. Extensive examinations and searches are then made and the publication may well arouse objections. Finally, after a process that can last four years, a patent will be granted. Under the European Patent Convention, to which the United Kingdom, Belgium, France, Germany, Holland, Italy, Norway, Spain, Sweden and Switzerland have signed up, the applicant can make a further application by a speeded-up process (co-ordinated by the European patent offices) for a bundled patent in any of the signatory countries within twelve months of the publication of the first filing.

An application can also be made for patents in many countries around the world, including the United States and Japan, under the Patent Co-operation Convention. Nevertheless, the patents are not international in themselves, only the process of application has international co-operative elements to it. The patents are granted by individual states for protection and rights within their jurisdiction. Patent protection is broadly similar in most countries.

Case study:
PROBLEMS INVOLVING INTELLECTUAL PROPERTY RIGHTS

In July 2001 Argos, Woolworth and their supplier Worlds Apart were found guilty of infringing the Ninja Corporation's design rights for a child's collapsible 'pop-up tent'. Worlds Apart supplied the offending items and Argos and Woolworth sold them. The Ninja Corporation claims to have lost between £15 million and £20 million over four years in lost revenue and is seeking an injunction to prevent further abuse of its intellectual property rights. (*The Times*, 16 July 2001.)

At the same time a US security company has developed what it claims to be a pirate-proof CD. When it is originally recorded the digital code is degraded with a series of tiny gaps causing white noise. A CD player or computer detects but overlooks them and the sound is normal. When the code is copied so are the tiny gaps, but in such a way that any CD player or computer cannot overlook them. The resulting hiss and distortion mean that the copy is of significantly poorer sound quality.

In February 2001 a San Francisco appeal court upheld a temporary injunction preventing Napster users from swapping copyrighted songs using a software format MP3. The practice was depriving record companies of copyright royalties on their 3 billion songs a month that were being exchanged for free in this way. Sony Universal, Warner, BMG and EMI in 2002 are offering various sorts of authorized downloads at full quality. See www.hmv.co.uk, http://www.msn.com and www.ondemanddistribution.com.

Dyson also won a breach of patent case in 2000 against Hoover, as its 'triple vortex' system was held to be a blatant copy of Dyson's patented 'dual cyclone' cleaner. (*The Times*, 4 October 2000.)

For considerably more detail on intellectual property rights and the e-world see Bainbridge (2000).

The English common law has long recognized the tort of *passing off* – the practice of representing one's goods or services as those of another. This can be by name or by get-up. There is no need to prove intention, merely a genuine and realistic likelihood of a proportion of the public being deceived. Examples include Reckitt and Colman *v.* Borden [1990] about the defendant's selling of lemon juice in a plastic lemon-shaped container, even though the brand name in no way resembled Reckitt's Jif brand; and United Biscuits *v.* Asda [1997], where Asda was allowed to keep the Puffin name for its chocolate-covered biscuits provided that the packaging design was altered so as not to resemble United Biscuits' well established Penguin brand. If the public are not likely to be confused the tort has not been committed, as in Stringfellow v. McCain Foods [1984] – no likely confusion between a night club and frozen chips – and Arsenal FC v. Reed [2000]. In this case, Reed's products were in Arsenal colours and used the words 'Gunners' and 'Arsenal', but the court was swayed by Reed's notices next to his stall disclaiming affiliation with official Arsenal merchandise and the argument that consumers were merely purchasing badges of allegiance and had not been misled from their brand loyalty. The European Court, however, ruled in 2002 that customers might be confused by his use of the words 'Arsenal' and 'Gunners' despite the disclaimer at the stall.

Cyber-squatting

Systems for the allocation of domain names have been discussed earlier in the chapter. 'Cyber-squatting' is the process of registering domain names with the intention of selling them to the trade mark owner; selling them to someone else with a commercial interest in the name; using them for deception or to belittle the trade mark owner; or retaining them to block the use by the trade mark owner in order to force up the price that they are prepared to pay for them. Such activities may well be actionable in the tort of passing off and/or as breaches of trade mark.

In Marks & Spencer and others v. One in a Million [1998], the latter had registered such domain names as marksandspencer.co.uk, since the policy for registration tends to be first-come-first-served and One in a Million had got in first. They wrote to Marks & Spencer, Ladbroke's, Sainsbury's, Virgin and British Telecom, offering to sell them the domain names, whilst also threatening to sell them to others and stop these trade mark owners from using the domain names if they would not buy. One in a Million had acted similarly with others in the past and was sued for passing off and breach of trade mark. An injunction was granted to restrain the threat of passing off and to order the transfer of the domain names to the claimants, since the only possible reason why a person unconnected with the trade mark owner would register a name closely connected with a well known business organization would be to pass off. With One in a Million's history and actions there was also a clear intention to infringe trade marks, since 'use in the course of trade' in the Act simply meant by way of business and not necessarily to trade under the name.

There is clearly an argument to be had over free trade and the stifling of competition issues associated with intellectual property rights and many owners of such rights are seen as unfairly exploiting their monopoly (e.g. multinational drug companies and the cost of medicines). Owners would argue that people should be fairly rewarded for the skill, effort, time and money put into research and development and if their intellectual property rights are not adequately protected, people would be loath to invest time and capital in the first place. This would stifle innovation and creativity.

INTERNET SERVICE PROVIDERS

By providing the means for their clients to put material on the Web, ISPs may be running risks in relation to both breach of copyright and defamation of character. In one sense the ISPs are publishers of the information, but clearly they do not have the knowledge or editorial control of a newspaper or traditional book publisher.

ISPs would be wise specifically to require, as a term of providing the service, that clients undertake to adhere to copyright and defamation laws, not to make infringing material available to others and to give an undertaking to the ISP to indemnify it for any liability that it incurs as a result of the client's actions. While these may be wise first steps, it is important to understand that although it is easy to give such undertakings it may well be far more difficult to enforce them in practice. This is particularly the case when dealing with a client who has few or no financial resources, and the aggrieved party may well have sued the ISP directly because the client could not be identified or did not appear financially to be worth suing.

Although ISPs may argue that it is unfair to make them liable for matters over which they have at best limited control, they are nevertheless providing the service as a business undertaking and must take the risks along with the profits. There would seem to be more equity in making the ISP liable than in allowing others to have their legal rights breached/their trade stolen/their reputations besmirched without any form of redress.

An ISP might be liable for secondary infringement under Section 24 (2) of the Copyright, Designs and Patents Act 1988 by transmitting a work without the copyright owner's licence by a telecommunication system, whilst knowing or having reason to believe copies would be made by reception in the United Kingdom or elsewhere. If someone posts, for example, pictures or text in breach of another's copyright on a Web site can the ISP be liable as secondary infringer?

The courts have also construed authorized infringement under Section 16 (2) quite widely to include in effect turning a blind eye. In Moorehouse v. University of New South Wales [1976] the university failed to display notices informing library users of the laws on copyright where there were photocopying facilities, and failed to supervise any copying that took place. This *laissez-faire* attitude led to them being held liable for authorized infringement.

This suggests that an ISP may need to warn its clients about copyright law, make spot checks/carry out random sampling to monitor compliance and take some action where non-compliance is discovered. Anything less would seem to be getting dangerously close to authorized infringement. Quite how realistic this idea is in practice, and indeed how desirable in the context of free speech and the Net as a worldwide open forum, is another matter.

Case study:
DEFAMATION AND INTERNET SERVICE PROVIDERS

In Godfrey *v.* Demon Internet [1999] the question of the possible liability of ISPs for defamation on sites for which they provide services was raised. The posting of the allegedly defamatory material was by an anonymous person in the United States and was about Godfrey, a UK resident. Godfrey complained more than once to Demon, the ISP concerned, about this allegedly obscene and defamatory material but to no avail. Godfrey therefore sued Demon, since the tort of libel (defamation in a permanent form as opposed to the spoken word or gestures) consists in publishing an untrue statement about a person which would cause right-thinking members of society to think less of them or to shun or avoid them. Publishing consists simply of making it known to anyone other than the person to whom it refers.

Byrne *v.* Deane [1937] is a precedent for saying that failure to remove from a physical notice board under one's control once one knew of the alleged defamation is, in fact, publishing. It would seem logical that the same should apply to a virtual notice board – especially in view of the vastly enhanced potential readership of the material – not just those persons who entered a private golf club – but anyone worldwide with an Internet connection.

Section 1 (3) of the Defamation Act 1996 says ISPs are not counted as publishers if they are involved only as the provider of access to the communications systems by which the statement was transmitted/made available by a person over whom they have no control.

For the Section 1 (3) innocent defamation defence to apply the ISP must prove:

- It was not the author of the statement.
- That it took reasonable care in respect of the publication.
- That it did not know/have reason to believe that what it did caused/contributed to the publication of the defamatory statement.

Until they were notified of the defamatory statement, that defence was open to Demon but not once it had been informed about it and took no action to remove the statement.

In Totalise *v.* Motley Fool and Interactive Investor [2001], Motley Fool operated a Web site as a discussion forum for various companies, including Totalise. Motley Fool's contract with its users included clauses committing it to respect and protect their privacy and not to disclose their identity or any information about them, except following legal process. Zeddust began posting defamatory comments about Totalise and after complaints Motley temporarily removed and then banned Zeddust. Posting then began to appear on Interactive Investor's Web site. Interactive removed them. Totalise sought disclosure of Zeddust's identity from both Motley and Interactive Investor, both of whom refused as per their contractual agreement with Zeddust.

Totalise relied on the precedent in Norwich Pharmacol Co. *v.* Customs and Excise Commission [1974] that innocent parties could be compelled to disclose the identity of wrongdoers. Interactive Investor's boards also carried statements that the contents did not represent the opinion of the Web site operator and that the operator was not the author of the opinions. The judge said, 'Zeddust had carried out a concerted campaign to a potentially vast audience of no geographical limit. The claimants were at risk of serious damage. Zeddust was hiding behind a cloak of anonymity and the claimants had no practical means of identifying Zeddust. The balance fell in favour of the claimants, otherwise one could defame with impunity on Web sites.' This decision, of course, does not make the ISP liable in defamation but simply orders disclosure of information about the ISP's clients. What, however, if those clients prove not to be persons of means and not worth suing? Godfrey *v.* Demon did establish that, in its particular circumstances, Demon did publish the statement in question, although thereafter the matter was settled out of court.

In 2002 the High Court of Australia decided that Joseph Gutnick could sue Dow Jones for defamation in Melbourne because an article on their Barons' Web site was downloaded and read in Australia. Dow Jones had tried to argue that the case should be tried in the United States, since that was where the story had been written and posted on the Internet. American publishers have freedom of speech under the First Amendment, so US libel laws are less favourable to claimants than those in Australia, or indeed England. It seems that Internet content is deemed to have been published in any place where it is viewed online, so a Web site publisher could face a whole series of actions in a variety of countries with the strictest libel laws.

After an application by Demon in July 2001, Dame Elizabeth Butler-Sloss, the President of the Family Division of the High Court, took account of the Section 1 (3) innocent defamation defence. She varied her injunction on all forms of media against publication of material likely to assist in the identification of the identity or whereabouts of Robert Thompson and Jon Venables, the killers of two-year-old James Bulger. The ban has been modified so that an ISP will be liable only if it knew that the material had been or was likely to be placed on, or accessed by, its server and 'failed to take all reasonable steps to prevent its publication' by removing the material from its server or by blocking access to it. In other words, ISPs will not be in breach of the order unless they, like Demon in the Godfrey case, knew/ought to have known it was there and did nothing in response. In the Thompson and Venables case by then the damage may well have been done. (*Times*, 11 July 2001.)

While one can understand the court's desire to provide an innocent victim of defamation with a remedy, the threat of an injunction might provide a perhaps not very deserving claimant with a weapon with which to cut off any discussion – even of a matter that perhaps deserves public investigation. Could this perhaps be a curb on investigative journalism or just on improper uses of it?

CHAPTER SUMMARY

This chapter has drawn the distinction between civil and criminal law, explored issues of jurisdiction and extraterritoriality and looked at the framework of English law, seeking to balance the competing interests of various parties in a variety of situations, within which organizations in the electronic age have to operate.

FURTHER READING

For the law surrounding business situations generally see A. Adams, *Law for Business Students*, 2nd edn, New York: Longman (2000). For law and computing see D. I. Bainbridge, *Introduction to Computer Law*, 4th edn, New York: Longman (2000). For more specialist writings on law and the Internet see particularly Y. Akdeniz, C. Walker and D. Wall, *The Internet, Law and Society*, New York: Longman (2000).

BIBLIOGRAPHY

Akdeniz, Y., Walker, C. and Wall, D. (2000) *The Internet, Law and Society*, New York: Longman.

Arthur, C. (2001) 'Hacker learns Internet deception isn't child's play', *Independent*, 7 July.

Bainbridge, D. I. (2000) *Introduction to Computer Law*, 4th edn, New York: Longman.

Barker, S. A. and Hurst, P. R. (1998) *The Limits of Trust: Cryptography, Governments and Electronic Commerce*, The Hague: Kluwer.

De Freitas, I. (2001) 'Nazis on the Net', *Times*, 9 January.

HMSO (1999) *Building Confidence in Electronic Commerce*, House of Commons Select Committee on Trade and Industry, 91998–9 H.C.187, London: HMSO.

Howells, G. and Weatherill, S. (1995) *Consumer Protection Law,* Aldershot: Dartmouth.

Schlectriem, P. (1998) *Commentary on the UN Convention on International Sale of Goods,* 2nd edn, Oxford: Clarendon Press.

Spinello, R. (2000) *Cyber Ethics: Morality and Law in Cyberspace*, Sudbury MA: Jones & Bartlett.

Cases

American Library Association *v.* Pataki [1997] 969 F. Supp. 170.

Arsenal FC *v.* Reed [2000], *Times*, 26 April 2001.

Beale *v.* Taylor [1967] 3 All ER 253.

Boulton *v.* Jones [1857] 2 H & N 564.

Bow Street Magistrates *ex parte* US Goverment [2000] Cr App R 61.

Byrne *v.* Deane [1937] 1 KB 818.

Carlill *v.* Carbolic Smoke Ball Co. [1893] 1 QB 256.

Crowther *v.* Shannon Motor Co. [1975] 1 All ER 139.

Donnelly *v.* Rowlands [1970] 1 WLR 1600.

European Convention on Human Rights and Fundamental Freedoms E Con HR&FF 91553 (Cmd 8969).

Fisher *v.* Bell [1960] 3 All ER 731.

Fletcher *v.* Budgen [1974] 2 All ER 1243.

Garnett *v.* Boots [1980].

Godfrey *v.* Demon Internet [1999], *Times*, 20 April 1999.

Green *v.* Cade [1978] Lloyd Rep 602.

Griffiths *v.* Peter Conway [1939] 1 All ER 685.

Gutnick *v.* Dow Jones [2000] *Times*, 11 December 2002.

IBCOS Computers *v.* Barclay Highland Mercantile Finance [1994] FSR 275.

London Borough of Havering *v.* Stevenson [1970] 3 All ER 601.

Marks & Spencer *v.* One in a Million [1998], *Times*, 29 July 1998.

MGN *v.* Ritters [1997], *Times*, 30 July 1997.

Moorehouse *v.* University of New South Wales [1976] RPC 151.

Newspaper Licensing Agency *v.* Marks & Spencer [2001], *Times*, 13 July 2001.

Norwich Pharmacol *v.* Customs and Excise Commission [1974] 1 AC 133.

Pharmaceutical Society of Great Britain *v.* Boot's Cash Chemists (Southern) [1953] 1 QB 401.

Philips Electronics *v.* Remington Consumer Products [1998] RPC 283.

R. *v.* Carey [2002], *Times*, 19 September 2002.

R. *v.* Ford Motor Co. [1974] 1 WLR 1200.

R. *v.* Rymer [1993], *Times*, 21 December 1993.

Reckitt & Colman *v.* Borden [1990] 1 All ER 873.

Rogers *v.* Parish [1987] 2 All ER 232.

Routledge *v.* Ansa Motors [1980] RTR 1.

St Albans City Council *v.* ICL [1996] 4 All ER 481.

Stringfellow *v.* McCain Foods [1984], *Times*, 3 July 1984.

Totalise *v.* Motley Fool and Interactive Investor [2001], *Times*, 15 March 2001.

United Biscuits *v.* Asda [1997] CLY 4883.

Westminster City Council *v.* Ray Alan (Manshop) [1982].

Wings *v.* Ellis [1984] 3 All ER 577.

WEB LINKS

www.amazon.co.uk

www.argos.co.uk

www.thetimes.co.uk

www.independent.co.uk

Chapter 8

e-Commerce: a global overview

GERALDINE T. COHEN

KEY LEARNING POINTS

After completing this chapter you will have an understanding of:

- The global expansion of e-Commerce
- The opportunities and threats in international trade and the implications for global e-Commerce
- The importance of the STEP factors in global e-Commerce and in particular the role of socio-cultural influences
- Global e-Commerce strategies, in particular the problems involved in the globalization versus localization debate
- The channels conflict faced by e-Commerce organizations in deciding between direct selling and the distributor model

ORDERED LIST OF SUB TOPICS

- The importance of going global
  - Methods of entry into global markets
  - Opportunities and threats in global e-Marketing
  - Niche marketing
  - Understanding the global environment
- Socio-cultural environments for global e-Commerce
  - Definitions of culture
  - Symbols and symbolism
  - Incompatible software
  - Culturally sensitive Web design
  - Methods of payment

- Legal issues in e-Commerce
- e-Commerce global strategies
  - Local versus global
  - Standardization versus adaptation
- Changing patterns in global distribution
  - e-Commerce distribution system
  - Global exporting

The Internet is bringing about a profound change in the ways business is conducted worldwide and is considered to have become the conduit for change from a producer culture to a consumer culture. Lisa Harris and Nelarine Cornelius argued in Chapter 4 that e-Commerce organizations worldwide need to understand the necessity of moving to a consumer-centred business model essentially dependent on offering real value and superior service in order to succeed (Nolan 1998a). Communication methods between sellers and buyers worldwide have changed beyond recognition in only a few years, with the use of international electronic transactions, use of e-mail messaging and the setting up of interactive Web sites for the benefit of the global supply of information and e-Commerce. Newly set up 'dotcom' organizations, as well as small companies, are reaching out beyond their local and national confines, finding easy access to global markets without the financial burden of expensive sales forces or retail outlets. Established global organizations are acknowledging the importance of the Internet in providing huge opportunities to their existing operations but also in identifying worrying threats.

Online retail revenue in 1999 was estimated at $36.6 billion in the United States, $3.5 billion in Europe and $2.8 billion in Asia-Pacific. The United States has been the centre of e-Commerce, but this is viewed as changing rapidly. The technology research company Forrester predicts that 50 per cent of e-Commerce will be conducted outside the United States by 2005. In Europe, e-Commerce is growing at an annual rate of more than 100 per cent, with Forrester predicting online sales of $1.5 trillion by 2004, whereas e-Commerce in the Asia-Pacific region has been booming (Pleasants 2001a).

Reflecting on the above figures, Pleasants affirms that e-Commerce is in a period of rapid transition from a US-based phenomenon to a global one. His

TIP

The latest Internet trends and statistics can be found on www.nua.ie/surveys.

advice to e-Business is that if it has global potential then it should move aggressively in entering markets outside the United States. Therefore a thorough understanding of each market's product-specific e-Commerce potential is essential.

This chapter will start with an overview of the globalization process and examine the importance of going global for e-Commerce organizations worldwide. It will then review the advantages offered by the advent of the Internet to global trading and the implications for the directions that organizations take as they plan their global strategies. The next part of the chapter will focus on socio-cultural environments and examine the role various factors play in the process of deciding which markets to target and on the methods of entry. Consumer buying behaviour for a wide range of products marketed through the Internet is clearly influenced by culture. The understanding of this process by e-Commerce organizations is of the utmost importance. A review of global e-Commerce strategies will follow, centring in particular on the globalization versus localization debate. Finally, the changing patterns in global distribution are analysed, in particular the 'channels conflict' faced by e-Commerce organizations in deciding between direct selling and the distributor model.

THE IMPORTANCE OF GOING GLOBAL

Globalization involves the transfer of an existing business system to other countries or the management of another business system in other countries. The terms 'international', 'multinational', 'global' and 'transnational' have been used to describe different stages in the globalization ladder of business development (Jobber 2001). The decision of nationally based e-Commerce to go global will depend on factors such as demography, entry modes, socio-cultural diversity, as well as the approach and management style to be used when entering new markets.

The United States today represents the largest national market in the world, with roughly 25 per cent of the total world market for all products and services. The fact that 75 per cent of the world market potential is outside their national territory has been the force driving many US companies to 'go international' and even to extend further and 'go global'. With three-quarters of its revenue generated by its soft drink business outside the United States, Coca-Cola, acknowledged as the most successful global company, has driven the message of globalization further than anybody else. For non-US companies the incentive is even stronger. The two wealthiest countries after the United States, Japan and Germany, have 85 per cent and 94 per cent respectively of the world market potential.

Today there are only seven countries where English is the primary language spoken, by about half a billion people or 8 per cent of the total population, their combined economies representing only 30 per cent of the total world economy. e-Commerce companies that will continue to target this small percentage of the world market will miss out on capturing a much larger potential market.

193

The total global e-Commerce market is forecast to reach \$1.6 trillion by 2003, a very powerful incentive for companies entering this arena. If present e-businesses have been able to achieve year-upon-year growth in visitors, sales or members using only domestic focused Web sites, then in order to sustain or increase this growth it will be almost impossible to do so without entering and servicing new markets.

According to a Nua.com survey, almost 10 per cent of the world's population has access to the Internet. The global Internet audience had grown to 580.78 million people by the end of May 2002. The survey indicated that, for the first time ever, Europe has the highest number of Internet users in the world, with 185.83 million Europeans online, compared with 182.83 million in the United States and Canada, and 167.86 million in Asia-Pacific.

The survey's findings also indicate that the digital divide between developed and developing nations is as wide as ever. While Europeans account for 32 per cent of global Internet users, only 6 per cent of the world's Net users are based in Latin America. The Middle East and Africa combined account for just 2 per cent of global Internet users; the lack of telecommunications infrastructures in those regions means that most citizens remain unconnected. Nua forecasts that the number of worldwide Internet users will reach 1 billion by 2005.

Methods of entry into global markets

Until recently a traditional business has had the options of entering new geographical markets through direct or indirect exporting, new start-ups,

Table 8.1 Internet penetration in top ten countries (%)

Country	Internet penetration within population
Iceland	69.80
Sweden	64.68
Denmark	60.38
Hong Kong	59.58
United States	59.1
Netherlands	58.07
United Kingdom	56.88
Norway	54.4
Australia	54.38
Canada	52.79

Source: Nua.com (2002).

franchising, joint ventures, acquisitions, concessions or licensing, depending on the degrees of risk and the level of involvement they were prepared to accept. To these alternatives can be added now the virtual business via the Internet. The nationally based business will start with cautious testing of new markets, often selected with a similar culture, having a focus that is culturally and managerially 'ethnocentric' or centred around the home market. A multi-national business will have a 'polycentric' orientation, i.e. a focus based on the understanding and appreciation of different operating contexts (Keegan and Schlegelmilch 2001).

The global or transnational business will have a fully global strategy, focusing on maximizing the benefits obtained from economies of scale in sourcing, product standardization and marketing. Typical of global operators is their adaptable, geocentric approach, which allows them to 'think globally but act locally'.

ACTIVITY

1 Discuss the role of the Internet in the globalization process.
2 Which countries do you believe are left behind in the e-Commerce world and why?
3 How essential is the global race to get connected to the Internet for economic development and education? Does it really matter?
4 Select a company of your choice and research through the Internet its expansion into foreign markets.

Opportunities and threats in global e-Marketing

The Internet has already made a big difference in the way business operates glob-ally, offering substantial advantages to both buyers and sellers, because it can cope with a rapidly changing environment. Many industries have further motives for embracing the Web, as it offers huge savings on their marketing and distri-bution costs, which in certain cases, for example the airlines, can make up about a quarter of their total operating expenses.

The Internet has made a big difference to aviation, with portable computers becoming essential in the process of booking and buying air travel. Simplifying booking and cutting out the cumbersome process of issuing card tickets can be very attractive to customers. Since 2000, an increasing number of airlines, such as Northwest and Swissair, have been offering online facilities for seat selection and check-in, as well as for booking and paying for flights (*Economist* 2001).

e-Commerce will also allow businesses to learn more about their Web customers, so they can package offers tailored to their individual needs. This is what in marketing terms is called 'customer of one' and it applies to airlines, just as it does to cars or computers. 'Relationship marketing' is discussed in more depth in Chapter 4.

Continuing with the same example, there are distinguishing characteristics between the different levels of airline Web sites. The most basic are 'brochure sites' which offer simple static information, not much different from the printed brochures found in the bricks-and-mortar travel agents. At the next level are the constantly updated versions of the 'brochure sites'. The third level contains sites that obtain information from the customer as he logs on and builds a profile of his travel needs and preferences. It can answer requests for information, take bookings and issue e-mail confirmation of bookings. This sort of e-Commerce transaction is now quite common, especially for the no-frills, low-cost airlines. The next generation Web site will recognize and greet the customer by his or her name when s/he logs on and will know that s/he is a valuable customer. It will be able to analyse his travel history and suggest alternative itineraries that might suit him better.

Niche marketing

No-frills, low-fare carriers such as EasyJet and Ryanair have been using this low-cost, high service strategy to carve out successful niches. The emergence of these new companies has increased the level of competition in the industry, putting established carriers under increasing threat of loss of business on their traditional routes and ultimately bankruptcy. One notable example is Swissair, and even British Airways has felt the pinch with the threat of its shares losing their blue-chip status.

Other examples of industries that have made good use of the trend towards personalization through the Internet are the perfume and fashion industries. Custom fragrance marketers have been established, usually family-run businesses where the Internet has radically changed the direction of this niche market. In 2001 a number of new entrants have included Procter & Gamble with Reflect.com, Ashford.com, RomanceHer.com, Eleuria.com and Creativescent. com. The Internet is about to turn this niche market into a major profit-making category of prestige fragrance and force the major perfume companies to create custom divisions. Nevertheless these new ways of doing business are at risk for being untested and vulnerable to sudden market downturns or fashion changes (Grubbe 2001).

Small and medium-size enterprises are the main beneficiaries of the low-cost marketing possibilities offered by the Internet, which can turn them from small niche players into global ones. A fundamental change is happening in the world of Asian marketing that could prove a bonanza for struggling companies. The Internet is providing low-cost ways for small to medium-size businesses to get their advertising message across, focusing on specific audiences. Asia has been experiencing a phenomenal growth in Internet advertising, whose potential demand has been recognized by US Internet advertising agencies. DoubleClick Asia, a joint venture between New York-based Double Click and Hong Kong Web portal builder Asiacontent.com, has been able to track Internet users' movements by collecting 'cookies' or files embedded in users' Web browsers that log the pages they visit and for how long. This information allows marketing solution providers such as DotMedia China or Next Media to help their customers, which are local companies, to target their own local audience in a far more efficient way by posting relevant ads on their Web sites (Leary 2000).

Another interesting SME example is Charles Tyrwhitt, a UK manufacturer of mainly shirts, but also ties and other accessories, to the exclusive ABC1 men market. The company has adopted a 'clicks and mortar' strategy (see Chapter 4), which hopefully will turn this British niche player into a global one. It will also reduce its brochure and marketing costs. The company's strong customer service culture is being translated on to the Net, where this is so important. The firm's success lies in its ability to carry more than 3,000 lines of stock at any one time, with each shirt being offered in up to forty-eight combinations of size, cuff and sleeve. The company is able to maximize sales by targeting groups of people more effectively than could ever be done through mail order (Renton 2000).

The key to the success of niche e-businesses is first and foremost brand awareness. Second, expanding the customer base geographically is leading to the need for a greater product range to meet strong local preferences in style and fashion. The Internet has proved to be the perfect messenger for niche interests, serving individual tastes and diverse geographical demands.

In certain industries, such as national media, which were previously dedicated to mass markets, the Internet is offering for the first time the possibility of meeting specialist demands. As successful online newspapers in the United States reach less than 25 per cent of their local Net users, some have tried to add an interest-based niche to their regional focus. For example, the *San Jose Mercury* is concentrating its online energies to SiliconValley.com, a specialist site for technology news. The objective is to have a network of loyal users by meeting specialist demand with detailed information. In the United Kingdom the commercial site Fish4 (www.Fish4.co.uk), which is backed by local newspaper publishers, owned by the Guardian Media Group, is claiming to have reached the necessary critical mass of information to make a niche product. BBC News online is another example where the battle between general and niche is being fought. The way it uses its huge breadth of content, both broad-brush and localized, demonstrates the diversity of its users and their demands. In just one day 98,450 different stories were read, amounting to a staggering 20 per cent of all the stories the site has ever produced (Barkham 2000).

ACTIVITY

1 The Internet is offering unique advantages to SMEs in terms of low-cost global niche marketing. Discuss and substantiate your views.

2 Investigate further the perfume industry and the new opportunities created by the Internet. Visit the Web sites mentioned in the text.

3 Based on the examples given in the text above, as well as through your own research and personal experience, discuss the advantages and disadvantages offered by the Internet to the airline industry worldwide. Access the Web sites of the newer entrants such as Ryanair or EasyJet and compare them with those of the established national airlines.

4 Access the www.Fish4.co.uk Web site and investigate the extent of their activities. Discuss their chances of establishing themselves and being successful long-term.

Understanding the global environment

For the e-Commerce organization shaping the direction of its global expansion it is vitally important to understand the external environment as a means of identification of opportunities and threats. An analysis of the variety of factors and environmental influences is necessary in order to allow a balance of internal capabilities and resources with the opportunities offered externally that ultimately would affect business planning and implementation within the organization.

The elements of the external environment connected with the organization can be divided into four distinct groupings, known by the acronym STEP and shown in Figure 8.1.

SOCIO-CULTURAL ENVIRONMENTS FOR GLOBAL E-COMMERCE

Culture is particularly important for an internationally or globally oriented e-Business, especially in respect to the impact it has on buyer behaviour and all the implications related to the organization and its management.

Definitions of culture

Culture has been defined in a multiplicity of ways and because of its diversity, there is no one universally accepted definition. Anthropologists and sociologists alike have tried hard to produce the perfect definition, as seen in Box 8.1, which samples their opinions spanning more than a century. In very simple terms, *culture*

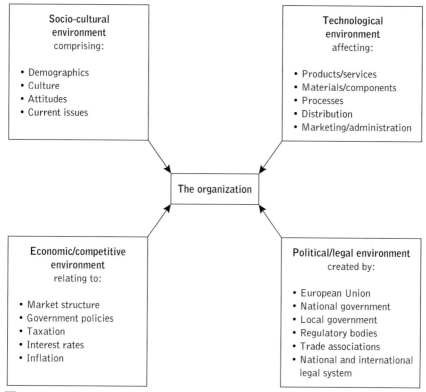

Figure 8.1 *STEP elements of the organization's external environment*
Source: adapted from Brassinton and Pettitt (2000)

is defined as 'ways of living, built by a group of human beings that are transmitted from one generation to another'.

Elements of culture

In 1999–2001, according to International Data Corporation, roughly 40 per cent of the people visiting the Internet have been seeking sites in languages other than English. Yet, according to the same study, 55 per cent of US companies have done nothing to customize their Web sites for non-English speaking users. With a total global potential e-Commerce market of $1.6 trillion by 2003, companies worldwide need to become experts fast on the cultural issues that must be met in order to make e-Commerce work (Rutherford www.cio.com).

For a successful e-Commerce operation, communication between a diversity of cultures with a multiplicity of languages involves far more than mere text translations. There are a variety of other cultural factors to consider, some of

Box 8.1:
WHAT IS CULTURE?

Culture ... is that complex whole which includes knowledge, belief, art, law, morals, custom, and any other capabilities and habits acquired by man as a member of society.

(Tylor 1891)

Culture is the socially inherited assemblage of practices and beliefs that determines the texture of our lives.

(Sapir 1949)

Culture is ... the collective programming of the mind that distinguishes the members of one category of people from those of another.

(Hofstede and Bond 1988)

Culture is an integrated system of learned behaviour patterns that are distinguishing characteristics of the members of any given society.

(Czinkota and Rokainen 1995)

Culture is defined as shared patterns of behaviour embedded in shared values, beliefs, meaning and understanding of a given group of people.

(Kitchen and Proctor 2001)

Source: Adapted from McCauley (2001).

which might appear inconsequential to a globally expanding e-Business but important enough to the consumer, and which could create significant problems if ignored (Pleasants 2001b).

Language

Today more than 50 per cent of all Internet users have a non-English mother tongue. With the dramatic expansion of the Internet, this number is expected to increase to 70 per cent by 2003. By contrast, more than two-thirds of Web pages are in English, with Japanese and German at a distant joint second position with almost 6 per cent each (Pleasants 2001b).

Nevertheless, past research has revealed that Web users are three times more likely to make purchases from Web sites in their own language and two-thirds of surfers will click away from a site in another language. It is expected that a fast increasing proportion of new Web sites will be in languages other than English. Asian languages, mainly Chinese, are poised for especially strong growth, owing to a fast increase in Internet penetration among Asian countries' population.

Aesthetics	Religion	Education
Beauty	Sacred objects	Formal education
Good taste	Philosophical systems	Primary education
Design	Beliefs and norms	Secondary education
Colour	Prayer	Higher education
Music	Taboos	Vocational training
Architecture	Holidays	Literacy level
Brand names	Rituals	HR planning

Law and politics		Values and attitudes
Home country law		Timekeeping
Foreign law		Achievement
International law	←— CULTURE —→	Work
Regulations		Health
Political risk		Process of change
Ideologies		Scientific progress
National interest		Risk taking

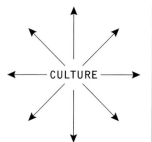

Language	Technology and material culture	Social organizations
Spoken language		Kinship
Written language		Social institutions
Official language	Transport	Authority structure
Linguistic pluralism	Energy	Interest groups
Language hierarchy	Tools and objects	Social mobility
International languages	Communications	Social stratification
Mass media	Urbanization	Status

 Figure 8.2 *Cultural environments*

Source: adapted from Chartered Institute of Marketing (1999)

There is also an increasing trend for companies worldwide to make their current English-language sites available in several other languages. The Internet is at present dominated by English and probably will continue to be for the foreseeable future, although it remains to be seen whether it will be the universally adopted language of the Net (as seen in Table 8.2).

> ## TIP
>
> For more information on languages on the Web, good sites to contact are Global Reach and CyberAtlas, which have information on Web pages by language.

Table 8.2 Primary languages of Web sites and Web users (%)

Language	Web page languages	Online population primary language
English	68.4	47.5
Japanese	5.9	8.6
German	5.8	6.1
Chinese	3.4	9.0
French	3.0	3.7
Spanish	2.4	4.5
Russian	1.9	2.1
Italian	1.6	3.1
Portuguese	1.4	2.5
Korean	1.3	4.4

Source: Adapted from Pleasants (2001b).

Case study:
LANGUAGE BARRIERS ON THE ASIAN NET

'All Your Base Are Belong to Us' is the enigmatic phrase that appears written on a number of public and private buildings thanks to the magic of Photoshop editing used by the creators of the online video that can be found on www.planetstarseige.com/allyourbase. The same phrase is used as the title of the video, going back to a quotation found on one of the early game consoles of a classic videogame called Zero Wing. Since most of the 16 bit console games were written in Japan, the phrase not only looks odd but is grammatically incorrect.

The use of deliberately or inadvertently poor English translations is quite common in Asia. Movies, signs, menus, adverts, clothing labels and now Web sites provide myriad examples of funny, cute or just plain bizarre jargon. Westerners and Asians who grew up with English as their native language tend to accept such mistranslations as part of the local charm. Nevertheless, the reverse translation of these expressions back into the local Asian language would be met with consternation.

The Internet has increased the exposure of the written word exponentially, and is dispersing these 'chopsocky' translations (a term used to describe Hong Kong martial arts films which are quickly made and distributed) faster and to a far wider audience. Generally, English native speakers tend to attribute spelling and grammar mistakes to lack of education, at best, or to a low level of intelligence, at worst. Chinese people in Asia, on the other hand, tend to place less emphasis on the correct spelling and grammar, as long as the correct message is being conveyed. This stems basically from the Chinese iconic text system, which is used by one-fifth of the world's population. Many Chinese people, who cannot understand each other verbally owing to the variety of existing dialects, can nevertheless read and understand each other's writings. People who are used to reading and writing symbols within a contextual linguistic framework tend to see the finicky English adherence to spelling and grammar as annoying and minor.

Ion Global, a leading e-Business integrator offering Internet strategies and solutions for global companies and a wholly owned subsidiary of china.com, has acquired extensive experience by testing Asian sites and is a strong promoter of common standards for the use and display of Asian languages on computer screens. The Chinese have several text coding systems for the Internet, named Big 5, GB and Unicode. A simple mistake of using the wrong browser or plug-in would render the text unreadable, which requires Chinese Net users to know in what system the Web sites are written in order to set their computers accordingly. Similarly, Korean, Thai, Nepalese, Cambodian and Burmese users need to download plug-ins and settings in order to make their alphabets legible on browsers.

Ion Global people believe that the problems with alphabet and character usability are a stumbling block for getting more Asian users on the Internet. When the digital divide between East and West will be bridged, and whether or not the Internet will become Chinese owing to the sheer number of potential users, remains unclear. One thing is certain, that in the future 'all your Net site are cater to us'.

Case study questions

1 Discuss the future of the English language as the universally adopted language on the Internet.
2 What are the implications of raising Asian use of the Internet for the future of hardware and software solutions?
3 What are the factors which need to be considered when translating an English Web site into a Web site used by Asian-speaking users such as Chinese, Korean or Japanese?
4 What elements of culture are more relevant when doing e-Commerce in Asia?

Source: Adapted from Yu (2001).

Translations on the Web

Literal translations of Web sites are a minefield. Machine translations have been an attractive option for some e-Commerce organizations because they are cheap, but they have severe limitations. In circumstances where speed has been the most critical factor, machine translations have been used to understand the general idea of a received message and to send an acknowledgement of its reception with a promise of follow-up. This has been acceptable in the early years of e-Commerce development, as a strategy designed to generate goodwill and buy time. To use it for a permanent Web site is a strategy fraught with danger.

Handing the text to computer-aided translators is not enough to ensure that the meaning and scope of the Web site are achieved. Here is an example of machine-translated text which has gone seriously wrong. A news item was taken in 1998 from the German version of MSNBC about the famous round-the-world balloon race, which was about to become an international incident if not properly understood by the Chinese. It was translated with the help of a computer-aided translation service supplied by Systran and sounded like this: 'One of the urgent problems of the Weltumrunder in the balloon "global challenge" solve itself now: China gave on Tuesday an overflight/flyover permission to the three balloon drivers on their Weltumseglung the message in Peking, British after information.' It is clear from this example that human translation and adaptation are required when interfacing with international customers and the correct understanding of critical messages is required (Nolan 1998c).

Box 8.2:
TRANSLATIONS THAT WENT BADLY WRONG

- Sign in a Hong Kong tailor: 'Ladies may have a fit upstairs.'
- Moscow guide to a Russian Orthodox monastery: 'You are welcome to visit the cemetery where famous Russian and Soviet composers, artists and writers are buried daily, except Thursdays.'
- Back of a jacket in Japan: 'Vigorous throw up. Go on a journey.'

Hotel signs across the world

- Paris: 'Please leave your values at the front desk.'
- Romania: 'The lift is being fixed for the next day. During that time we regret that you will be unbearable.'

Badly translated adverts

- 'Come alive with Pepsi' → 'Rise from the grave with Pepsi' (German).
- 'Avoid embarrassment, use Parker pens' → 'Avoid pregnancy, use Parker pens' (Spanish).
- 'Body by Fisher' → 'Corpse by Fisher' (Flemish).
- 'Tropicana orange juice' → 'Tropicana Chinese juice' (Spanish, in Cuba).

Sources: Jobber (2001); Keegan and Green (1997).

The content of a Web site needs to be localized not only in terms of meaning, but also in terms of its relevance. Almost certainly the editorial content will have to be adapted in terms of products and services relevant to the population targeted and in the dialects used locally. For example, when developing a Web site in Spanish, it has to be made specific to Spanish-speaking users in Spain, the United States, Mexico or Argentina.

In certain circumstances the site will have to be completely rebuilt from scratch to comply with the demands of the particular market or type of business. The decision between a culturally sensitive translation and a total remake of the site depends on the e-Business commitment to enter global markets. In markets with dual languages such as Canada, where a quarter of the population has French as primary language and a proportion of it is uncomfortable with English, the Web site should offer a choice of English or French.

Determining Web users' primary language without identifying the country where they live is again fraught with problems. For example, almost 50 per cent of US Hispanics are now online. Some may have Spanish as their language of choice; however, their cultural and business requirements might be completely different from Spanish-speaking users elsewhere. Additionally, there is no reason to believe that third-generation US Hispanics necessarily use Spanish as their primary language, or, if they fill in a computer form in English, that they don't want Spanish to be used for e-mail communications (Pleasants 2001b).

TIP

Ion Global, eTranslate, ITP and WorldPoint Interactive are consultancies which translate and localize content. Others such as GlobalSight, Idiom and Uniscape supply software that distributes translated content into different country-specific sites and allows users to combine their language preferences with regional sites.

Source: Rutherford (2000).

Case study:
AIRLINES MARKETING ONLINE

It seems that airlines are finding it a challenge to deliver personalized service to passengers, but it appears to be an even greater challenge for their Web marketers to accommodate international visitors to their Web sites.

Although the American airlines have received a lot of publicity regarding how well developed their Web sites are, in reality not many of them can provide information in foreign languages or even clear instructions on how to find out routes, prices, deals and destinations.

British Airways, on the other hand, have been praised for adapting their Web site to local conditions. Through their multi-nation site they have shown a deep understanding of the Internet needs of the international flyer. This is seen in the ways it markets itself locally, as well as in the languages offered on its sites. In this way it has established itself in a leadership position internationally, not only offline but also online.

The British Airways front page has forty-one countries listed on its drop-down menu and localizes the content from the country's point of view, whether it is Sri Lanka or the Czech Republic, or even English-speaking markets like South Africa, Ireland or the United States. On each local site it offers, in the native language, a wealth of information on schedules, arrivals, departures and airports on top of flights, fares and ways of booking from anywhere in the world to any possible destination.

As is usual on the Web, not only big companies are making the right moves. A small carrier compared to British Airways, Icelandair has parts of its site translated into twelve different languages. It has gone beyond the usual mono-language site, or possibly English plus one other language, of some of the American carriers. Icelandair thinks in global terms, showing clearly that it wants the international traveller's business, and it will probably get it!

Web sites: www.british-airways.com, www.icelandair.com.

Case study activities

1 Access the Web sites listed above.
2 Do a comparative analysis of their Web site design from the point of view of cultural sensitivity and ease of navigation for foreign users.
3 Suggest possible improvements to their respective Web sites.
4 Summarize the factors specific to the airline industry that affect their e-Commerce operations.

Source: Adapted from Nolan (1999).

Tone and formality of the language

Business culture and etiquette used on the Net, or 'Netiquette', need to be carefully researched and understood in order to avoid embarrassing mistakes. For example in the United States it is common to see Web sites which use informal greetings for their registered users, such as: 'Welcome back, Frank!' To address using first names might be appropriate to Anglo-Saxon cultures, but it would be unacceptable in Japan, where a registered Japanese visitor to the site would take offence at such a casual greeting. A culturally sensitive business would ensure that it used a significantly more formal greeting such as 'We are honoured by your return visit to our site, Mr Takahashi' (Hanrahan and Kwok 2001).

A survey undertaken by Ion Global which focused on the level of formality expected by different cultures in Asian and Pacific countries placed Japan and South Korea at the highest end, whereas Australia and the United States were the least formal, as seen in Figure 8.3.

Symbols and symbolism

The use of symbols on Web sites is widespread, owing to space saving requirements. Web designers frequently use icons and images; however, not all of them are exportable. For example, hand gestures could be a minefield to the uninitiated, and as they are natural they are perceived to be universal. In effect, they are culturally transmitted from one generation to another. The commonly used 'A-OK' of a circle formed with the thumb and forefinger, with the other fingers extended, is widely used in the United States, where it is considered a friendly

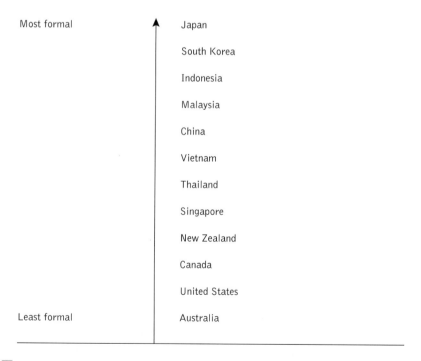

Figure 8.3 Levels of business formality expected in Asian and Pacific countries
Source: adapted from Kwok (2001)

gesture, whereas in Brazil it is considered obscene. Similarly the 'thumbs up' sign is considered highly offensive in Iran. A palm-forward wave is a nasty gesture in Greece and Nigeria (Hanrahan and Kwok 2001).

Some very successful Web sites are designed around a particular theme which has a specific symbolic significance (such as a compass or an animal). Special attention needs to be given to the choice of symbols, as their meanings might have different connotations in other cultures. For example, flowers have a strong symbolic significance in many cultures around the world. The rose is considered almost universally the symbol of love, although a hand holding a red rose is the symbol of socialism in Europe. The white lily is a symbol of purity, although in other cultures it is associated with death (Hanrahan and Kwok 2001).

Colours

Similarly, colours must be chosen with care in designing a Web site for global audiences. Colours such as black, white and red have different symbolic or religious meanings throughout the world. A Web site with a black background can appear 'cool' and 'sophisticated' to an American audience, but black is linked with death and bad luck in Chinese culture. Purple has religious significance in Catholicism, as does green in the Islamic world. User feedback during the design phase is necessary in order to avoid culturally insensitive choices (Hanrahan and Kwok 2001).

TIP

A number of consultancies such as IBM Institute for Business Value (www-923.ibm.com) perform 'cultural audits' on sites destined for global audiences, to make sure mistakes don't endanger the e-Business global expansion.

Source: Rutherford (2000).

Incompatible software

Rutherford also mentions a Forrester report entitled *The Multilingual Site Blueprint*, which surveyed twenty-seven US-based multilingual site operators and found that the greatest challenge encountered was adapting software to work with other languages. She gives the example that, to make Web software work with Asian languages, which contain up to 6,000 characters, site operators must install Unicode, a character coding system that supports written texts in different languages (www.unicode.org).

Culturally sensitive Web design

The way a home page is designed determines whether the user will stay on the site or abandon it out of frustration. There are a number of commonsense Web site development methods which will ensure the building of a loyal and satisfied customer base.

As a matter of practice, the first thing a non-English-speaking Net user will do when reaching a Web home page is to look for navigation leading to the site in a familiar language. According to Hanrahan and Kwok, the presentation of the language selector navigation is one of the key elements of the global user experience. A popular form of this type of navigation is a pull-down menu with a list of languages and the title such as 'Language selector' or 'Choose a country'. This method might be problematic, as a foreign visitor might not be able to understand the instructions designed to lead to the pull-down menu on a page in English that might be full of information and navigation options.

Another commonly used method suggested by Hanrahan and Kwok is to show a selection of country flags representing the different Web site versions. This method is acceptable if the Web sites contain country-specific content as opposed to language-specific content, as flags represent countries and not languages. As discussed previously, certain languages, such as Spanish for example, are used by majority or minority populations in a number of diverse countries. Using the flag representing Spain to represent Spanish might confuse users from Mexico, the United States or Argentina, who do not identify with the Spanish flag. The use of flags is appropriate when the target is a specific national market and not all speakers of a specific language.

When the target market is language-specific, one recommended way to address these problems is to design navigational images and buttons showing the name of each language available written in that language and with the appropriate script. This is known as 'good user experience'.

Another aspect related to language specificity is 'text swell', which describes what happens when the translation of a word from one language to another necessitates extended (or contracted) display space. Text swell can have a considerable effect on the layout of a Web page and should be an important consideration in the design of an international Web site.

Both HTML text and text within an image can be affected by text swell, as well as the size of pop-up windows. German tends to take up more horizontal space than English, while Chinese and Japanese take up less, but need taller spaces than languages based on the Latin alphabet (Hanrahan and Kwok 2001).

Methods of payment

Payment preferences vary considerably from country to country. For example, in the United States or the United Kingdom the overwhelmingly preferred method

209

of payment is the credit card, whereas in China cash on delivery (COD) is the prevailing method. In Japan, purchases through the Internet can be dispatched to and paid for at the convenience stores called *conbini* (see Case Study on p. 213). From a Web design point of view, it is therefore important to understand what payment options are used in the target market. No matter how appealing the product or service might appear to the consumer, if s/he is not given the right options of payment the purchasing sequence will be aborted.

Along with payment options, the online sales effort should also take into account the variety of currencies and country-linked value-added tax (VAT) systems. Research shows that customers are reluctant to commit to an online transaction in a 'foreign' currency owing to the uncertainty presented by the daily fluctuation of exchange rates.

A simple solution is to add an interactive currency calculator to the site, which will give a rough idea of the cost of the product or service and give an indication if it is worth proceeding with the purchase. A better solution includes payment systems that not only perform currency calculations but also calculate VAT (value-added tax or sales tax) by country and product or service category. The best systems currently available automatically update the currency conversion and tax rates, relieving the e-Commerce Web site operator of a daily burden, and can be used with any payment systems on the market. An example of a multi-currency payment system is WorldPay, launched in the United States, which offers the Web site operator the facility of offering products or services in more than 100 currencies (Nolan 1998b).

With the exchange rate updated daily, customers will have the certainty of seeing the real cost of their purchases, which will give them the ability of meaningful comparison with what they can find in local stores. These customer-sensitive methods are reducing the often painful order cancellations or goods being returned, owing to customers' shocked realization when checking their credit card bills. For example, having such a system implemented will allow the French or the Italian customer to see in euros exactly what has been charged on their Visa card, whereas the UK-based e-Commerce retailer will receive the equivalent amount in pounds sterling or, if US-based, the equivalent amount in US dollars.

Taxware is offering a system solution that calculates the appropriate local sales tax (VAT) for purchases based on geographical location and type of goods or services. It can even supply VAT records to be used by customers for tax return calculations (Nolan 1998b).

The combination of the two system solutions showing prices in the local currency and the local VAT provides the international customer with the complete picture, enabling a rapid and informed purchase decision online. The e-Commerce retailer offering such a facility is showing care towards the target market needs, leading to a satisfied, thus loyal customer base.

Box 8.3:
TEN EXPERT TIPS FOR GOING GLOBAL ONLINE

When developing a global e-Commerce Web site, it is imperative to pay close attention to how users around the world are going to interact and experience the process of finding products, the reading and understanding of product descriptions, the process of adding the products chosen to the shopping cart and finally concluding the purchase. Here are ten tips from the experts:

- Use local experts for advice on culturally, technically and legally sensitive issues and the overall development of the Web site. If necessary, establish partnerships with local e-businesses to ensure that the message is appropriate to the target market.
- Conduct usability tests on the Web sites in target markets at several stages of the development process. The site needs to be tested not only for ease of use but also for cultural appropriateness, adherence to technical requirements and legal compliance in the target markets.
- The home page design should include a clear and easy method for global users on how to find the version not only in their own language but also tailored to their country.
- All product descriptions should use the appropriate measurement terms and scales for weights and sizes (feet versus metres, pounds versus kilograms, etc.).
- Product descriptions should be written in a clear and easy-to-understand style, appropriate to the target market. If product information is written in English, but is destined for a global audience, it should be clear, precise and free of jargon, abbreviations, acronyms, slang or country-specific terms.
- A product information glossary should be provided, as well as a Help feature.
- International shipping information and country options should be clearly made available early on in the product selection process. e-Commerce users feel cheated spending time choosing and filling their shopping baskets only to find out at the end that shipment will not be available to the location requested. Differences in price, terms and conditions should be clearly stated.
- Payment options should be culturally sensitive and appropriate to the target market.
- Form fields used in the checkout process should allow for different formats for international addresses, telephone numbers and postal codes.
- And finally . . . offer a currency converter!

Source: Adapted from Hanrahan and Kwok (2001).

ACTIVITY

Visit the Web sites of the following groups of companies. Within the industry groups presented below, decide which of the companies is offering a more accessible and navigable Web site for the global user:

Soft drinks

- Coca-Cola   www.cocacola.com
- Pepsi-Cola   www.pepsi.com

Books

- Amazon   www.amazon.com
- Blackwell's   www.blackwell.co.uk
- W. H. Smith   www.whsmith.co.uk

Airlines

- EasyJet   www.easyjet.com
- British Airways   www.britishairways.com
- Icelandair   www.icelandair.com

Sport footwear

- Adidas   www.adidas.com
- Nike   www.nike.com
- Reebok   www.reebok.com

LEGAL ISSUES IN e-COMMERCE

A comprehensive international legislation system for global e-Commerce does not exist at present and it is not expected in the foreseeable future. Even within the United States, which is so advanced in its use of the Internet, certain e-Commerce legal issues have caused significant disagreements, such as the validity of digital signatures. While waiting for federal legislation, many states have set up their own laws, which have been widely different in substance from state to state. Organizations such as the UN conference on international trade law have been actively calling for global co-ordination of appropriate legal structures. The most important issues are copyright protection, contractual agreements and privacy laws. See Chapter 7 – 'e-Business and the Law', by Dave Wadsworth – for a more in-depth discussion of the legal issues in e-Commerce.

ACTIVITY

You are asked to make an assessment on the cultural sensitivity of the companies whose Web sites are listed below. Visit the sites and rank them according to the range of criteria discussed in this chapter.

- Marriott   www.marriott.com
- Virgin   www.virgin.com
- Sony   www.sony.com
- Carlsberg   www.carlsberg.com
- Air Miles   www.airmiles.co.uk
- Tesco   www.tesco.com
- UK government Consumer Gateway   www.consumer.gov.uk
- Multimaps   www.multimaps.com
- Nestlé   www.nestle.com

Case study:
CONBINI: THE JAPANESE STYLE OF B2C

According to a domain survey undertaken by the Internet Software Consortium in January 2000, Japan has the highest number of hosts worldwide (3.6 per cent) after the United States (73.4 per cent). In terms of Internet population, Japan had 27 million users by the end of 1999. Unique to Japan, the highest growth, of 59 per cent over the previous year, was in the user category accessing the Internet through mobile phones, video-game devices and Internet appliances.

Another unique aspect of e-Commerce in Japan is the role played by the *conbini* or convenience stores in promoting this new growth area among consumers. *Conbini* in Japan are much more than the convenience stores used by consumers in the United States or United Kingdom for out-of-hours local shopping. They are very much a part of the Japanese way of life, far more so than in the West.

The spread of the *conbini* in Japan is universal, with one *conbini* for every 2,000 Japanese. There are more than 50,000 *conbini*, open twenty-four hours a day, seven days a week. With an average of 149 m² (1,600 sq ft) of space, they sell a wide variety of fast moving consumer goods on top of the packaged snacks, drinks, newspapers, videos and games traditionally retailed in the West. Moreover, *conbini* offer customers the facilities for paying their utility bills, making insurance payments, sending packages, mail and fax, colour printing, booking tickets for films, concerts and exhibitions. An increasing number of *conbini* have cash dispensing and video rental machines. Apart from the sophisticated computer expertise, *conbini* chains have also substantial distribution expertise.

213

With the use of credit cards still very limited in Japan owing to consumer reluctance to use them for online shopping, *conbini* fill the gap between online retailers and consumers and play a key role in Japan-style e-Commerce. The *conbini* are heavily competing for becoming the main place consumers will use to pay in cash for products ordered online.

Conbini fulfil a vital role in the distribution of goods ordered online by busy Japanese consumers who work long hours and are unable to have their orders delivered at home. Delivery services will not leave packages unattended outside front doors, which is considered irresponsible in the security-conscious Japanese culture. *Conbini* are helping to solve this problem. Picking up their orders at the *conbini* is seen as convenient, not only for consumers but also for the online retailers who are able to consolidate their package deliveries and therefore reduce costs. Furthermore, for consumers who do not have access to the Internet either at home or at work, the *conbini* are now offering online shopping terminals on their premises, allowing easy access and payment facilities under one roof.

Lawson, the second largest *conbini* chain in Japan after Seven-Eleven, has been the first to install online shopping terminals, called Loppi, in its 7,200 stores. Shoppers can log on to the Lawson's Loppi terminals to scan for product information, select the products or services of their choice and, when they finish, receive a printed paper receipt from the store counter. The terminals are also connected to the in-store POS registers where customers can take their receipts and pay for their purchases. The orders will be delivered a few days later to the stores, where they will be kept ready for collection.

Seven-Eleven Japan Company, the largest *conbini* chain, has entered e-Commerce by joining efforts in 1999 with Softbank and Yahoo Japan in order to sell books, CDs and videos online. Like Lawson's Loppi, Seven-Eleven is installing online multimedia terminals in all its 8,000 stores in Japan. Its 7dream.com site is providing travel-related services, ticket booking facilities, music CDs, books, car rental reservation services, lifestyle information, gifts and the company is even planning to sell mobile phones online.

Seven-Meal Service Company is another Seven-Eleven venture that is being linked with 7dream.com to provide take-away meals online, meal deliveries and even medical services. The retail industry is closely watching these developments, as they will be affecting the traditional retail system in Japan.

The Japanese have gradually adopted the Internet into their own, existing culture, creating a unique business model that simply works better in the Japanese environment.

Case study questions

1 What factors should be taken into account when designing a Web site for the Japanese market?
2 What are the cultural differences between e-Commerce practices in Japan compared with the United States or the United Kingdom?

3 Discuss the joint venture strategies adopted by the *conbini* chains in their efforts to adapt in the new e-Commerce era. Are there any similarities with changes in e-tailing practices in Western countries, such as the United Kingdom?

4 What changes do you foresee happening to the Japanese retail industry?

Sources: Osborn (1998); Clark (1999); Landers (1999, 2000); Sekizawa (2000); *We@lth Monthly*, June 2000, all in Chen (2000).

e-COMMERCE GLOBAL STRATEGIES

The organizations practising in the area of e-Commerce are facing a number of decisions regarding their global activities. Having analysed the characteristics of the target foreign market, they now face the next stage of developing an international marketing programme. This would include defining and selecting target segments, positioning the product or service and making the decision to modify the elements of the marketing mix to suit the conditions of the foreign market. For physical goods, the marketing mix is composed of four elements: product, price, place (distribution) and promotion. For services, the marketing mix extends to seven elements with the addition of people, processes and physical evidence.

Given the diversity of the global environment, with differing cultures, customs and competition, the decision facing the e-Commerce marketer is the degree of change necessary within the elements of the marketing mix. There are a number of pressures affecting this decision, which can be summarized as (1) staying local versus going global, (2) standardization or adaptation.

Local versus global

Ten years ago 'pan-European' advertising was all the rage among direct marketing companies in the United Kingdom. A precursor of global communication, it was based on a simple idea, namely that consumers in various countries fall into the same socio-demographic categories, with similar if not identical buying habits and tastes brought about by low-cost cross-border travel. It uses the same imagery, messages, product and brand positioning across all campaigns and all markets. Economies of scale could be achieved and global brands built up, as campaigns could be extended from one country to another.

More recently, globalization has received a few hard knocks, due to changes in customer tastes and timing. Some products achieved global status because they required very little effort in terms of product development in order to be successful in new markets. Others needed extensive redevelopment in order to localize their marketing mix.

A good example is basic office software such as Microsoft Word, which works equally well in most countries, once it has been localized for language

215

characteristics. Other examples are soft drinks like Coca-Cola or imaging products like Kodak, which need only minimal changes of their global campaigns to adapt to local taste. Alternatively, cars are more of a 'lifestyle' purchase. Consumer tastes in cars vary more widely between the United States, Germany, Japan, Italy, the United Kingdom and India. Achieving substantial economies of scale either in product development or in advertising is more difficult.

Ford has been one of the manufacturers most successful in using a modular approach to car manufacturing and marketing. Recognizing that there are strong differences in consumer preferences, Ford has reduced the number of components – and thereby has achieved economies of scale – without affecting the number of options available to customers in each of the seventy-five different national markets in which Ford sells cars. Ford manages to use a modular approach also in its advertising messages, emphasizing safety in Scandinavia, performance in Italy, design in France and handling in Germany. The Ford brand may be global, but the product and its supporting marketing effort are very much local.

For e-Commerce marketers with global ambitions, the requirements are to find out if the product or service they represent and the way of doing business can be exported in their 'domestic' forms or they will encounter consumer resistance and will need substantial adaptation to suit consumer tastes.

Box 8.4:
THE RISKS OF GLOBAL WEB MARKETING

For companies that have an established global distribution system the decision to exploit the Internet as a marketing tool needs to be considered with care. Once a Web site is established which has an online purchase facility, there is the risk that overseas customers will cut out the local distributor, place orders electronically and expect price discounts. This was the case of Millipore Corporation of Bedford, Massachusetts, a company with annual sales of $600 million specializing in filtration products for water purification for laboratories and the detection of contaminants in semiconductor manufacturing. With a 'blue chip' list of customers worldwide the Internet clearly offered an effective medium to both communicate information and provide the customer with a purchasing mechanism. However, Millipore faced a massive complication in that, similar to many other multinationals, it charges higher prices overseas in order to cover the additional cost of support services. Having faced the potential dilemma associated with inter-country pricing differentials, Millipore decided to postpone offering an online ordering facility and instead restrict its Web site to providing information with supporting pre- and post-purchase service activities.

Source: Adapted from Jobber (2001: 756).

Standardization versus adaptation

The decision whether to standardize or adapt the marketing mix elements is a major one for any organization operating outside its home environment. Standardization allows the organization to maintain a consistent image and identity throughout the world. It provides economies of scale and is particularly valuable for maximizing impact with the internationally mobile customer. It works best within an identified international segment and with a product of well defined complexity. Global branding and the transfer of new product ideas across boundaries are both possible with standardization.

Standardization has been used successfully in running global promotional campaigns. Transferring campaigns from one country to another is almost impossible, owing to language and cultural differences. Nevertheless, the clever use of pop music as a universal language has allowed Levi's advertising to be successful where others have failed. Coca-Cola has also succeeded with its 'one sound, one sight, one appeal' philosophy which brings it closer to a full standardization position. Benetton is still running their 'United Colours of Benetton' global campaign based on multi-cultural, universal images that appeal globally (Jobber 2001).

Adaptation is nevertheless necessary if the organization is under pressure to satisfy the multiplicity of needs of the global customer to the extent to which it will have to change the elements of the marketing mix.

ACTIVITY

1 Give examples of companies that have decided to standardize their e-Commerce marketing and companies that have a locally adapted approach.
2 Select a local marketing campaign from a Web site you are familiar with, and assess the extent to which it needs adaptation for another country of your choice. Do the same exercise for adaptation to a multicultural society within the same country.
3 Examine the pricing methods used by a company of your choice which is involved in global e-Commerce.

CHANGING PATTERNS IN GLOBAL DISTRIBUTION

Distribution is the process by which all consumer and industrial goods are transferred from the producers to the end users. The process includes not only the physical handling and distribution of goods and the transfer of ownership from producer to consumer, but also the whole range of buying and selling negotiations between producers and intermediaries, and between intermediaries and

217

consumers. Distribution channels are the ways and means by which goods are distributed from the producer to the end user. The traditional distribution model has been linear, as can be seen from Figure 8.4.

The producer is the originator of the products, which it builds or manufactures. Wholesalers and distributors bring together the products from a number of manufacturers, then divide them and transport them in small lots to resellers or retailers who deal directly with the consumers. The value added of the distribution chain has been in the dispatch, warehousing and delivering of products. Sometimes distributors undertake the repackaging and marketing of the products.

The chain of intermediaries, who are the wholesalers, distributors and retailers, adds substantial costs to the value chain, which can make the prices to the end user significantly higher than those of the producers. The Internet has been unique in its potential to revolutionize the value chain, as it enables producers to reach the end users directly.

As e-Commerce firms are developing, they will be choosing their entry and distribution modes on the basis of reducing their transaction costs even to the point of internalizing certain activities which have been traditionally performed by intermediaries. The Internet has raised expectations that, in time, producers will sell directly to end users and, in turn, end users will prefer buying direct from the producers. What is actually happening is that value chains are being deconstructed,

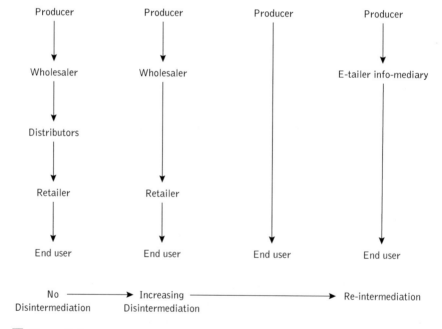

Figure 8.4 *Traditional and e-Commerce distribution channels*

Source: adapted from Hollensen (2001)

reconstructed and transformed into value webs, giving rise to a new class of inter-mediaries, which are the collecting and distributing of information. For example, companies like Yahoo! or Netscape act as information collectors and dissemina-tors, offering e-Commerce new possibilities of doing business.

e-Commerce distribution system

For Web-based businesses focused on competing in global markets, there is every indication that representatives in the field are necessary in order to facilitate dis-patch, the handling of returns and servicing. Companies that deal with consumer goods and have relatively low international volumes that require little service assis-tance may be able to dispense with any on-the-spot distribution requirements and rely on a global integrated carrier, such as DHL. Advice on global distribution can be found on International Trade Administration's Web site (www.ita.doc.gov).

Case study:
WILL e-COMMERCE CHANGE JAPAN'S TRADITIONAL DISTRIBUTION SYSTEM?

Distribution systems can vary enormously from one country to another. Only four centralized wholesalers cover the whole market for most products in Finland. At the other extreme, there are over 300,000 wholesalers and 1.6 million retailers in Japan. Customers' buying habits and cultural characteristics are at the heart of such differ-ences. Whereas UK shoppers might make once-a-month purchases by car in an out-of-town hypermarket, secure in the knowledge of being able to store them in their spacious homes, their Japanese counterparts have serious constraints in terms of living and storage space. They have to make frequent trips to local stores, and because of Japan's narrow roads and lack of parking facilities all these shopping trips will be made on foot. Land prices are very high in Japan, so local shops have to keep renewing their inventories on a daily basis.

The distribution system in Japan is one of the longest value channels in the world, with lots of wholesalers selling to other wholesalers. The Japanese system is based on a network of distributors and of subservient links between them and the manufac-turers. This distribution network, called *ryatsu-keiretsuka*, is in effect a political hierarchy in which wholesalers are locked in hierarchical layers and where the power resides at the 'commanding heights' of the larger *keiretsus*. Distributors at the lower layers in the vertical structure are tied to the *keiretsu* network by bonds of loyalty, mutual obligation, trust and power that extend throughout existing distribution struc-tures. Whilst this arrangement guarantees members some degree of security, it deprives them of economic freedom. Distributors that choose to deal with firms outside the

219

established group risk severing their ties with the group. On the other hand, smaller distributors are protected from tying up their cash in inventories that do not sell and can rely on reliable delivery and financial help, when necessary.

With the advent of the Internet and the growing number of independent B2B operators, the whole of the traditional distribution system is in jeopardy and with it the economic stability of Japan. e-Commerce will in effect make the majority of wholesalers redundant and as there are 4 million jobs at stake, this could exacerbate Japan's unemployment level, which is already very high. The *keiretsu* system has traditionally limited competition among suppliers. The Internet's transparent price mechanism and the loosening of the *keiretsu* ties are expected to fuel competitive dynamics in the e-Commerce market. Slowly but surely, Japan's distribution system is going to be dismantled beyond recognition.

Case study questions

1 Undertake an Internet search of the food distribution system in your own country.
2 Compare it with the distribution systems in Japan and Finland. Can you define similarities and discrepancies between your own domestic system and the other two distribution systems?
3 What are the implications of the expansion of B2C on the Japanese distribution system?
4 Similarly, what are the implications of the expansion of B2C on your domestic distribution system?

Source: Adapted from Doole and Lowe (1999); Hollensen (2001).

Global exporting

The European Union in its present form has a larger population than the United States. Nevertheless, most of its producers and consumers live and work in a radius of 800 km, equivalent to 12 per cent of the land area of the United States, and for historical and economic reasons, transport in the European countries has been burdened with rules and regulations. For example, a trucker transporting goods from Glasgow to Athens used to spend 30 per cent of his time at border crossings, waiting and filling in up to 200 forms. These inefficiencies are mercifully now a thing of the past. In order to move goods between EU member states only one simplified transit document is required and many of the custom formalities have been eliminated. However, consignment to countries outside the European Union is still burdened with an array of obstacles, cultural and linguistic, which lead to many companies failing to exploit the opportunities offered by overseas markets. The SME sector is affected in particular, as such companies do not have the resources to spend on overseas sales teams and trade-related computer systems.

CHAPTER SUMMARY

e-Commerce is in rapid transition from a US-based phenomenon to a global one. e-Commerce organizations need to evaluate their global potential in order to maintain their competitiveness in the face of increasing moves towards globalization.

It is becoming obvious that e-Commerce is developing in distinctly different ways in each country, especially in culturally diverse regions such as Europe and the Far East. Organizations involved with business online need to research and comprehend the product-specific e-Commerce potential, together with a thorough understanding of the markets these products are to be offered.

A key issue is the culturally sensitive approach to global e-Business and the development of global strategies that will take into account the socio-cultural factors specific to each target market. Another key issue in the development of these strategies is the degree of standardization or adaptation of the marketing mix.

Expanding operations globally for any organization including those involved in e-Commerce requires understanding of exporting complexities and making decisions on the provision of product support.

FURTHER READING

Cateora, P. and Graham, J. L. (2002) *International Marketing*, 11th edn, New York: McGraw-Hill.

Keegan, W. J. and Green, M. C. (2003) *Global Marketing*, 3rd edn, Englewood Cliffs NJ: Prentice Hall.

BIBLIOGRAPHY

Andrews, K. J. (1999) 'Integrating your Web efforts', *Target Marketing* (Philadelphia), 22, 12 (December): 68–70.

Barkham, P. (2000) 'New media: why Tunbridge Wells matters Net talk is all about building global communities . . .', *Guardian*, 14 February.

Brassington, F. and Pettitt, S. (2000) *Principles of Marketing*, Harlow: Pearson.

221

Cateora, P. R. and Ghauri, P. N. (1999) *International Marketing*, European edn, New York: McGraw-Hill.

Cateora, P. R. and Graham, J. L. (1999) *International Marketing*, 10th edn, Burr Ridge IL: Irwin McGraw-Hill.

Chartered Institute of Marketing (1999) *Study Text: International Marketing Strategy*, London: BPP.

Chen, P. (2000) 'Successful Models of Business to Consumer e-Commerce Organizations in both Western and Asian Business Environments', unpublished dissertation, London: Brunel University.

Clark, T. (1999) 'What is the difference between e-tailing and mail order?' *Japan Internet Report*, 40 (July/August), www.jir.net.

Clawson, T. (2001) 'Trading places', *e.business*, July.

De Mooij, M. (1994) *Advertising Worldwide: Concepts, Theories and Practice of International, Multinational and Global Advertising*, 2nd edn, Englewood Cliffs NJ: Prentice Hall.

Doole, I. and Lowe, R. (1999) *International Marketing Strategy*, London: ITP.

Economist (2001) 'Webbed wings', *Economist* (London), 358, 8212 (10 March): S20–1.

Forrester Research. Online. Available http: www.forrester.com.

Grubbe, L. (2001) 'Uncommon scents', *Global Cosmetic Industry* (New York), 168, 4 (April): 36–42.

Hanrahan, M. and Kwok, W-T. (2001) 'Globalising the Web: how to refine the international user experience to create business results', draft chapter, unpublished, London: Ion Global, June.

Hollensen, S. (2001) *Global Marketing: a Market-responsive Approach*, Englewood Cliffs NJ: Prentice Hall.

Jacob, T. (2000) 'The Web and mortgage banking: keeping the faith', *Mortgage Banking* (Washington DC), 61, 3 (December): 15–16.

Jobber, D. (2001) *Principles and Practice of Marketing*, New York: McGraw-Hill.

Keegan, W. J. and Green, M. C. (1997) *Principles of Global Marketing*, Englewood Cliffs NJ: Prentice Hall.

Keegan, W. J. and Schlegelmilch, B. B. (2001) *Global Marketing Management: a European Perspective*, Englewood Cliffs NJ: Prentice Hall.

Kwok, W-T. (2001) 'Going Global Online: an Overview of Everything you need to Know in Thirty-five Minutes Flat', presentation to the American Academy of Advertising conference, 29 March.

Landers, P. (1999) 'In Japan, the hub of e-Commerce is a Seven-eleven', *Wall Street Journal*, 1 November.

Landers, P. (2000) 'Seven-eleven Japan: Sony set e-Commerce plan', *Wall Street Journal*, 7 January.

Leary, A. (2000) 'Counting on technology', *Asian Business* (Hong Kong), 36, 2 (February): 20.

McCauley, A. (2001) *International Marketing: Consuming Globally, Thinking Locally*, New York: Wiley.

McClelland, S. (2000) 'iGlobal: the Internet innovator', *Telecommunications* (Dedham), 34, 5 (May): S2–S3.

Nolan, S. (1998a) 'With the Net, no country is an island'. Online. Available HTTP: www.clickz.com (accessed 18 November 1998).

Nolan, S. (1998b) 'Drachmas accepted here!'. Online. Available HTTP: www.clickz. com (accessed 9 December 1998).

Nolan, S. (1998c) 'Translation gone awry'. Online. Available HTTP: www.clickz.com (accessed 23 December 1998).

Nolan, S. (1999) 'Not so friendly cyber skies'. Online. Available HTTP: www.clickz.com (accessed 24 March 1999).

Nua.com (2002) *Surveys.* Online. Available HTTP: www.nua.ie/surveys/how_ many_online /index.html (accessed 13 August 2002).

Osborn, K. (1998) 'We have seen the future and it is *conbini*', *Computer Japan,* October. Online. Available HTTP: www.cjmag.co.jp (accessed October 1998).

Pleasants, N. (2001a) 'Online purchasing by country/region', *Global Marketing.* Online. Available HTTP: www.clickz.com (accessed 27 April 2001).

Pleasants, N. (2001b) 'The language of the Web', *Global Marketing.* Online. Available HTTP: www.clickz.com (accessed 11 May 2001).

Porter, M. E. (1985) *Competitive Advantage. Creating and Sustaining Superior Performance,* New York: Free Press.

Renton, J. (2000) 'Shirtmaker measures up for selling over the Internet', *Sunday Times* (London), 13 February.

Rutherford, E. (2000) 'How to avoid Global Web site Disasters', Globalization Research Center, www.cio.com, posted 14 November 2000.

Schulz, W. E. (1999) 'Internet: a low investment can produce big returns', *Practical Accountant* (Boston MA, pp. 10–11).

Sekizawa, T. (2000), World Information Technology Conference, Taiwan, *Global Views Monthly*, July.

Smith, T. (2000) 'Online sales take off for low-fare airlines', *Internetweek* (Manhasset NY), 6 March, p. 8.

Speer, R. N. Jr (2000) 'Raising the bar', *Banking Strategies* (Chicago), 76, 6 (November–December): 129–36.

Usunier, J-C. (1996) *Marketing across Cultures,* Harlow: Prentice Hall.

We@lth Monthly (2000) 'Traditional old companies take over the "e" era', *We@lth Monthly* (Taiwan), June.

Yu, F. (2001) ' "All your base are belong to us": the barriers of language on the Asian Web'. Online. Available HTTP: www.ion-global.com (accessed March 2001).

Part V

The public sector

e-Government

NOAH CURTHOYS, PETER M. ECKERSLEY AND PAUL JACKSON

KEY LEARNING POINTS

After completing this chapter you will have an understanding of:

- The theoretical and political antecedents of 'e-Government'
- The similarities and differences between e-Government and e-Business
- e-Government programmes in a number of countries, concentrating particularly on the United Kingdom
- Non-technical issues related to e-Government and public sector 'modernization'

ORDERED LIST OF SUB TOPICS

- e-Government: origins of the concept
- e-Government and e-Governance
- e-Government programmes
- Joined-up (e)-Government
- Management of change
- Ethical and privacy issues

E-GOVERNMENT: ORIGINS OF THE CONCEPT

From 'digital government' to 'e-Government'

Whilst e-Government has become a recognized concept within public sector circles, and is increasingly understood by citizens, it has a relatively short history.

It appears to have started with the National Science Foundation's (NSF) various research projects based in the United States; in this case the key report published in 1997 – *Toward a Digital Government in the Twenty-first Century* – started consideration of what was in effect e-Government. The NSF wanted to look at the US federal government's use of Internet technology to enhance service provision. To this end, digital government was initially an approach to public administration that incorporated the questions of improved effectiveness and better governmental performance.

Next came rhetorical changes, corporate realization of an emerging market, and ultimately some rapid rebranding. Over the late 1990s, the term 'digital government' effectively gave way to the more businesslike 'e-Government'. This appears to have been inspired as an extension of the e-Commerce language and a parallel to e-Business; it also served to popularize the concepts of e-Government within government itself.

Following this link with private sector technologies and changes, and the emergence of an infrastructure to allow it, e-Government has spread outwards through the industrialized world. It has filtered into different political cultures, technological infrastructures and even management systems. There is the Singaporean island-wide, broadband-supported e-Government, publicized through the use of online census returns; the UKOnline portal designed around 'life episodes'; Sweden's 24/7 plan for automated and permanently available e-Government services; or the e-Europe agenda, launched at the Lisbon EU summit in 2000. America has FirstGov and Project QuickSilver, and both Australia and New Zealand have national e-Government agendas. Worldwide, digital government has moved from the confines of academic debate to the corporate and political world of e-Government.

The UK modernization agenda

With the arrival of the 1997 Blair government, technology assumed a greater role generally in the 'modernization' of the UK public sector. This coincided, of course, with the dotcom 'bubble'. Whilst with hindsight we can see that many things were overdone and over-hyped around this time (leading to the collapse of many dotcom companies and Internet stocks), the events left a policy legacy in which technology was to play a central role.

From 1997 onwards, the renewal of the UK public sector was inseparably linked with the notion of 'Information Age government', as set out in the Modernization White Paper, which is discussed later in this chapter. It is important to recognize, however, that the employment of new technology was itself influenced by a range of other factors, not least the principles of New Public Management, which dominated the way much of the public sector was organized.

New Public Management

e-Government found itself at the end of a string of reforms and changes in the machinery of governments across the Western world which had been progressing for almost twenty years. Privatization, accountability, decentralization and the rolling back of the state are commonplace public sector terms now. With considerable political backing they have radically reshaped Britain, much of Scandinavia, Australia, New Zealand and the United States. In a weaker form, the key concepts of this so-called 'Anglo-Saxon' model of government have even started to transfer to France and Germany, albeit with local adaptation. In sum, New Public Management (NPM) has established a corporate culture and management structure within government that allows radical change and emphasizes private sector skills and experience. In the late 1990s e-Government connected with this agenda.

In some accounts, NPM derives from two main sources: business managerialism and its effect on public sector management, and the literature on the broader economics of public choice (Foster and Plowden 1996). The logic is that these two 'forces' have helped establish a 'hollowed out' state within which modern government is shifting from a role that incorporated production and provision to one of regulation alone. This change is a result of NPM's impact on administrative structures, particularly following the establishment of outside agencies and private bodies, and can be seen occurring continuously over a twenty-year period (Rhodes and Weller 2001).

In some ways, these management reforms go further. It has been argued that the NPM is the type of change that demonstrates transformative qualities, based on six indicators (Ferlie *et al.* 1996): the existence of multiple and interrelated changes system-wide; the creation of new, collective organizational forms; the development of individual level 'multi-layered' changes; change in service provision; reconfiguration of power relations, and finally the evolution of new cultures and ideology. Interestingly, Ferlie concludes, 'transformation, on our evidence, has not meant the total acceptance of the replacement of the old system by a market-based system, but rather a blend of old and new which produces something radically different' (Ferlie *et al.* 1996: 114).

As a follow-up, e-Government and the New Public Management are in many ways similar to the relationship between business process re-engineering and e-Business. Both share similar core goals, yet e-Government and e-Business incorporate a stronger technological agenda than their predecessors. As far as government can go in its efforts to establish e-Government, it seems to be none the less dependent on the existing NPM structures, without which success is perhaps uncertain.

E-GOVERNMENT AND E-GOVERNANCE

The public sector is different . . .

One of the drawbacks of comparing e-Government with e-Business is the residual difference between government and the private sector. Whilst there has been much blurring of the line – government agencies run as businesses, corporate entities operating public services, even mixed public and private funding – the distinction between the two is very real. Fundamentally speaking, government does not have to operate with shareholders in mind, it has a monopoly of official power, and it is ultimately the lender (and financer) of last resort. Even after the reforms of the NPM, the private sector – and consequently e-Business too – cannot be seen as comparable to the public sector because it has fundamentally different resources and roles.

Globalization and the rise of multinational business operations are changing the scale and focus of governmental activity, and in corporatist-leaning states (like Japan and much of South East Asia) the balance between government and business power may well be tilted in favour of the companies. None the less, no matter who delivers public services, the traditional role of government is very different from that of the private sector. With this in mind, e-Government can also be said to have divergent aims from e-Business.

One example is useful: taxation. It is not yet mandatory to participate in an e-Government system by providing online tax returns, although interacting with the Inland Revenue on this issue is compulsory. Envisaging a more sophisticated and embedded form of e-Government, however, leads to a quandary – just as offline tax returns are now compulsory, so too may online returns become obligatory. In other words, what happens offline, where government maintains a monopoly of services, could be mirrored in the online world. In contrast, the need to buy books at Amazon.com is not mandatory (although price and market position may say otherwise). We will return to this issue later in the chapter.

Accountability

Naturally, if e-Government has a monopolistic role, there are much greater ethical concerns to consider. Some of this will be examined below, but a key issue is relevant here: *accountability*. Without a central regulator like the state, or competitive market pressures to compel fair practice (in theory), it is crucial for e-Government to be accountable. So who watches the Web masters? Currently, the level of e-Government accountability is at best slim.

On one level, parliamentary oversight committees play a role. For example, the Committee of Public Accounts may examine some funding issues, while the Select Committee on the Modernization of the House of Commons could deal with e-Democracy. But the nature of NPM and the centralizing effects of an increasingly presidential executive mean that access and power are less potent than in the past. Whilst Ministers are accountable for e-Government, Parliament is not necessarily strong enough to make that mean anything on a day-to-day basis.

Alternative institutions feed into the governance aspect. The National Audit Office is increasingly interested and focused on e-Government, albeit largely on a case-by-case basis. Its reports have some 'teeth', though its recommendations are by no means binding on the Treasury or government as a whole. Yet it is one of the few arbiters of independent analysis and official accountability.

At a more traditional level, Ministers (who are increasingly less accountable, or more accurately, responsible) make executive heads accountable to them. In an age of modernization and effectiveness of delivery, success means internal accountability. This is evidenced by the establishment of 'e-champions' in central government departments, who 'own' the reform process and push changes through. Such individuals are accountable to the Cabinet and to their respective Ministers, and as senior civil servants are powerful government figures.

Legitimacy

Whilst accountability could be seen as the primary layer of public interaction with e-Government – perhaps even the most important – it is also bound up in questions of legitimacy. Whilst broadly speaking this could apply to the hotly disputed validity of a political programme (for example following the US presidential elections of 2000), on a more day-to-day level it is also about use. Who uses e-Government?

As the main targets of e-Government are citizens, the legitimacy of the service depends in large part on its popular support, and the public good it conveys or provides. Unlike comprehensive health care coverage or emergency services, e-Government provides no immediate or blatant improvement in what the state offers: it is not necessarily a social 'killer app'. This is not to say that it does not improve government itself, just that existing services can work well without being 'e-enabled'.

As a result, the core argument behind implementing e-Government must be the same in the public sector as e-Business reformers adopt in the private sector: to improve operational performance. An e-Government should transform the state into a more effective and hopefully more efficient machine or, more

231

accurately, organism. This fits in well with the goals of NPM but is also similar to e-Business, in which the goal is to streamline and transform activities, organization and basic roles within the company. So why do this if existing structures already work? In business, the profit motive or shareholder financial interests may be a key driver. In government there is no such pressure. Instead, political issues – for example, the delivery of a manifesto commitment – and managerial issues, like the smooth running of the state, are the primary drivers.

Essential services

Where the state has most legitimacy is where essential services can be fundamentally transformed, arguably for the better. Again policy differences may distort what has been achieved, but e-Government offers the chance to improve the quality of what the state does and provides for its citizens. If government can be joined-up and save lives (for example, with the co-ordination of ambulance, police and fire services) or improve living situations (for example, welfare provision combined with health care needs), then in some ways e-Government provides the glue to bind departments together. (Joined-up working in the public sector is discussed later in the chapter.) Essential services can be improved by e-Government in the same way that core business competences can be sharpened through good e-Business.

Of course, this means that e-Government has to be part of a clearly defined, funded and regulated project and incorporate change management. It is a process of reform with a goal in mind: in some ways 'e-Government' will have succeeded in this area when it becomes simply 'government' again. Yet to suggest a comprehensive e-Government in which key state services are clarified, speeded up, made easier and basically run better is to suggest the correct delivery of essential services. And what are those essential services?

The world of government in the 1980s would suggest a stripped out, neo-Victorian model in which the state does little and the private sector – the grand market – is 'king'. Perhaps in this view e-Government is a regression down Hayek's 'road to serfdom', in which government is strengthened and enabled. Essential services could well be more loosely defined. Is it essential to provide basic health care? Housing? Transport? Food and clothes? Holidays abroad? Where is the line drawn? It has been said that e-Government is the use of technology to enhance the delivery of government services (Silcock 2001). Knowing the boundaries of e-Government first requires a definition of what those services are: to know exactly what the state itself does – and does not – do.

Access

Perhaps most important, the public sector must ensure that its services are available to all, through whichever access channel the citizen wishes to use. Private companies are able to decommission older channels they see as unprofitable and concentrate on those aspects of their business that will deliver the greatest return for their shareholders. Consequently, banks in rural areas have closed down and cheaper, online financial services have replaced them, even if their account holders in the countryside do not have access to the Internet.

In contrast, the public sector must continue to use traditional methods until they are no longer wanted, something which is likely to result in a long and expensive process of delivering services through a variety of channels. The full benefits of e-Government will be realized only if the older delivery mechanisms can be closed down, and a substantial marketing campaign will be required to ensure sufficient take-up of online services for that to happen. Recognizing this, a number of local authorities (including Liverpool City Council) have concentrated on service delivery via call centres rather than the Internet, since a far higher proportion of their citizens can use a telephone than the Web. As a result, they will probably be able to close down older channels earlier than other councils.

e-Democracy

Voter turnout at elections dipped to a pitiful 59 per cent in the United Kingdom's 2001 general election and far fewer citizens have bothered to choose their local and European representatives in recent years. The figures are even lower for younger voters. However, as Kearns *et al*. (2002) have pointed out, young people are not necessarily disaffected with politics and issues, only with traditional political processes and parties.

Perhaps in response to this, the government published a consultation document on e-Democracy in July 2002, pledging 'to give individuals more choice about how they can participate in the political process' (HM Government 2002: 4). The paper acknowledges that the government bears a responsibility for low turnouts and highlighted how e-Participation and e-Voting could empower citizens, particularly the young.

Although, as Bend (2002) argues, the introduction of technology into traditional political practices is not a panacea for the problem of people not turning up at the polls, many believe it will provide new ways of involving citizens in the democratic process *in between* elections. Indeed, it has the potential to transform the relationship between government and governed, through easier access to information, increased transparency, and discussion and feedback mechanisms.

e-Government revitalizing

In spite of much criticism that concentrating on making public services available online is a case of poor prioritization, this process will empower citizens by allowing them to access information quickly and easily. Civil society organizations can now download government consultation papers or legislation from the Web as soon as they are ready, rather than having to wait for a hard copy to be published and sent to them in the post.

In the 2002 Local Government Bill, the government said it would like to see local authorities perform a greater role in the leadership and revitalization of their communities. The best way to ensure that this leadership is representative is by increasing communication between the council and its citizens, and new technology can play an important part in achieving this. Councils also have a vital role to play in providing local people with access to the technology and in explaining how it is used – in libraries, community centres and other public buildings. The e-Envoy (the government's principal 'e-Champion') has said that 98 per cent of all UK citizens should be within a few miles of one of these centres by the end of 2002 (PAC 2002).

e-Consultation

One of the easiest ways to engage citizens in the political process is to allow for online consultation. This can occur prior to decisions being made, to ensure that all relevant parties can have their say on probable outcomes or, when new laws are enacted, to assess how effective they have been. The UK government already allows (and in many cases prefers) opinions on draft legislation or policies to be sent via e-mail and many local authorities take a similar position on potentially controversial planning or licensing applications, for example. Many citizens find this way of registering their opinions far more convenient than writing a letter, putting it in an envelope and posting it. Most Western democracies give e-mail petitions the same weight as paper versions. The European Union, not generally regarded as one of the most democratic institutions in the world, often arranges for its commissioners to answer online queries in real time and thus discuss issues with people in all member states simultaneously.

In the same way, individual MPs, MEPs or councillors can be contacted electronically, if they make their e-mail addresses publicly available. Although recent research has found that a majority of MPs are reluctant to embrace this new form of communication (Parity 2002) and the majority still do not have their own Web sites (Hansard Society 2002), it nevertheless provides citizens with a quicker and easier way of contacting their representatives.

e-Voting

Most e-Democracy activity and discussion in the United Kingdom has concentrated on electronic voting. This covers voting via the Internet, e-mail, a kiosk, mobile phone or text message. In May 2002 a number of English local authorities piloted these different kinds of e-Voting and turnout increased in each area

234

that was involved, although some wards were more successful than others. Central government and the local authorities concerned cautiously welcomed the results, although a number of councils also piloted all-postal voting, and this proved to be more successful in improving turnout figures.

Although a number of security and anonymity concerns still exist (Communications – Electronic Security Group 2002), government Ministers have expressed their wish to see an e-enabled general election some time after 2006.

The business of government

As discussed earlier, the nature of government is different from business, despite commonalities. The core role of public sector activity is hard to define, and has been debated, at least in recorded form, since Plato and Aristotle. What is the nature of the state – the business of government? What is the end – or *telos* – of the government? To understand e-Government, it is perhaps useful to first set out the context of government itself as it relates to these issues.

Public administration

A natural conclusion is that the state exists to provide security and well-being, a buffer against Thomas Hobbes's 'state of nature'. As a result, it is necessarily part coercive, part administrative. In terms of e-Government it is mainly the administrative element that is of interest. Public administration is the governing of a state by an organization, in this case the government, which in the modern world is a bureaucratic organization. The modern state would be recognizable to the likes of Max Weber, who outlined the first theories of bureaucracy and organizational behaviour over a hundred years ago. In this way, the nature of e-Government is to extend and improve the bureaucracy of public administration, by merging ICT capabilities with existing management systems. Just as e-Business takes the organization of corporate administration and automates, reorganizes and streamlines, so too e-Government revolutionizes the tools of government. It does not, however, change the reason for government.

Public services

Further on from this, the emerging focus on public service delivery has led to a strengthening of existing government services. With increased financial support for core policy areas like health, education, defence and transport, the role of public services in Britain has undergone a quiet but significant shift since the late 1990s. As this has shifted attention from markets to networks (Rhodes and Weller 2001), it has also apparently led to a greater strategic demand for e-Government as a means of adapting to an Internet Age.

As a service in itself, e-Government can also be regarded as a paradigm shift in government thinking. Just as modern computing was adopted by government, so too the joined-up world of e-Governance and e-Government has built upon the acceptance of ICT in everyday administration. Public services now include Charter Marks and Open Government scrutiny; as such, e-Government has itself become a public service, as an information provider on the activities of government. With the use of information portals and searchable data archives, programmes like the online posting of the 1901 census, though often subdued by poor ICT architecture, are increasingly connecting people with government. As an information service this is a step forward – with the parallel but separate use of transactional services, e-Government has firmly emerged as a core public service.

Central and local government

However, as a catalyst of change, or a technology of itself, one significant problem has been the role it plays within different tiers of government. As devolution starts to absorb greater levels of policy making and delivery, and local government increasingly signs up to the modernization programme, the divide between central and local government services is stark. Whilst local initiatives and duties like waste disposal, buying various permits and Council Tax collection are frequently e-enabled, local e-Government is focused more practically on transactions and direct interaction with citizens.

The technological ramifications obscure this point. Because much low-level online government activity can be done locally, the transactional nature of local e-Government clouds the picture of what central government reform is achieving. Organizational changes leading to greater flexibility, *ad hoc* network formation and virtual working are happening from a top-down approach within central government; local e-Government initiatives are aimed less at these kind of managerial reforms than on what can be done in terms of interaction with citizens. Thus local initiatives are more pragmatic and aimed at government-to-citizen (G2C) or government-to-business (G2B) transactions, whereas national approaches are more strategic and focused on government-to-government (G2G) relationships.

Health

Owing to the fact that it is funded by general taxation, rather than social insurance schemes (as in France or Germany) or the private sector (as in the United States), health tends to be a hotter political potato in the United Kingdom than in other Western democracies. Central government is held responsible for the health service, since all NHS staff ultimately answer to the Secretary of State. Consequently, British governments are especially keen to maintain and improve the NHS, and 'e-Health' is an obvious way to do this.

236

In April 2002 the government altered the structure of the NHS, replacing the old regional offices, ninety-five local health authorities and 481 primary care groups with twenty-eight 'strategic' health authorities and 302 Primary Care Trusts (PCTs). Although this represented a significant devolution of power, Ministers in central government will still make the important decisions and the public will ultimately praise or blame them for successes and failures.

As a result, the NHS is characterized by 'top-down' policy implementation, which has advantages (in that it ensures standards are kept the same across the country) as well as disadvantages (it fails to take account of local differences). In areas like IT, where interoperability of systems is paramount, this can obviously be seen as a bonus. However, along with the lack of a comparable 'Pathfinder' system for primary care trusts, this deters significant local innovation, which could result in solutions that are relevant across the service. The government's promise to grant 'Foundation' status to those hospitals that are deemed to be the best performing could correct this. Foundation hospitals will have greater freedom from central government, including the right to borrow money for investment.

E-GOVERNMENT PROGRAMMES

Nearly every country around the globe has taken up the challenge of implementing e-Government, using various approaches. Some states are more concerned with changing external rather than internal communications systems, and often the strategy may reflect the country's characteristics (such as whether it is centralized or federal, large or small, a democracy or a dictatorship, and has a high or low level of technological advancement).

United Kingdom

The UK government has instructed most public sector organizations to set out the details of their strategies for e-Enablement. They were originally given a target of making all services available electronically by 2008; this was then brought forward to 2005. 'Electronically' has also been defined to mean via telephone if the person being called is using an electronic device, such as a computer interface or call centre database. These targets have been criticized for being too blunt an instrument, since they mean organizations can just transfer all their delivery mechanisms to the Internet or a call centre, without fundamentally reforming them. In addition, they do not address related matters, such as making the electronic services easy to use or relevant to the citizen. No target exists to encourage the take-up of online services.

THINK POINT

What types of government services could be transferred to the Web?

A fair number of 'transactional' services require citizens to sign documentation, and this can create difficulties, as many organizations have problems authenticating the user. For example, UK citizens cannot complete the process of applying for a passport online, since a signature and photograph are required, as well as payment of a fee. Alternatively some advice may be better given by telephone or face to face, especially if it concerns issues that citizens want to keep private. On the other hand, the United Kingdom was the first country to allow minor crimes to be reported on the Web. This process does not require financial transactions and authentication is not a major issue – indeed, some victims may prefer the relative anonymity of the Internet to entering a police station. e-Government can reap the greatest benefits in service areas that are used most often by citizens and require the least state input, such as repeat requests for prescriptions, registering on the electoral roll and paying Council Tax.

The modernization White Paper

The 1999 White Paper *Modernising Government* helped to set the agenda for e-Government in the United Kingdom and led directly to a range of subsequent 'e'-related policies and projects. *Modernising Government* laid out the main tenets of the government's approach to public sector change. Among these was the creation of 'responsive public services', built around citizens' needs (rather than fragmented, supplier-driven structures). As well as responsive services, *improved quality of services* featured highly. Targets for efficiency and effectiveness were to be proposed, backed up by a new inspection regime.

The galvanizing issue for e-Government came from the putative contribution of technology to modernization and change. And indeed, it was the White Paper that first laid out the targets for Electronic Service Delivery (ESD). In March 1999, however, the talk was still of 'Information Age government'. The (synonymous) notion of 'electronic government' received its first major outing a year later with the Cabinet Office report *e-Government: a Strategic Framework for Public Services in the Information Age*.

Right from the outset, then, the modernization and Information Age/ e-Government agendas were inextricably linked. A modern public sector required – among other things – the strategic and widespread adoption of information technologies (IT) and the new ways of doing things that went with them.

In 2001 English councils were asked to produce Implementing Electronic Government (IEGs) statements and Scottish authorities had to draft Twenty-first Century Government Action Plans (GAPs) to outline how they would reach ESD targets. Central government departments were required to produce 'e-Business strategies'. These moves were intended to deliver a more systematic look at the role of e-Government and the broader contributions it could make to public sector modernization.

e-Strategies

In many ways, the correlation between e-Business and e-Government allows the direct comparison of private sector strategies with public sector strategies. It is noticeable that the adoption of a core e-Business strategy in central and local government has been somewhat institutionalized. For example, the formal and not so formal connections between direct Whitehall funding and the meeting of the 2005 targets for online service delivery are just one context of the use of e-Business strategies, IEGs and so on.

To deliver results (and consequently receive central funding for key projects), it has become accepted practice – perhaps even 'best practice' – to base the business plan on a core e-Business strategy. Each central government department has one, is developing one or maintains a more general (but comparable) plan. For local government, e-Business strategies have been even more clearly tied to government action.

On the face of it, this is a clear example of 'stick and carrot': without the presence of the strategy documents, there is apparently no reward. Perhaps it makes sense to see e-Business strategy documents, and the thinking behind them, as one of the cornerstones of emerging e-Government. They exist not because they have to, but because they can be used as tools of government to achieve specific ends – in this case, clear performance targets, and the broader adoption of e-Government ideas, management practices, and technology.

IEGs and the national strategy for local e-Government

All local authorities in England were asked to submit Implementing Electronic Government statements to central government in the autumns of 2001 and 2002. The first of these was supposed to explain how the council would deliver 100 per cent ESD by 2005. This fitted in with the Best Value performance indicator (BVPI) 157, which was designed to assess the extent of e-Enablement in individual local authorities by looking at the percentage of services available online.

The 2002 IEGs were for authorities to provide an update on their progress and frame their programme within the Office of the Deputy Prime Minister's

239

(ODPM) national strategy document, a draft of which was published in April 2002 and the final version later in the year. On receiving a satisfactory IEG, the ODPM gave the council concerned a £200,000 grant for its e-Government programme. Nearly every authority received this money in the 2001 process, although a few had to re-submit their statements. English fire brigades were asked to produce similar strategies for the first time in 2002, with the promise of £25,000 in funding for those deemed satisfactory. Thus far, police authorities have not been required to do so.

The Scottish Executive asked councils north of the border to produce Twenty-first Century Government Action Plans to outline how they intended to achieve 100 per cent ESD by 2005. Although they shared the same *raison d'être* as IEGs, *Modernising Government* grants from the Scottish Executive were not dependent on producing 'satisfactory' documents. In addition, English authorities were provided with more detailed guidance than their Scottish counterparts in drafting their documents and so care should be taken when comparing the two.

The ODPM's national strategy document, *egov@local,* built on the modernization White Paper and attempted to outline a clear national framework of priorities and standards whilst not preventing local innovation (ODPM 2002). It included the following checklist, so that practitioners could assess the extent to which their council services are:

- 'Joined-up'
- Accessible to customers when and where they are most convenient
- Delivered or supported electronically
- Delivered by partnerships, where appropriate
- Delivered 'seamlessly'
- Open and accountable
- Used by 'e-Citizens'

The strategy saw e-Government as an intrinsic part of the overall drive to improve public services. It also posited that e-Government could help to deliver better democratic accountability and tackle social exclusion, by enabling greater community input into political decisions, particularly at the local level.

The National Health Service Information Authority

The National Health Service Information Authority (NHSIA) performs a similar function for the NHS as the Office of the e-Envoy does for the rest of the public sector. Essentially, it is charged with replacing paper-based systems with electronic patient records and an electronic library of health information by 2005. In 1998 the government published its *Information for Health* strategy, which stated that it wanted to see the following by 2005 (NHSIA 1998):

240

- Electronic health records for every person in the country
- NHS staff able to access patient records and information about best clinical practice online
- 'Seamless' care for patients, facilitated by patient information sharing between GPs, hospitals and community services
- Online and telephone information services accessible to the public round the clock, to encourage patients to treat themselves at home where appropriate

Progress on a number of these targets has been good. NHS Direct, which provides patients with 24/7 access to health advice by telephone or the Internet, was completed on schedule and has proved to be one of the most successful e-Government projects (NAO 2002a). By March 2002, 95 per cent of all GPs' surgeries had e-mail facilities and were connected to the NHS intranet, and by September that year the NHSIA had improved the search facility of its online library and allowed patients the same right as medical staff to access the information. However, some targets for implementation in 2002 were not met, such as allowing online GP bookings and referrals, or having electronic patient records in 35 per cent of all health authorities.

Structural differences in the NHS when compared with government are reflected by the fact that primary care trusts did not produce IEGs or similar documents. Responsibility for implementing local e-Health lies at a much higher level than it does for local e-Government.

Audit reports on progress

During 2002 public sector watchdogs, the Audit Commission (AC) and National Audit Office (NAO), produced three reports into e-Government's progress. They emphasized that a great deal has been achieved, with a number of councils and agencies delivering the vision. However, they also identified the following difficulties:

- Many projects have not concentrated on delivering real value – they look at delivering ESD rather than taking the opportunity to change processes. This 'tick box' approach (doing what is required but nothing else) could seriously threaten the chances of delivering the full benefits of e-Government.
- A number of public sector organizations have poorly prioritized their e-Government projects and set unrealistic targets for delivery.
- There is a possibility that services will be available online but nobody will want to use them, owing to poor marketing, lack of incentives for the public to opt for newer access channels, or poor choice of channel for the delivery of services.

241

- Low-income groups and the elderly may have access problems and therefore not use online services.
- Internal cultural barriers to change and lack of ICT skills could prove problematic in e-enabling internal processes.

Although central departments and local authorities are confident of reaching the 2005 target, the House of Commons Public Accounts Committee (PAC) has echoed the above concerns (PAC 2002).

The true outcome will not be known for some time, since those services which are currently available electronically have tended to be the easiest to e-enable, often using simple Web publishing tools to make information available via the Internet. Transactional services, where most of the benefits of e-Government can be realized, are much more difficult to make electronically available, since distributing or receiving money online requires authentication and additional security tools.

Case study:
WEST LOTHIAN COUNCIL

Prior to beginning any e-Government projects, West Lothian Council consulted a cross-section of its population to find out how they wished to access local services. The overwhelming response was for a greater number of access channels, availability outside normal 'office hours' and joined-up delivery. The council established a number of one-stop shops around the area, which are open at weekends, as well as a single portal Web site (www.wlonline.org.uk) for the whole community.

By providing a choice of access channel, the authority does not exclude those members of the community who might not wish or be able to use the Internet straight away. One-stop shops reduce the need for citizens to visit a plethora of institutions if they need information or a complex service. Scottish local government reorganization played an important role in realizing this, by allowing the council to examine the legacy information silos and integrate them where possible.

As a result of the original consultation, West Lothian has avoided many of the pitfalls highlighted by the AC and NAO. Its prioritization of e-Government goals and projects have most recently led to the introduction of an online payment system for Council Tax, business rates, rents, service accounts and parking fines. Such developments will ensure that the authority can reap the many benefits of e-Government in the medium and longer term.

Sources: Leitch (2002); Scottish Executive (2002).

Other countries

Whilst the United Kingdom is an excellent example for analysis of e-Government, there are lessons to be learned from international experience. Of course, the pool to draw from is very deep, and the three states cited below – the United States, Germany and Sweden – demonstrate aspects of e-Government that are especially relevant here. This is not to say other prominent e-Governments like Australia, New Zealand or Singapore are less useful, but that these three have some unique qualities which are worth examining.

It is worth noting that as the technology of e-Government has spread far, covering diverse political structures in Russia, Japan, Brazil and Malaysia, it is still predominantly an Atlantic and Antipodean affair. EU member states, along with the United States, Canada, New Zealand and Australia, are consistently identified as pioneers in e-Government, with Singapore being a notable exception. Whilst budgetary funding has much to do with this, the Anglocentric nature of e-Government is one possible area worth further research; for a further look at this, Geraldine Cohen discussed the problems of language and character recognition in Chapter 8. Do Japan and China, for example, suffer from less e-Government as a result of language difficulties in software? Would emerging technologies like accurate voice recognition significantly shift the way e-Business has been applied there? More fundamentally, is successful e-Government predicated on the existence of NPM reforms? Ultimately, there is much still to look into; yet the three countries cited below offer a good range for discussion.

United States

To provide some explicit contrast, one useful comparison is with the United States. As the founder country of the Internet, digital (and therefore electronic) government, and even much of the e-Business practices overshadowed by the dotcom era, there is much to look at. However, it is worth noting a few crucial differences. Unlike the United Kingdom, the US government system is decentralized in a manner that has considerably influenced the composition and delivery of e-Government. Constitutionally, culturally and managerially, there is much difference between the two countries.

US central government and state government have very different delivery agendas, and this has affected the emphasis on e-Government services. Many of the services offered in the United Kingdom by central government (e.g. the issuing of driving licences) are devolved to state level in the United States, whilst the central services are fundamentally geared up towards more internal issues like information sharing and e-Business management systems. The degree of centralization that powers much of UK e-Government policy is absent in the United States. Interestingly, this has had an effect on the management behind e-Government.

243

The focus on transactional services at a central level is not as clear in the United States as it is in the United Kingdom. Whilst the key FirstGov portal (www.firstgov.gov) has largely delivered a government information search engine, the real changes have been occurring internally, as key projects like Quicksilver have focused on management changes. Indeed, the cornerstone Bush administration document 'The President's Management Agenda' sets the tone of e-Government by placing it squarely within a policy designed to reform public sector bureaucracy, not simply deliver services online.

Case Study: FIRSTGOV

Developed within a ninety-day time-period as part of the Clinton administration's commitment to swift adoption of Internet technology within government, FirstGov started life as a central information resource in 2000. The model was to provide information, links and a 'front door' to all US federal, state and local government information. As such, private data were not collected (for example, as cookies), and documents themselves were indexed but not stored or archived. Transactional e-Government was not part of the original plan.

Having now undergone a change of administration in 2001, and after witnessing a range of similar efforts in other countries, FirstGov is redesigning itself. It is increasingly a part of the President's management agenda, and is therefore moving towards a more interactive role: whilst it is not yet offering the same service as UKOnline, for example, it involves twenty-two agencies, and has a model of 'franchising' its brand across the private sector. The US government describes FirstGov as the 'catalyst of a growing e-Government'.

Germany

Much different in style to both the United States and the United Kingdom, the e-Government emerging in Germany is traditionally seen as 'behind' the Anglo-American policies and achievements. In some ways there is a degree of evidence for this, with little budgetary funding supporting the German changes, and the announcement of targets that mirror those in colleague EU states like the United Kingdom, rather than being unique to the German government structure.

However, this can be misleading. Unlike the United Kingdom, but with a direct similarity to the United States, the federal system has led to much transactional e-Government being pioneered at local level. With the bulk of services delivered within the sixteen *Länder*, the demand for central oversight is not as overt as in the United Kingdom. Welfare payments, online tax filing and the plethora of environmental and local permits and regulatory issues which need authorization are all increasingly seeping into e-Government systems, and in a manner devoid of the United Kingdom's frequent rhetorical 'branding' of initiatives.

Yet federal e-Government is not resting in Germany, and as with the US FirstGov idea, the key portals (for example www.deutschland.de) are increasingly acting as linkages between the different political strata. As an information source it is also akin to the pre-UKOnline 'OpenGov' portal, acting as an impartial first step to information sources only. The difference in Germany is that this has been achieved deliberately as a result of a clear strategy, rather than in the evolutionary way of the United Kingdom's offerings. Coming late to the e-Government agenda, Germany has had the benefit of watching 'market leaders' like the United States and United Kingdom work out their own models.

Sweden

Sweden is in many ways closer to the United Kingdom than the United States or Germany on the issue of e-Government. With a similar system of uneven devolution, established but relatively weak local service delivery and much New Public Management, the Swedish state also has a context of parliamentary democracy, which can be compared directly with that of the United Kingdom. This has filtered into Swedish e-Government as well, as centrally defined targets, management and funding have shaped the evolution of policy.

Though not as focused on e-Business, the nature of public sector management has already been so amended to utilize private sector methodology that e-Government has been taken up almost as a corollary to its corporate sister practice of e-Business. As with the United Kingdom, e-Government is created within a context of previous radical change, and openness to further management reforms. Sweden does not have the same rigidly centralized e-Government apparatus as that found in Germany, or the constitutionally restricted federal governance practised in the United States. It is consequently operating e-Government in a similar manner to the United Kingdom.

Yet there are differences. Two key examples are notable. First, Sweden has decentralized to a degree not planned in the United Kingdom. With the extension of New Public Management across executive government, e-Government is being implemented within a network of over 100 separate 'agencies', each run effectively as a not-for-profit organization. In contrast, the political – more specifically, ministerial – control in the United Kingdom over e-Government is far stronger and more traditional. Swedish e-Government is therefore far more geared to executive than to ministerial or departmental delivery. In this way it shares much commonality with the executive offices of the US presidency.

245

Second, Swedish e-Government has been implemented within an extremely developed governmental and corporate ICT environment. Unlike the United Kingdom or Germany, and ahead of the United States, Sweden had highly funded and developed mobile communications, Internet and IT systems in place and running prior to the explosion in popularity of Internet services. In many ways, because of the advanced state of technology and existing decentralization, Sweden provides an example of e-Government in a country that has practically removed the need to even use 'e' as a description. Government is automatically 'e-Government', albeit in an existing – and less modern – manner.

JOINED-UP (e)-GOVERNMENT

Despite being a long-held aim of UK policy makers, achieving 'joined-up government' (integrated working between and across government departments, levels and agencies) has largely proved to be a chimera. However, e-Government provides an opportunity to turn this into reality, since questioning and changing the way the public sector operates will help break down traditional barriers to sharing departmental information and the 'silo mentality'.

More recently, traditional advocates of identity cards have seen their arguments strengthened by proposals that they should include personal information, thus allowing card holders to use government services more easily. These 'entitlement' cards could include details of citizens' health records and the benefits they receive, as well as more standard data such as name, address and date of birth. This would enable quicker access to services in hospitals, benefit agencies and other government buildings and would be facilitated by the sharing of information across departments.

Such changes would obviously have implications for individual freedoms and therefore the Home Office released a consultation paper on the issue in July 2002. Similarly, the Cabinet Office's Performance and Innovation Unit published a report into data sharing, something that is essential for the full realization of e-Government but controversial in terms of personal privacy, in April 2002. Privacy issues are dealt with in more detail later in the chapter.

Many public sector organizations have been pushed rather than pulled into e-Government partnerships, owing to the financial attractions. As will be explained later, this is particularly the case with local authorities. However, forming these partnerships with other public sector organizations can often be the first step towards true joined-up working, in which public services are designed around the needs of the user, not the deliverer. A good example of this is UKOnline.

Being radical: the re-engineering philosophy

e-Government seeks the radical reworking and transformation of traditional public sector structures and processes. In the United Kingdom, Prime Minister Tony

Blair has said that he wants to shape public services around the needs of their users (the 'citizen-as-customer'), rather than the wishes of the service provider. This makes it different from previous change programmes or IT projects, which have been seen as just an 'add-on' to current practices. UKOnline demonstrates this by providing the user with navigational tools to help with various 'life episodes' (moving home, having a baby, finding a job, etc.), rather than orga-nizing its content on a departmental basis. Many local authorities and other national governments have followed this lead, resulting in a far more logical user experience than would be the case if it followed traditional departmental lines.

Working across boundaries

UKOnline showed that it was possible for departments to work with one another. The 'joined-up' rhetoric has increased since its launch and a number of projects in central and local government have proved to be successful. Central govern-ment has urged other public sector bodies to form partnerships with one another; this will reduce expenditure on IT (and other) infrastructure through economies of scale, make transacting with government easier for the citizen, help to iden-tify common goals and assist with the sharing of best practice.

One of the first attempts to join up central government responsibilities involved job centres and benefit agencies. Despite staff resistance, the two services were merged. This had benefits from both government and citizen perspectives. For the government it resulted in economies of scale, since fewer buildings and staff were required. In addition, the new, unified computer system was far better equipped to identify claimants and deal with potential fraud than the previous paper-based processes that linked the two agencies. For users, most people who visited one of the buildings would also go to the other and consequently they were now able to deal with more than one issue at once.

Achieving properly joined-up systems is not easy, as many staff members feel threatened by outside influence on their working patterns. Chapter 4 listed a number of barriers to e-Business organizational change and most of these can also be applied to e-Government. The section 'Management of change' later in this chapter (p. 250) will deal with some of these problems.

Intra-agency

Many public sector bodies do not have good systems for the dissemination of information across the institution. This often results in unnecessary duplica-tion, poor quality data and a frustrating user experience. The NHS is a prime example of this and therefore has been set a target date of 2005 for getting all patients' medical records into an interoperable electronic format. Although health is an area where personal privacy is paramount, internal joining up of systems with proper security provision to protect individuals should result in a much improved service.

THINK POINT

If you are taken to Casualty, how many times do you have to tell NHS staff what happened to you? Would they have access to your GP records?

Case study:
WEST SURREY HEALTH AUTHORITY

Most patients who arrive at Accident and Emergency (A&E) in an ambulance must first inform the paramedic of their symptoms (and other relevant medical information, such as allergies, dates of recent immunizations and possibly blood type), then tell a receptionist at the hospital and finally the doctor or nurse who treats them. If the patient is admitted, the casualty department relays the information to the patient's GP, who may later refer the case to a specialist.

In the majority of cases, therefore, the patient (who may not be in full control of their faculties) has to repeat this information several times to NHS staff. These staff members then write down the relevant details on paper, which is disseminated to a number of colleagues. This process can obviously result in a number of problems: the patient's account may differ each time they are asked about the problem, doctors are not known for the legibility of their handwriting, the plethora of forms can create audit problems and pieces of paper may get lost, torn, wet or delayed in transit.

West Surrey Health Authority now uses a single form that can be delivered electronically to the relevant people, thus removing any risk of copying errors and speeding up the whole process. The form is also much easier to audit than traditional mechanisms and interfaces with a database of illnesses so that paramedics can often identify ailments earlier while patients are still in the ambulance, rather than after they arrive at A&E. This offers the added advantage that, since conditions are diagnosed more quickly, lives are saved and the need for unnecessary 'blue light' alerts is reduced.

Source: Adapted from Navein and Jardine (2002).

Inter-agency

Since the United Kingdom's e-Government programme is not just limited to 'government' but affects the whole public sector, many different agencies are looking for similar solutions. A partnership between different tiers of local govern-ment (district and county authorities) is perhaps the most obvious way in which this can be done. Similar arrangements also exist between neighbouring author-ities, such as those in North Yorkshire, which have set up a portal that allows users to find information relevant to them, regardless of whether a unitary, district or county council is responsible for it.

Case study: ANGUSNET

Network infrastructure in the Angus area was deteriorating and unable to cope with the new demands of e-Government and the National Grid for Learning. Angus Council, together with Abertay College in Dundee, NHS Tayside, local colleges and voluntary organizations, approached Tayside Police with a view to jointly procuring and managing new broadband infrastructure. The police force already owned many spots on high ground in the area to assist with their radio communications. This meant the part-nership required planning permission for only one more mast to cover the entire area. Consequently all schools, libraries, hospitals, council offices, health centres and other public buildings in the area are now connected through 2 MB worth of their own broadband infrastructure. This has resulted in massive cost savings, since previously each agency was paying significantly more in total line rental than the cost of main-taining the shared infrastructure.

Source: Adapted from Cairns and Jennow (2002).

Public–private

Joined-up public–private working is undoubtedly the most controversial form of partnership, with the well rehearsed criticisms of the UK government's flagship Private Finance Initiative (PFI) policy accounting for only some of the opposi-tion. If government bodies share personal information with private companies, this may be even more controversial than one public sector organization passing on private details to another.

However, because e-Government by definition involves the integration of ICT into public sector processes, technology and communications companies need to play an essential role in realizing the vision. Furthermore, since e-Business prac-tices tend to be more established than those of e-Government, private companies can use their experience of implementing technological change to ensure that pub-lic sector organizations do not encounter the same problems they had to overcome.

249

Case study:
LIVERPOOL CITY COUNCIL AND BRITISH TELECOM

There are a number of examples of successful public–private working, such as Liverpool City Council's agreement with BT. In 2002 these two organizations formed the Liverpool Direct call centre, which deals with citizens' enquiries to the local authority. The centre is not outsourced to the company, but jointly run by both organizations, and the council therefore maintains contact with its citizens. Since the establishment of Liverpool Direct, the council and BT have formed a joint venture company, offering the use of the call centre to other organizations in return for cash. Interestingly, the deal does not prevent Liverpool from choosing other partners should a different company be successful in the tendering process.

Source: Adapted from Melville (2002).

MANAGEMENT OF CHANGE

Whilst e-Business and e-Government reflect both theoretical and philosophical developments, they also contain a practical agenda for change. How that change is managed is crucial to the outcome of successful electronic management, and as such e-Government can be seen as reforming existing administrative practice. What e-Government offers the public sector is similar to the lure of e-Business: radically improved management, control and adaptability. One such issue derived from this is the funding for change: the following section looks at how money and pilot projects have influenced the management of both e-Government and broader public sector management reform.

Dealing with public funds and essential services

Although opinion polls appear to suggest that the electorate is prepared to fund extra investment in public services through tax or National Insurance increases, the state tends to find it more difficult to pay for major projects than private companies. The 'e-Government and e-Governance' section pointed out that public sector organizations have to worry about far more stakeholders (principally their citizens) than private companies. This leads to the overriding conviction that the government may be spending 'our money' unwisely if a public sector project fails to deliver. Such failures trigger a far more emotional reaction than if a private business makes a poor investment decision. Regular customers of that company may not even associate themselves with its loss, even though some of the money wasted may have come directly from them.

250

Consequently the patchy history of public sector IT projects has raised many suspicions about the ability of state employees to invest in the right technology. High-profile failures include the attempt to make the results of the 1901 census available online, which resulted in the Web site crashing (and remaining inaccessible for months afterwards) when the organizers vastly underestimated demand, and the Individual Learning Accounts programme, which had to be abandoned owing to excessive fraud. Consequently, Whitehall feels justified in adopting a cautious approach to granting funding for e-Government.

Getting money and spending it

Many UK public sector institutions, particularly local authorities, argue that this prudence could prevent them from implementing e-Government in full. In response, the centre points to the fact that ESD will result in efficiency savings and therefore councils will eventually reap the returns from their investment in ICT.

Whichever way you look at it, however, the sources of funding for local authorities are limited. Councils have estimated that realizing local e-Government would cost around £2.5 billion. As has been explained, central government allocated each English council £200,000 on the production of a 'satisfactory' IEG statement in both 2001 and 2002. Money was also available for 'pathfinders', partnerships and through the Invest to Save budget, but it will not come close to the authorities' own estimate of their needs. Probably by design rather than accident, this has pushed many councils towards partnerships, either with other public bodies or with private companies, in an attempt to realize economies of scale or access additional funding.

The NHS is in comparatively better shape on this score, thanks in part to the massive increases in proposed health expenditure over the coming years, much of which will be invested in ICT. Perhaps more pertinently, central government is seen as responsible for the Health Service and so is far more enthusiastic to fund projects in this area than to assist with funding local services, for which local politicians tend to be held to account.

ETHICAL AND PRIVACY ISSUES

As has been touched upon throughout this chapter, there are considerable ethical and philosophical questions relating to e-Government. Whilst the privacy concerns of an emerging Information Age are always of relevance, the very involvement of the state in e-Business issues leads to serious questions concerning the viability, legitimacy and ethical basis of such organizational changes. Furthermore, back-office re-engineering might well offer considerable improvements in government capabilities, but is this desirable? One check upon

251

government is the limitations of surveillance technology as well as the will to use it: in many ways, e-Government upsets this balance.

Sharing data between agencies

Broadly speaking, a key privacy issue that is part of everyday Internet life concerns the collection of private data. Chapter 5 of this volume shows how such data can then be used by active e-Businesses. The approaches taken by existing e-Government structures have been no better than those of the private sector to date. In some cases, most notably in the United States, the constitutional and legal context of government precludes the holding of certain data, and critical tracking technologies – for example, setting software trackers or 'cookies' to monitor an Internet user's online journey – have proved to be impractical in most cases. In the United Kingdom the approach has been very different, with customizable portals requiring identification at some point during access to the e-Government service.

Either way, how data are stored leads to issues about who has access to the stored data, which is a much larger ethical question. Should health records be opened up to medical insurers? What about to pharmaceutical businesses pursuing statistical research? Alternatively, is it acceptable to allow access to a citizen's online voting record (assuming that the parallel realm of e-Democracy is achieved successfully) for personal viewing? Choices have to be made to determine the boundaries between a passive and an active data collection regime.

The Big Brother state

As governments begin to adopt the Internet-led technologies of information storage, control and dissemination, key ethical and political questions arise. Who controls access to electronic government? Who pays for it? Are revenue streams like advertising or market intelligence profiling acceptable areas of government activity? Indeed, are they acceptable areas of business activity if outsourced or privatized?

Given electoral habits, it is difficult to predict future government policy, and ICT-fuelled organizational change is no different. These questions are hard to answer – not because the technology is unpredictable (though this is a potential issue), but because the underlying management required by government is often affected by the electoral cycle and the different policies favoured by different politicians and parties.

The picture of an e-Government environment of deep, automated control is not yet reality; the problems of large IT projects, for example online tax filing in the United Kingdom, are symptomatic of incomplete e-Business. Whilst the films and fears depict a Big Brother environment made real, in which a government intent on developing an Orwellian form of public sector rule applies the tools of e-Business, such a reality has yet to appear. Too few households and taxpayers have access to efficient broadband services, let alone the omniscient remote surveillance software and hardware systems of a Big Brother state. Even the more authoritarian examples of sophisticated systems, such as Singapore, do not attempt to claim Orwell's forecasted role.

This is not to say that e-Government does not represent a threat to civil liberties, or the constitutional ideals favoured by many. Indeed, it is the very lack of regulation and legal standards surrounding the Internet which has led to the unfettered evolution of e-Business models within a public sector setting. Although this is by no means an unwelcome outcome, it demonstrates two clear issues that have yet to be addressed sufficiently: cryptography and architecture.

Cryptography and identification

The widespread adoption of previously classified encryption technology has enabled an Internet in which civilian data can be relatively safely secured from espionage. Whilst the trade-off appears to be greater identification of users, the availability of public-key encryption protocols (or Public Key Infrastructure, PKI) in software like OpenPGP offers the possibility of wide-scale electronic privacy. Existing e-Government can even benefit from such technology if a national infrastructure is in place. However, a critical mass needs to build prior to use, with enough citizens adopting PKI as a standard. With sufficient uptake, a PKI system would enable e-Government to become a secure and dependable part of the state.

With regard to e-Government however, there needs to be acceptance that such an outcome would require a degree of single-point identification, a *de facto* identity card. In states like Germany or France there is little political problem with this and PKI is often advanced in its adoption. For the United Kingdom and United States, however, the concept of single ID sources – for example, a biometric or standard smart card – is a very contentious political issue. For e-Government to work in this case depends more on social and political norms than on technology, funding or management.

The importance of architecture

Underlying even cryptography, the second key area of concern is the 'architecture' of a system. With e-Government, the basic code – like XML – regulates the nature of service provision. Yet traditionally that is the role of statute, policy and the courts. Indeed, the basis of e-Government seems to lack a constitutional setting that regulates it in any known manner. It is this realm of technical code prior to oversight that Lawrence Lessig refers to as the 'architecture' of cyberspace (Lessig 1999); what governs the code is no clearer within the public

253

realm than it is within the traditional e-Business setting. As a result, the archi-tecture of e-Government can be seen as playing a similar role to a constitution and its government: the one regulates the other.

Officially, the Internet technologies of servers, domains, mark-up languages, data protocols, virtual private networks or even HTML are all subject to a degree of informal control and governance. In most cases, this was originally set up by the US government through companies like ICANN. However, as Internet tech-nology becomes more sophisticated and e-Government evolves into a complex system, the underlying code, which has hitherto been loosely regulated, is increas-ingly subject to both corporate and proprietary government regulations.

As Lessig implies, where is the security in a citizen-wide data network that is run on proprietary but flawed network software? If the architecture of e-Government is broken or poorly designed then the outcomes of e-Government services will be dissatisfaction and failure. More sinisterly, the seemingly innocuous issues about privacy and data storage and sharing could well prove to be more serious when subjected to a more sinister e-Government architecture. That the political will is lacking in the present environment is no substitute for constitutional or legal protection against abuse: the architecture of e-Government is crucial in enabling future capabilities and service delivery.

THINK POINT

With the implementation of the Government Gateway in the United Kingdom, as well as the electronic Government Interoperability Framework (e-GIF), the United Kingdom is pioneering the use of proprietary e-Government architec-ture. Linked with Microsoft, and in direct competition with the Linux code frequently preferred in Germany, the Office of the e-Envoy (OeE) has devel-oped a structure that 'wires' together existing IT, and strategically reorients government facilities towards the 2005 online targets.

But is the use of XML and proprietary software a useful step within e-Government? If Lessig's notion of 'architecting' a new form of organization on the Internet is valid, then primary concern exists about access, security and control. In particular, there is a market opportunity for the United Kingdom to export its model of e-Government as a code-based solution for other states or local governments. Would an open-source system provide a better quality of e-Government in the long term? This is particularly relevant if the United Kingdom maintains proprietary control over other governments' e-Government architecture.

CHAPTER SUMMARY

We have seen that while e-Government bears many resemblances to e-Business generally, the nature of government and public administration presents a range of unique issues and challenges. e-Government has combined with a series of existing public sector reform programmes but has also become central to the main modernization agenda, in both central and local government, as well as in the NHS. The scope of the changes involved – particularly where 'joining up' across borders is concerned – suggests some radical developments, with major political, managerial and ethical implications. And it is these, rather than the narrow 'technical' issues, that are likely to prove the main challenges in the years ahead.

FURTHER READING

Dunleavy, P., Margetts, H., Bastow, S., Callaghan, R. and Yared, H. (2002) *Government on the Web* II, London: NAO.

Fountain, J. (2001) *Building the Virtual State*, Washington DC: Brookings Institution.

Heeks, R. (1999) *Reinventing Government in the Information Age*, New York: Routledge.

Margetts, H. (1999) *Information Technology in Government*, New York: Routledge.

Silcock, R. (2001) 'What is e-Government?' *Parliamentary Affairs*, 54: 88–101.

Stedman-Jones, D. and Crowe, B. (2001) *Transformation, not Automation*, London: Demos.

BIBLIOGRAPHY

Audit Commission (2002a) *Councils and e-Government: Research so far*. Online. Available HTTP: www.audit-commission.gov.uk/reports/AC-REPORT.asp?CatID=&Prod ID=7C1CF20B-1CDB-4890-99F4-A91072E11550 (accessed September 2002).

Audit Commission (2002b) *'Message beyond the Medium': Improving Local Government Services through e-Government*. Online. Available HTTP: www.audit-commission.gov.uk/reports/AC-REPORT.asp?CatID=ENGLISH^LG^SUBJECT^ LG-CROSS-CUT^REPORTS-AND-DATA^AC-REPORT&ProdID=83CAA7E8-EF10–4596-B8C3-DDA61C29E076 (accessed September 2002).

Bend, J. (2002) 'A red herring dressed as reform', *Public Finance*, 14 July 2002. Online. Available HTTP: www.cipfa.org.uk/pf_new/features_details.ihtml?news_ id=13254 (accessed September 2002).

Cairns, A. and Jennow, J. (2002) *'Joining up for Regional Broadband – the Partnership Model Developed in Angus'*, presentation given to CIPFA e-Government Forum workshop in Edinburgh on 30 April.

Communications – Electronics Security Group (2002) *e-Voting Security Study*. Online. Available HTTP: www.edemocracy.gov.uk/library/papers/study.pdf (accessed September 2002).

Computing Magazine (2002) 'Government and technology can work together, but the mindset must change', *Computing Magazine*, 12 September, p. 34.

Cross, M. (2002) 'Why do government IT projects go wrong?', *Computing Magazine*, 12 September, pp. 37–40.

DoH (2002) '*Appointment of the Director-General of NHS Information Technology*' (press release). Online. Available HTTP: www.tap.ukwebhost.eds.com/doh/Intpress.nsf/page/2002-0367?OpenDocument (accessed September 2002).

Ferlie, E., Ashburner, L., Fitzgerald, L. and Pettigrew, A. (1996) *The New Public Management in Action*, Oxford: Oxford University Press.

Foster, C. D. and Plowden, F. J. (1996) *The State under Stress*, Buckingham: Open University Press.

Hansard Society (2001) *Democracy Online: What do we want from MPs' Web sites?* Online. Available HTTP: www.hansard-society.org.uk/MPWEB.pdf (accessed September 2002).

HM Government (2002) *In the Service of Democracy*. Online. Available HTTP: www.edemocracy.gov.uk/downloads/e-Democracy.pdf (accessed September 2002).

Kearns, I., Bend, J. and Stern, B. (2002) *e-Participation in Local Government*. Online. Available HTTP: www.ippr.org.uk/research/files/team34/project80/eparticipation.pdf (accessed October 2002).

Leitch, A. (2002) '*Partnership Working to deliver Better Services*', presentation given to CIPFA e-Government Forum workshop in Edinburgh on 30 April.

Lessig, L. (1999) *Code*, New York: Basic Books.

Melville, A. (2002) *e-Government and Organizational Transformation: Lessons from Liverpool and Hampshire*, London: NLGN/IDeA.

NAO (2002a) *NHS Direct in England*. Online. Available HTTP: www.nao.gov.uk/publications/nao_reports/01-02/0102505.pdf (accessed January 2002).

NAO (2002b) *Better Public Services through e-Government*. Online. Available HTTP: www.nao.gov.uk/publications/nao_reports/01-02/0102704-I.pdf (accessed April 2002).

NAO (2002c) *Government on the Web*. Online. Available HTTP: www.nao.gov.uk/publications/nao_reports/01-02/0102764.pdf (accessed April 2002).

Navein, J. and Jardine, J. (2002) '*e-Health as a Catalyst for Health Service Re-engineering*', presentation given to CIPFA e-Government Forum seminar in London on 21 May.

NHSIA (1998) *An Information Strategy for the Modern NHS 1998–2005: A National Strategy for Local Implementation*. Online. Available HTTP: www.nhsia.nhs.uk/def/pages/info4health/contents.asp (accessed June 2002).

NHSIA (2002) NHS Information Authority Annual report 2001–2. Online. Available HTTP: www.nhsia.nhs.uk/pdf/annrep2002.pdf (accessed 7 October 2002).

ODPM (2002) *eGov@local: Towards a National Strategy for Local e-Government*. Online. Available HTTP: www.local-regions.odpm.gov.uk/consult/egov/pdf/lgo_main.pdf (accessed April 2002).

PAC (2002) *Improving Public Services through e-Government*. Online. Available HTTP: www.publications.parliament.uk/pa/cm200102/cmselect/cmpubacc/845/845.pdf (accessed August 2002).

Parity (2002) *MPs Just Want to be Faxed*. Online. Available HTTP: www.parity.net/news/15_08_02mp.htm (accessed September 2002).

Rhodes, R. A. W. and Weller, P. (2001) *The Changing World of Top Officials*, Buckingham: Open University Press.

Scottish Executive (2002) 'West Lothian wires up its citizens' (press release). Online. Available HTTP: www.scotland.gov.uk/pages/news/2002/09/SEFD094a.aspx (accessed October 2002).

WEB LINKS

UKOnline
www.ukonline.gov.uk

North Yorkshire Portal
www.findinyorkshire.org.uk

FirstGov Portal
www.firstgov.gov

UK e-Democracy Portal
www.edemocracy.gov.uk

ODPM Local e-Government homepage
www.localegov.gov.uk

Index

Note: Where a page number is followed by a '*t*' it indicates the reference is to a table; where the page number is followed by an '*f*' it indicates a figure.

All legal cases can be found under the heading 'case law'; UK legislation is under the heading 'UK (legislation)'.

265